PRAISE FOR *NIMBLE, FOCUSED, FEISTY*

"Having worked with Sara over the years, I have learned that fostering a strong culture is THE key ingredient for a business to adapt to ever changing market dynamics and challenges. *Nimble, Focused, Feisty* is a fantastic and straightforward guide to driving your own vibrant culture and succinctly clarifies why culture is critical to your success as a contemporary leader."

—PAUL ROGERS, president and chief executive officer
at GE Wurldtech

"As a strategy leader in a large complex organization tasked with driving transformation, I have found that culture work is tricky business. Roberts's emphasis on mindset, connected leadership, and the feisty spark is the right recipe to begin the cultural change journey. She gets down to the brass tacks of what it takes to steer a big ship onto a better, more enlightened course."

—ERIN SELLMAN, senior vice president
and head of strategy, insights, and planning
at Lowe's Companies, Inc.

"What is company culture? It's something you can't afford to ignore. It's the difference between sinking or swimming in today's consumer-driven marketplace. *Nimble, Focused, Feisty* is the ultimate guide to staying afloat by learning from the best. And I speak from first-hand experience having worked with Sara and her team."

—CYNTHIA STODDARD, senior vice president
and chief information officer at NetApp

"Innovation gets all the buzz, but that's not what's going to save your company. We live in a new world. You need to transform your culture to thrive...to have impact. Sara Roberts shows you how."

—BRANT COOPER, founder of Moves the Needle
and author of the *New York Times* bestseller
The Lean Entrepreneur

"There is no Wizard of Oz curtain between how customers perceive you and how your employees think, collaborate, execute, and maneuver change. The only way to sustainably and authentically deliver great experiences to customers in today's complex environment is to create a company culture that enables people to contribute fearlessly and connect passionately to the organization's purpose. Nimble, Focused, Feisty will shift your thinking about how to lead and thrive in a marketplace, and a world, exploding with change."

—ROBIN BEERS, head of customer experience insights
at Wells Fargo Bank

"*Nimble, Focused, Feisty* shines an important light on company culture. Chilling to those who would ignore culture and inspiring to those wishing to build it, Sara Roberts's words are vital to those who care about the future of their companies."

—DAN ADAMS, founder of the AIM Institute
and author of *New Product Blueprinting*

"Sara astutely synthesizes, in a meaningful and actionable way, the most powerful trends facing corporations. It's a great introduction for executives who are trying to understand why this crazy thing called culture is so important, while providing a layer of depth for current cultural change agents. *Nimble, Focused, Feisty* explores the importance of creating a corporate culture that empowers employees. She demonstrates how companies that have embraced collaboration have been able to adapt and thrive, and how the lack of attention to culture has led to the downfall of corporate giants. Sara makes the case for why 21st century leaders need to be both self-aware and responsive to an increasingly quickening environment. Sara brings together all of the current thought leadership around the importance of new models for corporate culture—the winning strategy for companies interested in adapting to survive. She provides concrete, actionable steps, and thought provoking questions to kickstart the journey of organizational transformation, which arguably all companies will need to embrace."

—SHANNON LUCAS, change agent and director
of innovation at Vodafone Global Enterprise

"What is the difference between a great company and all the others? In a word, culture. Sara Roberts has cracked the code on what a great culture looks like...and offers practical guidelines on how you can build a great one in your company."

—DAN WARD, U.S. Air Force Lieutenant Colonel
and author of *F.I.R.E.: How Fast, Inexpensive, Restrained,
and Elegant Methods Ignite Innovation*
and *The Simplicity Cycle*

SARA ROBERTS

NIMBLE FOCUSED FEISTY

Organizational Cultures
That Win in the New Era
and How to Create Them

BENBELLA BOOKS, INC.
Dallas, TX

BenBella Books, Inc.
10300 N. Central Expy., #530
Dallas, TX 75231
www.benbellabooks.com
Send feedback to feedback@benbellabooks.com

Printed in the United States of America
10 9 8 7 6 5 4 3 2 1

Library of Congress Cataloging-in-Publication Data is available upon request.
LCCN: 2016011919
978-1-942952-13-8 (hardback)
978-1-942952-14-5 (e-book)

Editing by Debbie Harmsen
Copyediting by Brian Buchanan
Proofreading by James Fraleigh and Brittney Martinez
Indexing by Jigsaw Information
Text design and composition by John Reinhardt Book Design
Cover illustration and design by Joel Holland
Jacket design by Sarah Dombrowsky

Distributed by Perseus Distribution
www.perseusdistribution.com
To place orders through Perseus Distribution:
Tel: (800) 343-4499
Fax: (800) 351-5073
E-mail: orderentry@perseusbooks.com

Special discounts for bulk sales (minimum of 25 copies) are available.
Please contact Aida Herrera at aida@benbellabooks.com.

For Vinn and Joerg.
I'm beyond blessed for the life
I get to share with you two.

CONTENTS

FOREWORD

HOW DO TWENTIETH-CENTURY COMPANIES become nimble, focused, and feisty? That's a question Sara Roberts asks and answers in this book, and it's a problem I grappled with firsthand while leading a coaching community as Innovation Leader at GE.

In 2013, I initially thought the challenge of rolling out an organization-wide innovation methodology through a large group of willing and eager team members would be relatively straightforward. We had a bevy of supportive tools and templates at our disposal and a century of confidence in the company's track record of reinvention. Yet, we encountered the sort of widespread and subconscious resistance to change that brings to mind Peter Drucker's famous observation that "Culture eats strategy for lunch."

My role was to get several hundred internal coaches aligned around that strategy and equip them to lead their teams through new external offerings and internal processes. I soon discovered that I could not simply rely on templates and methodology to make this happen; there were other, unspoken barriers in the mindset of the coaching team holding us back. Essentially, we were running into an invisible fence called culture. Sara and her group helped make that invisible fence far more visible.

What did that fence look like? Occasionally, for example, we encountered well-intentioned but sometimes over-engineered and limiting processes that hampered our coaches who were trying to guide their teams to think outside the box within volatile markets. We also needed people to take ownership of total outcomes and give up the luxury of being able to say, "I executed on and was in compliance with what that other team told me, so it's not my fault if we didn't hit the mark."

Exposing such mindsets and getting people to be honest with themselves was difficult and even emotional work. More than once I heard a leader say, "I didn't come here to think about me; just give me what I need to help me drive my people." Yet self-awareness and a conscious decision to change mindsets and behaviors is what it takes, we found, to go beyond the current paradigm and understand what kind of culture is necessary at GE for coaches to drive innovation.

Sometimes that honesty provoked hard questions, such as, "Am I the right coach or leader to see this change through?" It's also easy to drift back to familiar comfort zones and risk becoming the kind of manager each of us quietly despises. Sara helped us understand the premise of personal change as a means to culture change, as well as the possibility that we needed more heterogeneity in the people we selected. A mix of personality types and outlooks was important in creating a team of early adopters capable of taking on large-scale organizational change.

We were motivated by the discovery that we were being chartered for a higher purpose than just refashioning internal processes to reap market benefits. Our job was to be courageous leaders able to pivot toward fresh ideas and leverage opportunities for our employees to "play big," deliver more, and have the license to do something amazing. To get there, we needed to implement the roots of a new culture—something that you, the readers of this book, will now have the opportunity to learn how to do.

Simeon Sessley, Innovation Leader, GE

INTRODUCTION

WHY HOW BEATS WHAT

WHAT WOULD YOUR REACTION be if I told you that some of the biggest and most successful organizations today are walking dinosaurs? I'll throw out some candidates, but you could take your pick from any number of major corporations that are familiar household names. General Motors. Yahoo!. Radio Shack. (Oops, already gone.) Best Buy. Sears. Target. Each of these companies was a category maker or leader in its day. Each grew to be a large enterprise that outpaced most competitors. And each has been caught flat-footed in this new era.

You may look at that list and think that's crazy talk. Flat-footed? Some of these companies continue to do very well. And yes, some of them are still very successful in purely financial terms. General Motors is #6 on the Fortune 100 list, Best Buy is #72. But look beyond those rankings and you'll see that more nimble and adaptive organizations are nipping at their heels with disruptive services and approaches that are doing better at meeting customer needs. Irrelevancy is much closer than any of them would prefer to believe, and there's a good chance they'll be too siloed, stuck, and slow to respond in the face of even the most dire threat.

Today we're seeing a great shift in the organizations that win now versus those that won in the past. Companies like Google, Amazon, Netflix, and Facebook have joined the Fortune 500, while many of the old guard— Kodak, the *New York Times*, and Compaq—have been unceremoniously pushed out. And, that turnover is happening much more quickly than anyone might have predicted. Fifty years ago, most firms were expected to last seventy-five years on the Fortune 500 list; today the average life

1

expectancy is down to fifteen years. In 2014, only sixty-one companies from the Fortune 500 list in 1955 remain. At the current turnover rate, it's safe to say the list fifty years from now will be entirely made up of companies that don't currently exist.[1]

Shouldn't that shake the confidence of anyone who leads, works for, or invests in a company today?

I've spent the best and most creative years of my career trying to figure out why some organizations thrive and manage to change their markets and the world while others—even those with great promise, visionary leaders, amazing products, and periods of success—struggle to matter, frequently get in their own way, frustrate customers more often than they delight them, and thwart or stifle talented people rather than develop and inspire them. I've worked at or worked with both kinds of organizations, and the differences can be subtle. Across the board, the CEOs and executives are invariably intelligent and capable; there are heaps of talented and committed people throughout the ranks; products and services are often compelling; and overall intentions are good. Yet in struggling organizations there's something missing.

To a critical but observant eye, organizations that struggle seem to lack the zest, vibrancy, and collective will needed to consistently solve problems, surmount obstacles, and innovate in big ways and small. That energy may be there in pockets, but unfortunately, it is usually stifled or squashed for confusing and complex reasons. Sometimes the leadership gets in the way, but more often than not the organization itself seems to be the problem. It's as though the energy inherent in talented people and creative ideas is out of sync with deeper priorities, including the way decisions are made, how successes and failures are handled, how workflow is planned, and resources are allocated.

When I analyze struggling organizations as a consultant, I find it easy to point out the processes or approaches that bog down efficiency or get in the way of meeting customer needs, or to call out individual leaders or managers who are having a toxic effect on colleagues or reports, or to identify gaps between strategy or innovation and the demands of the market. Yet, I've come to realize that the root cause is more fundamental. The difference most often comes down to an emphasis on "What" versus "How."

The business of the organization is its "What"—*what* goods it produces, *what* services it provides, *what* solutions it offers. The culture of the organization is its "How"—*how* it makes decisions, *how* it views customers, *how* it thinks and feels, *how* it treats people. All organizations balance these two modes in order to function in the world—much as human beings rely on both sides of the brain. But in most organizations, *what* is an urgent priority, while *how* is usually taken for granted.

In most organizations, *what* is an urgent priority, while *how* is usually taken for granted.

In this book, I want to explain why *how* matters far more than *what* and has a much bigger impact on strategy, innovation, and performance than most realize. Along the way, I'll show you what organizations with winning cultures do differently and what you can do to make the culture of your organization the Difference Maker in your own success.

SWITCHING FROM DEFENSE TO OFFENSE

Leaders in most organizations don't see culture as an urgent priority the way they view strategy, innovation, efficiency, customer satisfaction, financial discipline, or any number of other business concerns. Their *what* is the focus of all their hard work and long meetings; their *how* is more likely to be celebrated after the hard work has paid off.

I'm not saying that culture is completely overlooked in such organizations. Indeed, people may be genuinely proud of their organizational culture, and leadership may speak eloquently about the importance of treasuring the legacy of culture or acting as stewards in service of it. Yet even in organizations where culture is valued, it likely functions as little more than a means of defining the organization's special character. Perhaps it also helps the organization resist change and create alignment; or it may serve as a touchstone for decisions as to who belongs or who doesn't, what's acceptable and what isn't, and which direction should be taken or which shouldn't.

In other organizations—often the new and vibrant startups taking the world by storm but also some of the largest, most established, and most prosperous organizations ever—the *how* of culture has a different level of urgency and importance. In these organizations culture is not relied on to play defense but offense. It's not a passive force but an active discipline with a set of deliberate practices and mindsets. It does not preserve the organization from the forces of change but makes it resilient, adaptable, and always moving forward. It is not taken for granted but is relied upon to develop people, overcome setbacks, beat competitors, execute strategy, and innovate.

Culture is not a passive force but an active discipline with a set of deliberate practices and mindsets. It does not preserve the organization from the forces of change but makes it resilient, adaptable, and always moving forward.

Those organizations see *what* as an important tactical challenge, but they believe it's not enough to do *what* exceptionally well in order to succeed. Why not? Because *what* can change at the drop of a hat. Markets shift. Competition gets crowded. Technology alters the game that's being played. If *what* is all you know how to do, then you're likely to continue struggling to do that *what* even when it no longer makes sense. In contrast, if *how* is the source of your resiliency and growth, then you are more likely to know when change and innovation is needed and may even have a pretty good inkling of what needs to be done next.

Effects of Well-Managed Culture

Many have struggled to measure the impact of culture over the years, but recently there have been some important advances in looking at how culture drives an organization's ability to execute. One such study on corporate culture and performance led by James Heskett and John Kotter outlined results for 207 large companies in twenty-two industries over an eleven-year period.[2] Heskett and Kotter reported that companies that managed their cultures well saw revenue increases of 682 percent versus 166 percent for the companies that did not manage their cultures well; stock price increases of 901 percent versus 74 percent; and net income increases of 756 percent versus 1 percent.

CONSTANT VIGILANCE, ALWAYS CHANGING

And yet, developing a winning culture is not the eternal answer to all of your challenges. In fact, just like a winning strategy, a winning product, or a winning approach to customers, success through culture can ultimately make an organization vulnerable to disruption and competition.

Books that proclaim the value of culture often inadvertently point this out. Years later, the organizations that have been showcased start to falter. Sometimes they even fail miserably. What went wrong? Were the metrics used in Jim Collins and Larry Porras' *Built to Last* or Tom Peters and Robert Waterman's *In Search of Excellence* incorrect? I don't think that was the true nature of the problem, even though some of the companies in *Built to Last* have also come upon hard times, and Tom Peters once admitted to "faking the data" when selecting companies like NCR, Wang, or Xerox over a GE.[3] Rather, the decline or downfall of once-heralded organizations is a powerful indicator of just how hard the work of developing and fostering a successful culture can be.

Companies that grow and succeed on the wave of a strong culture are ultimately susceptible to the belief that their culture is sacrosanct and untouchable. Organizations that were once experimental in their evolution and vigilant about their markets, customers, and competitors often become calcified around their culture and resistant to new ideas and new opportunities. They even begin to reject people with different points of view or backgrounds, or who speak out of turn, point out problems, or try to shake things up. They prefer to protect their dominant position and grow in a steady and incremental way, rather than risk change or play bold. Ironically, that's when a once-great culture can actually hold an organization and its people back. Most of us have experienced an environment in which culture actually gets in the way of the organization's goals despite brilliant people, great strategies, and solid operations.

Some leaders believe that culture does not change. Once established by the founders, it is Holy Writ and remains the same forever. Others concede that culture does change but argue that its evolution should and must be organic. In their view, culture is like a slow-moving glacier or a trickle of water in the Grand Canyon—a powerful but subtle force, shaping the landscape of the organization gradually and magnificently over time.

Yet, those cherished myths around culture don't withstand much examination. I have found that cultures:

1. are not immutable and do change over time;
2. can in fact change dramatically and suddenly in a short period of time;
3. are strongly influenced and shaped, for good or ill, deliberately or unintentionally, by the leader.

Just think about GE. One of the original dozen companies on the Dow Jones Industrial Average in 1896, GE is the only company that remains on that list today. As former CEO Jack Welch said, "The reason why GE has been the only company to remain in the Dow Jones from the beginning to the present is that it has changed with the times."[4]

Despite being very well-known and thoroughly studied, GE is not a particularly well-understood company. In my own experience working closely with several of its many high-performing groups, the GE culture is subtle but pervasive. It doesn't scream at you from posters so much as it permeates the way people work and the decisions that get made, big and small. In fact, GE is one of my favorite environments. Each business is very autonomous from corporate and held in high regard, but there's a consistency across what could otherwise have been a sprawling enterprise. The people I've met there are some of the brightest and most aggressive I've known—they're "mad hustlers" when it comes to execution and getting things done. But they're also kind and passionate, generative with ideas rather than skeptical about them, and intensely curious and open-minded.

I asked some prominent people in the organization how much GE culture has changed over the decades, particularly in the transition between CEOs Jack Welch and Jeff Immelt. They said that the culture has shown both remarkable consistency and noticeable shifts as the company has adapted to market forces and new ways of working. Welch's GE was hard-nosed and bottom-line oriented. In a short time, Immelt has shaped GE according to the needs of an era marked by rapid change, global competition, and constant innovation. He's moved decision-making closer to the point of customer interactions and he's challenged overly engineered processes, which have made it harder to meet or respond to customer needs. This has had a big impact on culture. As Vijay Govindarajan says in the *New York Times* of that ongoing change effort, "'Jeff Immelt will have totally remade GE . . . It's a different company for a different time.'"[5]

Raghu Krishnamoorthy, GE's vice president of executive development and chief learning officer, wrote a fascinating piece in the *Harvard Business Review* recently about that imperative of culture change at GE. Everyone knows that product life cycles are getting shorter, Krishnamoorthy explained, but few know that culture also has a life cycle that's getting shorter as well. Indeed, many organizations "get in trouble because of a frozen culture."[6] Significant strategic shifts require shifts in culture too. As Krishnamoorthy put it, "a constant reengineering of our business portfolio, operating model, and culture has been a key to our evolution."[7]

Like all visionary and effective leaders, Welch and Immelt both understand that culture is a tool and a resource to be used deftly and sometimes forcefully to move the company in the direction the leader believes in. If the culture isn't right for the times, that culture needs to shift, too, in ways that reinforce what's working, and to pivot toward what would achieve even better results.

Eric Schmidt, chairman of Google, and Jonathan Rosenberg, former SVP of Products, argue the same belief in their book, *How Google Works*. "Most companies' culture just happens; no one plans it," Schmidt and Rosenberg write. "That can work, but it means leaving a critical component of your success to chance."[8] They warn that even strong cultures may have to change with circumstances for a company to continue being successful. Their advice is to take a hard look at culture and ask, "What problems has this culture caused with the business? It is important not to simply criticize the existing culture, which will just insult people, but rather to draw a connection between business failures and how the culture may have played a hand in those situations. Then articulate the new culture you envision."[9]

I guess we shouldn't be too surprised that a company filled with hyperbright engineers is not afraid to tinker with what's working. In truth, they believe that's the only way it will continue to work.

PUTTING CULTURE INTO ACTION

Organizations need healthy, dynamic cultures and disciplined cultural practices to thrive as circumstances change. In this book, I am going to show you how culture is architected or reconfigured in the first place, and which levers need to be pulled and which measures need to be tracked in order to maintain that dynamism and discipline over time.

In Part I, I am going to do a deeper dive on the importance of culture—why *how* beats *what*—and tell stories of companies that have deliberately architected their cultures to succeed. I'm going to explain why the mindsets of those organizations are critical differentiators and explore the attributes that make the most dynamic companies today "nimble, focused, and feisty." To give you a primer on those terms:

- Nimble companies are much faster and more agile than ordinary organizations.
- Focused companies use their sense of purpose as a lens to understand and meet the needs of customers and markets.
- Feisty companies play big and act bold in order to capitalize on advantages and out-muscle the competition.

In Part II, I'm going to show you how you can architect your own culture to bring the same dynamism and discipline to your organization. I'll start with purpose because that is how you focus your organization on what your people have been brought together to do. Then I'll look at the structures and processes you will need to be nimble, and at the attitudes and practices that enable you to be feisty.

There is no such thing as a permanent advantage anymore—not in a world changing this quickly. But if you build your organization to be nimble, focused, and feisty you will be far more resilient to the chaos and turmoil of our time, and much more likely to be leading disruption rather than being disrupted and outperformed by others.

1

HOW CULTURE MAKES OR BREAKS YOU

ON NOVEMBER 6, 2013, the death knell rang for Blockbuster Video. The floundering organization announced that it would close its 300 remaining US stores by January 2014 and terminate its DVD-by-mail rental service.

Even in an age of disruption, this was a remarkable downfall. In 2004, less than a decade earlier, Blockbuster had thoroughly dominated the video-rental business and was one of the most visible and well-known retail brands in the country with 10,000 stores, more than 60,000 employees, and a market value of $5 billion.

So, what happened? How could a thriving company at the top of its game go extinct so quickly?

That question is at the heart of this book, and it's one that every leader needs to ask about his or her own organization. How do we keep our businesses vital, innovative, and ahead of competitors when yesterday's success means next to nothing in whatever world we'll face tomorrow?

The answer is culture.

How do we keep our businesses vital, innovative, and ahead of competitors when yesterday's success means next to nothing in whatever world we'll face tomorrow?

The answer is culture.

THE ICEBERG THEORY

I chose the story of Blockbuster to open this book because it provides a stark example of the fate of a company when its market and competitive landscape suddenly change, and the organization is unable to successfully respond. At the same time, Blockbuster will also show us how easy it is to point to those changes and say that strategy or operations or leadership or technology is the reason for the collapse, allowing us to overlook the larger and more fundamental question of culture that lurks, like the invisible portion of an iceberg, below the surface.

The easiest way to explain the fall of Blockbuster is to point to Netflix and Redbox. That's what happened on the surface. The business press chalked up Blockbuster's demise to a "failure to innovate," and Blockbuster became a case study in the way market leaders grow complacent and overlook the disruptions of pesky upstart competitors.

The story stuck because it makes sense and fits our growing understanding of how challenging the global economy has become. Blockbuster—like McDonald's, Sony, or Best Buy—represented the traditional approach to long-term growth and success: achieve a dominant market position and leverage the advantages of scale and brand to lock in customers, accrue revenue, and perpetuate success. Once upon a time, that strategy, if decently executed, seemed unassailable. But no one is surprised anymore when the story ends with Goliath encountering some David wielding a new slingshot. The deeper question is why companies like Blockbuster that appear so formidable and solid by traditional measures become unexpectedly vulnerable to disruptive competition.

When we dig into the details of the innovation explanation, it's easy to understand why it's so compelling. Blockbuster was attacked on two fronts at once. One assault came on the ground when Redbox arrived in 2002 with a new retail strategy that was deceptively old-fashioned. Instead of stand-alone stores, Redbox put DVD vending machines in other retail outlets. To Blockbuster, a few hundred DVDs in a kiosk probably didn't seem like much of a threat given the giant inventory of movies at a single Blockbuster retail store. Yet, with lower overhead, Redbox was able to slash DVD rental costs to one dollar and compete with Blockbuster on price and convenience. Within five years, Redbox had more US locations than Blockbuster.

The second and ultimately more significant assault came from the air. Netflix started as a subscription-based DVD mail-delivery service. What Netflix lacked in convenience, it made up for with a large catalogue of movies, an easy way to organize and order rentals online, and a lack of late fees. Famously, the idea for the business arose after co-founder and CEO Reed Hastings was forced to pay forty dollars in late fees to Blockbuster for a copy of *Apollo 13*. Hastings knew that the dissatisfaction he felt over that penalty was something just about every Blockbuster customer could relate to, so he came up with a revenue model that didn't rely on making customers angry.

Capitalizing on pent-up customer frustration is a classic path to disruptive innovation, and Netflix made that impulse part of its core. In 2007, the same year Redbox surpassed Blockbuster in retail outlets, Netflix took pre-emptive steps to disrupt its own delivery model and introduced a streaming service. This, many believe, was the final nail in Blockbuster's coffin. Blockbuster was not too big to fail; it was too big to respond.

Or so the story goes.

At a strategic level, the explanation that disruptive innovation from new competitors killed Blockbuster is a good lesson to absorb. Dominant companies rise and fall all the time, and Davids often slay Goliaths. To stay on top, companies need to aggressively reinvent themselves in line with changing customer needs. In the famous words of Andy Grove, "Only the paranoid survive."

The problem, however, is that in Blockbuster's case that narrative is wrong. It wasn't innovation, change, or a pesky competitor that did Blockbuster in. That was just the tip of the iceberg. Below the surface of the water, Blockbuster collided with the culture that it had relied upon to become so dominant in the first place.

THE REST OF THE ICEBERG

Blockbuster came to rule the retail movie-rental market by improving customer experience and offering the kind of ubiquity, convenience, and access to movies that independent video stores couldn't deliver. Its revenue model was strong, the brand was powerful, performance was excellent, and by the time John Antioco became CEO in 1997, just as the dot-com boom was beginning, the company was in an enviable position. Even so, Antioco knew that Blockbuster couldn't stand pat. He wanted to change the company at its core by making it more responsive to customer needs and more agile with new technology, while continuing to innovate its business model. Blockbuster only had about 25 percent market share then and plenty of room to grow. Indeed, it would grow to about 40 percent before Antioco was done.

Antioco was an accomplished turnaround expert who'd been raised in the world of retail. He'd helped 7-Eleven achieve prominence and had been instrumental in returning Circle K and Taco Bell to profitability. When he was tapped to head Blockbuster, he was excited because it gave him the opportunity to give "customers what they want while still making money for the company."[1] Much of the success Antioco did achieve with Blockbuster came from this customer focus.

Indeed, one of the things customers wanted was newly released movies. At the time, however, movie studios charged rental companies sixty-five dollars per VHS tape, and that upfront investment was too large to stock enough titles to give customers easy access, especially when demand would drop off within a few weeks. So Antioco went to movie studios and persuaded them to flip that business model—take less up front for more on the back end—and Blockbuster began a policy of guaranteeing the availability of new releases, which helped sales and market share grow. Chalk up one big win for innovation.

Video-on-demand was a worry but not yet technically feasible to achieve at scale. Instead, it was the arrival of DVDs that proved to be the Trojan horse that allowed Redbox and Netflix to challenge the video-rental giant. Unlike VHS tapes, DVDs could be easily stocked in kiosks or delivered in inexpensive mailers. Nevertheless, though Blockbuster was a little slow to switch to DVDs, once it did respond, the company continued to thrive because of its market dominance. Daunted by his overwhelming foe, Netflix CEO Hastings proposed a partnership with Blockbuster in 2000 in which Netflix would leverage its internet-delivery prowess to manage Blockbuster's online brand while Blockbuster would promote Netflix in its stores. Blockbuster refused in part because it had its own web strategy in mind.

Antioco didn't see new technology as a threat to Blockbuster so much as an opportunity. He decided to build a fairly radical model for the time—called Blockbuster Total Access—in which customers could choose to do business in one of the company's retail stores or online through Blockbuster.com. By the mid-2000s, Total Access dominated the video-rental market. Around the same time, Blockbuster also decided to eliminate late fees even though they accounted for 16 percent of total revenues. Antioco knew that penalizing customers was no way to thrive long-term.

Soon, Blockbuster was on the march again, stealing nearly a million customers from Netflix each year. By 2007, things were so bleak for Netflix that Hastings sought and obtained permission from his board to begin merger talks with Blockbuster.[2]

On the brink of total victory, however, everything changed for Blockbuster. The board put a full stop to the direction Blockbuster was engaged in and forced out Antioco because they disliked many of the changes he had made, such as cutting out 16 percent of revenue by rescinding late fees. In Antioco's place, they hired James Keyes. Keyes had been the CEO of 7-Eleven from 2000 to 2005, presiding over a remarkable thirty-six consecutive quarters of same-store sales growth, which by 2004, had resulted in global revenues of $41 billion. To the board, Keyes seemed like the perfect candidate to lead the company into the future because he more closely resembled the Blockbuster of the past.[3] He had the experience of scaling and stabilizing a highly successful retailer that seemed to be on every street corner throughout the United States. That was the Blockbuster the board knew and understood.

Keyes' vision was to make Blockbuster the 7-Eleven of video stores. He believed that stable growth in retail locations and expanded products within those locations would make Blockbuster successful.

Keyes' vision was to make Blockbuster the 7-Eleven of video stores. He believed that stable growth in retail locations and expanded products within those locations would make Blockbuster successful.

After being named CEO, he quickly restructured his team, ridding the company of Antioco's lieutenants as though they were a virus and promptly naming a new CFO, CIO, general counsel, and vice president of merchandising, distribution, and logistics.[4] Then he redirected Blockbuster's online business strategy to an in-store, retail-oriented model because he couldn't see the potential value of a DVD-by-mail service, nor the relevance and opportunities that Blockbuster.com may have presented. "The Internet is worthless, and we're getting out of it," he declared.[5] "I've been frankly confused by this fascination that everybody has with Netflix . . . Netflix doesn't really have or do anything that we can't or don't already do ourselves."[6]

Antioco had compressed some of the hierarchy at Blockbuster as part of his approach to modernizing the company and given retail clerks a lot of freedom to solve customer problems and see to their needs. Keyes put that hierarchy back in, reestablishing many layers of management between the top team and the customer. As a result, decisions were increasingly made without any direct experience of customer needs or their frustrations with the Blockbuster experience.[7] Thus, employees at the prized retail stores—who had briefly enjoyed how good it felt to satisfy customers—became intensely frustrated by policies that got in their way. For example, to take breaks, under Keyes' reign, retail employees had to clock in and out under extraordinarily strict guidelines, regardless of how busy the store may have been at the time. They also were mandated to restock damaged DVDs despite customer complaints and, to cut costs, were deliberately understaffed on peak weekend nights, so they did not even have time to restock or tidy shelves. They knew, better than anyone insulated at the top, that Blockbuster customers were eager for better alternatives, yet they were not allowed to do anything about it.[8]

Keyes was blind to these problems and probably believed his own words when he said, "Blockbuster is a turnaround explosion just waiting for a spark. If we exceed the expectations of our customers, we will in turn exceed the expectations of our shareholders."

Of course, this statement reads like a bad joke today now that Blockbuster is gone and Netflix is worth more than ten times what Blockbuster was at its peak.

OLD WAY VS. NEW WAY

Why did Keyes stop Blockbuster from attempting a new way? I believe it was because he saw the traditional Blockbuster culture—a brick-and-mortar business model built to leverage scale and brand—as a permanent strength, and structured the organization and its strategy accordingly. But it was this same locked-in culture that didn't allow the company to react and innovate when it needed to adapt. Keyes and his team refused to look at or internalize the current truths they faced in the marketplace, and they wouldn't take the time to understand emerging technologies or shifting consumer behaviors that threatened to completely disrupt the home-entertainment industry. Keyes' personal leadership style, best characterized as a "don't question me and let's execute" mentality, made it easy for everyone to put on blinders and plow ahead. And, whenever employees got glimpses of market truth, the company wasn't positioned or structured to respond. In the end, changing its business model to survive in a new reality was going to cost money, resources, and creative energy that Blockbuster was unwilling and unable to spend.

As we all know, this narrative is not an isolated one. Many big companies that were incredibly successful in the twentieth century are failing and floundering in the twenty-first. Pundits and journalists usually point to a lack of execution and innovation. Yet it's the organizational culture that large companies built in the process of becoming successful and powerful in the twentieth century that is now defeating them in this new era. Many such companies continue to fixate on doing more or better at *what* has made them successful in the past—offering a particular product or service at scale—while not yet recognizing that today the *how* of a company—what it stands for, what matters to it, how it tends to the changing needs of its people and customers—is infinitely more important.

Many companies fixate on doing more or better at *what* has made them successful in the past—offering a particular product or service at scale—while not yet recognizing that today the *how* of a company— what it stands for, what matters to it, how it tends to the changing needs of its people and customers—is infinitely more important.

Much of the inertia of traditional companies can be traced back to their cultural roots. Who were they when they first started? What were their goals? What was the mindset of these formidable pioneers? What worked in the twentieth century?

Winning in the twentieth century required getting big and then managing for stability. Companies were focused on the *what*—their strategy or their product. And they had plenty of time and resources to do the *what* well. The world moved much more slowly than it does today, so in general it was possible to pick a strategy, execute it well, and become successful as a result. Accordingly, twentieth-century companies built their organizations to meet quality, quantity, and cost drivers, and they produced products to meet clear demand, while distributing in a mass market, and standardizing all processes and outputs to maximize efficiency.

Enterprises operating this way today are clinging to the same mindset that James Keyes held on to—a belief that scale, mass, and efficiency will provide an eternal advantage. In contrast, Netflix has actually developed a theory to describe why success in business eventually leads to failure.[9] Netflix believes that growth increases organizational complexity and the potential for chaos, and that companies naturally respond by specializing on a narrower range of success factors and putting more processes in place to dampen the chaos. However, this restricts what makes working for a particular organization interesting, creative, and engaging and drives talent and diversity of thinking out. The long-term outcome of failure isn't seen at first because as this is all happening, the business continues to perform well or even better, and short-term outcomes are improved. But when the market shifts—as it is bound to do—the company is left without the talented people, emotional commitment, or creative range to respond. A focus on *what* has smothered the reliance on *how*.

Mark Parker, the CEO of Nike, sees cultural inertia as a very deadly, self-perpetuating, and existential threat. He says, "One of my fears is being this big, slow, constipated, bureaucratic company that's happy with its success. Companies fall apart when their model is so successful that it stifles thinking that challenges it. It's like what the Joker said—'This town needs an enema.' When needed, you've got to apply that enema, so to speak."[10]

While that may be a more vivid depiction than many care to imagine, it's critical that we understand how culture can cause a company to resist, adapt, or lead in this new environment.

It's easy to think that companies like Apple and Google are "winning" now because they're smarter at product, packaging, and positioning. In reality, it's their *how* that propels their unique *what*. It's their culture—the principles behind how they do what they do, and think what they think, as an organization—that makes them successful.

Dig more deeply into these organizations and you'll see that for them culture is a *verb*, not a *noun*. It isn't about ping-pong tables and Happy Hour Fridays. It's about leveraging culture as the key driver to success. Culture is how they operate and consciously create an environment and organization that enables them to innovate according to market needs, execute the strategy they think is best, and deliver on their purpose.

Cracking the code on that *how* and reinforcing it in everything the organization does is the most important thing any leader can do today to help his or her organization survive and thrive.

THE CULTURE DIFFERENCE IN A COMPLEX WORLD

If culture is so critical to the performance of the most successful organizations today, why isn't that more self-evident to people working in business?

I believe it's because culture is highly intangible and abstract compared with other business concerns. Hard-nosed business leaders—and all of us with pressing challenges and urgent priorities who are under stress to "make the numbers"—can easily overlook culture because it is difficult to observe, measure, and manage, and frankly touchy-feely in nature.

Even the concept of culture is abstract. I think of it as the set of tacit understandings and beliefs that drive behaviors, ways of thinking, and ways of talking and interacting that the people within a particular group perceive are right or normal. These, in turn, shape the practices of the group, the outputs of its work, and its reputation or brand. In other words, I see culture most tangibly in *how* people act, including *how* they make decisions, *how* they treat colleagues and customers, *how* they define and reward success, talk about problems, view the world, plan for the future, develop products, etc.

We're exiting a world in which culture was largely left untended to grow organically. The culture of a society—whether it's a small tribe or a church group or a modern nation-state—often forms in this way. Slowly, over time, due in part to the insular nature of the group and its identification as being separate from the rest of the world, distinctions form, get reinforced, and become marks of uniqueness. That uniqueness is the culture's particular *how*—how it thinks, how it acts, how it defines what's right.

When you think of culture as developing through a slow, organic process, it's easy to grasp how that particular approach mapped well with the rise of the twentieth-century organization. Traditionally, organizations were founded for a *what*—to mass-produce an automobile or a computer, to deliver oil or electricity, to provide a specific restaurant or hotel experience anywhere the customer happened to go, and they were built to do basically the same thing over and over as efficiently as possible in order to meet an ever-expanding market need while fending off others who tried to do much the same thing. The culture—the *how*—may have been instilled by a particularly intentional founder or leader, but it grew out of the processes and approaches that defined success within that model.

The more success accrued, the more that culture was reinforced. Indeed, we have seen throughout history that organizations with the "strongest" cultures are the ones that have been, in Jim Collins' words, "Built to Last." Collins' research was based on the long-term success of definitive market leaders that had bested rivals with similar processes. Culture, to Collins, was the critical difference between those comparison companies. And this rings true to our understanding of twentieth-century organizations. Over decades, reinforced by success, the culture of lasting companies becomes locked-in and distinct. It was said, in the *Mad Men* era, that you could always tell someone who worked at an IBM or a GM by how he dressed, how he talked and acted, even how he thought.

We've entered a world in which companies come and go, break up and reform, and change direction at a much more dynamic rate. This started to happen in the early 1990s, when the big companies of the twentieth century, such as IBM or GE, began to divest themselves of major business lines and lay off tens of thousands of employees in response to market and financial pressures. And it accelerated as capital markets became attracted to the new technology startups of the dot-com era, when companies were formed and grew dramatically in valuation almost overnight.

The US military coined a term in the 1990s to describe the increasingly unsettled political, social, and economic environment: VUCA, which stands for volatile, uncertain, complex, and ambiguous. Today, it feels as though the pressures of VUCA have become even more daunting and real.

What are the root causes of this change? The suspects comprise a familiar lineup—technology, consumer expectations, globalization, capital markets, and employee expectations (you know those Millennials). However, it's helpful to understand the influence of each in the context of the effect on corporate culture.

Technology and Consumer Expectations

Let's start with technology. When information technology first began to change our world, it seemed as though its impact would be felt mostly in what companies could do and how people worked. Today, it's clear that technology has had an even more radical impact on consumer expectations and habits. People now expect technology to deliver them whatever they want, whenever they want it, as cheaply as possible with no more effort than a swipe of a finger on a smartphone. This has led to incredible malleability in how and what we consume. Consumers are now willing to shift product loyalties or delivery mechanisms at the drop of a hat. Indeed, more than 60 percent of consumers who interact with brands today do so through multiple channels.[11] Social media has normalized real-time responses, and consumers expect that immediacy in all aspects of their lives. They want consistency and quality regardless of time, place, device, or medium. Companies, meanwhile, are in a race to figure out how to reconfigure themselves to meet those insatiable needs and extremely high expectations.

Globalization

Globalization is another force that has affected how and what we expect from businesses. Once upon a time, products and services had a strong regional basis. Now, they can be delivered and consumed anywhere, any time, 24/7. Competitors are no longer next door; they're all over the world and able to leverage lower overhead and a just-in-time global delivery system to beat you at whatever game you choose to play. This further reduces the value of the *what* and puts a premium on the *how*.

Capital Markets

Capital markets have the same global freedom. Once, relationships with investors and bankers were long-term, intimate, and clubby. Today, trillions of dollars zip from one side of the global economy to another in response to exciting new investment opportunities, thus abandoning less-promising ones without mercy. The appeal of "what" is more fleeting than ever; only "how" can sustain the interest of fickle capital.

Employee Expectations

Employee expectations have also changed dramatically. While people can't move about quite as easily as goods, services, or capital yet, they are no longer as tied to geographic regions for employment. Working remotely or virtually is now unremarkable. Teams all over the world can collaborate in real time. And Millennials, in particular, are drawn to places of work that engage and stimulate them, and they enjoy the freedom to be choosy. As a group, they are adaptive and innovative by nature and prefer their employer to be so, as well. They aren't attracted to traditional hierarchical structures, and they want to work for businesses that support innovation and thrive on change. In fact, according to Deloitte's third annual Millennial Survey, 78 percent of Millennials are influenced by how innovative a company is when deciding whether they want to work there, and most say their current employer does not encourage them to think creatively.[12]

Millennials also care about company purpose and culture like no other generation before them. *Forbes* reports that 60 percent of Millennials leave their companies in less than three years, with the primary reason tied to the lack of a good cultural fit.[13] And they consume products with the values of the companies making those products in mind. All of this points, once again, to the importance of "how" over what.

Can twentieth-century culture evolve to meet the demands and pressures of the twenty-first century VUCA reality?

The difference between old-era culture and new-era culture is striking. A winning culture in the twentieth century was methodical, efficient, and hierarchical. It was built with industrial needs in mind to cohere around simple processes that could be scaled. It benefited from squeezing out variation as a way of reducing noise and controlling chaos. It won by focusing relentlessly on the *what*, and doing that same *what* over and over again. It changed when it had to, but only after long deliberation, exhaustive analysis, and as little course correction as possible.

Indeed, that description is one of the reasons why culture—so vaunted in the 1990s by the likes of Jim Collins and Tom Peters, among others—is under attack today as a force actually holding companies back. UC Berkeley's Jennifer Chatman, a thought leader in research on organizational culture, acknowledges this when she writes, "Conventionally, researchers have argued that strong cultures that align employee behavior with organizational objectives should boost performance. More recently, research has shown that a strong culture can actually stifle creativity and innovation in dynamic environments because people are adhering too closely to routines creating behavioral uniformity, inertia, and an inward focus."[14]

In other words, in a VUCA world, some believe that a strong culture can limit or hamstring an organization rather than bolster and protect it. And certainly this holds true when we think of a Blockbuster or similar behemoth. But Chatman's research actually shows that a strong culture, in and of itself, is not disadvantageous today if—and it's a big *IF*—that culture prizes adaptability and innovation over stability and process while also relying on strong alignment with values to direct people, rather than enforced adherence to rigid policies and rules. In fact, such companies— the ones with strong, cohesive, adaptive, innovative cultures—are performing better financially today and growing faster over time in spite of the turbulence of a VUCA world.

In essence, Chatman is saying that a strong culture reinforces a vigorous company's direction because that company can successfully adapt or change depending on strategic needs or market forces. If the culture is too weak, people will not know what to do or how to act in tumultuous circumstances, and the organization will lose its way. But companies can go too far. If the culture is too calcified and inflexible, the company will be unable to adapt and innovate effectively.

I think of culture as the guide and the glue of an organization. When culture provides the kind of clarity and intentionality that support its "why" or purpose and the characteristics of its "how," it helps people see and understand where they need to go. At the same time, when cultural values and characteristics are fully integrated into the fabric of how the organization operates, culture serves as the glue that binds everyone together around norms, expectations, mindsets, and behaviors. In the best organizations, this sense of cohesion and direction is aligned with programs, practices, and processes that reinforce a sense of rightness and shared passion in directing energies toward common goals.

When culture provides the kind of clarity and intentionality that support its "why" or purpose and the characteristics of its "how," it helps people see and understand where they need to go.

Chatman describes companies that are highly adaptable, innovative, and values-driven as characterized by "risk-taking, willingness to experiment, initiative-taking, along with the ability to be fast-moving and quick to take advantage of opportunities."

NIMBLE, FOCUSED, AND FEISTY

When I consider Chatman's research through the lens of my own and add my experience working directly with organizations that thrive or struggle, I see the types of companies she's talking about as ones that have a very particular type of culture: one that is "nimble, focused, and feisty." These are the companies that win in the twenty-first century.

Let's look at each of these traits in turn.

Nimble

Companies that are nimble have structures and processes to guide them, but they encourage and foster adaptability, innovation, and risk-taking rather than impede it. This flexibility allows them to respond quickly to new developments, market shifts, opportunities, learnings, or customer demands.

Focused

Companies that are focused are not free-for-alls without limits. Instead, they work hard to build consensus and alignment around the culture as a way of binding employees together in the pursuit of common goals and mutual passions. That shared mission is reinforced by how the members of the culture communicate, work together, make decisions, and plan, among other activities. The unified sense of purpose that results helps people focus like a laser on the customer and understand how their individual contributions make a difference.

Feisty

And companies that are feisty have leaders and team members who are oriented toward making a major difference in the world and are eager to act bold and play big. They hire, promote, and reward accordingly, and they reject people who are not exceptional, creative, or driven enough to meet those expectations or who do not fit the culture and play well with others.

Throughout the chapters of part one of the book, I will share how these companies bring these characteristics to life through each of these three lenses.

SHARING PASSION

Brian Chesky, the CEO and co-founder of Airbnb, published a famous memo in 2013 that he sent to all the employees of his firm as a reminder to keep culture front and center. The memo was titled "Don't Fuck Up the Culture" and it was based on advice given to the senior team by noted venture capitalist Peter Thiel. Thiel had just given Airbnb $150 million in additional funding, and Chesky asked him for his single most important piece of advice for their continued success. Chesky was surprised that Thiel would emphasize culture, but Thiel knew that culture had been critical in Airbnb's success so far and would continue to be in the future so long as that culture did not become stale, bureaucratic, and stifling. Airbnb, after all, had a nifty idea and a good approach, but it owned no tangible assets, just like Uber, Facebook, and Alibaba, some of the biggest companies in the world today. What Airbnb did have that would be more difficult to replicate or compete against was its culture or its *how*.

Chesky did a nice job summing up why that was important. "Culture," he wrote, "is simply a shared way of doing something with passion." Airbnb has very deliberately established a particular culture—one that supports creativity, individual decision-making, problem-solving, customer closeness, collaboration across fluid teams, and fun.[15] The danger, according to Thiel, is that as Airbnb continues to grow and reaches a certain size, the need to develop processes that "control the chaos" and help achieve short-term outcomes that meet growth expectations (as Netflix also noted) will begin to overwhelm what matters to the people in the business. Chesky knew that if Airbnb's culture stayed strong, there would be less need for corporate processes, more trust and engagement, and more of the autonomy and freedom needed to surface and pursue entrepreneurial ideas. He acknowledged that Airbnb would probably not always be in the same business, but would need to grow and change with new opportunities and market demands. A strong culture—not a brilliant strategy, more market share, or a better website—would make that possible. And he believed that such a culture could be "defended" and reinforced through how Airbnb hired and how its employees went about their work and related to one another.

In contrast, Myspace is an example of a company that did not defend its culture well. Once upon a time, Myspace was a dominant social-networking platform. In 2005, it was acquired by News Corp for $580 million. While it is understandable that the Myspace founders, Chris DeWolfe and Tom Anderson, took Rupert Murdoch's money, and they clearly cared enough about the company to stay on, this new development did little to keep the Myspace culture strong. DeWolfe talks about how the added bureaucracy of a big company was particularly a shock to Myspace. "There are more meetings during the day with a big company,"

DeWolfe said. "There are three different levels of finance that you need to go through . . . you end up taking your eye off the ball."[16] And new priorities came into play that overwhelmed the user experience, engineering quality, innovation, and sense of fun that had typified the Myspace culture. There was extreme pressure to monetize the site and drive revenue at the cost of the user experience, the quality of the engineering, the level of innovation, and the fun for all involved.[17] Though the money started rolling in and the number of users continued to rise, News Corp persisted in driving changes that not only impeded future growth but also frustrated or turned off customers, employees, and partners who had very different cultural expectations for Myspace.

Myspace reached its peak of popularity three years later in December 2008, when it attracted 75.9 million unique visitors per month. But by April 2009, Myspace had started losing about a million US users each month and its ad revenue was dropping as a result. DeWolfe and Anderson were kicked to the curb. Within two years, News Corp began looking for a buyer to take Myspace off its hands. By May 2011, the user number had dropped to half its peak at about 34.8 million. In June 2011, it was purchased for $35 million, more than half a billion less than when it first sold in 2005.

The companies that are thriving in this new era, the ones we think of as category makers or market leaders, have founders or leaders who are very deliberate, purposeful, and even tactical about developing an organizational culture they believe will be a Difference Maker in their success. They recognize that culture was a winning formula for companies in the past and is today too. But instead of waiting for culture to form slowly over many years, these companies have learned how to accelerate that development by architecting it deliberately, and they see safeguarding it with a vengeance as one of their primary responsibilities.

Think back on the Netflix vs. Blockbuster story at the beginning of this chapter. By 2001, Netflix was on the ropes competitively with Blockbuster, but it was also starting to grow dramatically. It needed to add a tremendous number of employees to keep up with that growth, and it knew that it needed the right people to do so. So Netflix focused on reaching highly talented people who fit the culture.

Reed Hastings and Patty McCord, Netflix's talent manager, sat down and wrote out all the things that mattered to Netflix from a culture, process, and people perspective, and put it in a 124-slide PowerPoint deck called "Netflix Culture: Freedom & Responsibilities." Sheryl Sandberg, Facebook's COO, and the author of *Lean In,* said, "It may well be the most important document ever to come out of the Valley."[18]

In it, Hastings and McCord laid out a definition of the Netflix culture, why it mattered, and why it actually needed to be a lived set of values, not just a bunch of meaningless words. It defined the characteristics that led to success at Netflix, and what the environment of Netflix needed to be to foster and leverage those characteristics. And it talked about the vital importance of culture and alignment over rules and procedures. As slide forty-two put it, "Our model is to *increase* employee freedom as we grow, rather than limit it, to continue to attract and nourish innovative people, so we have better chance of sustained success."[19] The deck ended with, "We keep improving our culture as we grow."

That's a radically different approach to culture, people, and processes than most companies born and bred in the twentieth century. Such a deck wouldn't get past an HR manager let alone legal at a twentieth-century company. But it's the "most important document ever to come out of the Valley" to those who understand the value of nimble, focused, and feisty. And it's a choice that's being consciously and deliberately made by the most vital companies and most successful CEOs working today.

OLD WAY VS. NEW WAY VS. RIGHT WAY

This discussion of culture is not just a way of glorifying new-economy companies and kicking twentieth century market leaders while they're down. In fact, very few companies—old or new—are sufficiently nimble, focused, and feisty across the board. All companies have work to do. All companies must continue to work at their culture in an engaged, determined, and conscientious way—forever. The world is too dynamic—too VUCA—to take a break on culture.

Moreover, any company—even one with a twentieth-century culture— can become nimble, focused, and feisty. It is possible to both architect such a culture and to shape and mold it. This book has been written to help all types of companies—from the startup still being planned in a basement apartment, to the Fortune 500 at the top of its game.

To illustrate how culture change can revitalize a stagnant organization, I want to look at the evolution of a company we all know well—Apple. While many hold Apple up as a model company because of its incredible success and market value, it's worth looking at the journey Apple took to get where it is today.

Apple's Journey

When Apple was launched in 1976, it was the Facebook, Airbnb, or Netflix of its day. The founders were passionate and they took the world by storm.

Then Apple started to get big, and it faced intense new demands to "grow up." In a twentieth-century world, this meant adopting discipline and processes. Steve Jobs valued the culture of innovation and passion that made Apple special; and he wanted to put most of his attention on the part of the company that embodied such culture—its product development and design. But he wanted someone else—a grown-up—to take over the operations side and give Apple the discipline it needed to satisfy investors. So he asked John Sculley, who had been president of Pepsi-Cola, to be CEO. Like Keyes at Blockbuster, Sculley was a classic twentieth-century culture leader, and Jobs and he clashed badly, until Jobs was ousted in the spring of 1985.

Apple was lost in the years that followed. Its culture was rudderless. It tried to adhere to the discipline of industrial production but had no spark, passion, or innovation. Steve Jobs returned as interim CEO. The turnaround began. Apple resumed its iconic status and took that a million miles farther, reinventing modern life as we know it and becoming the most profitable and valuable company in the world by the time of Jobs' death.

How that turnaround was engineered, however, had everything to do with culture.

It's fascinating to watch the early speeches Jobs made to employees upon his return. He talked about getting back to the basics of great products, great marketing, and great distribution. The distribution piece showed that he had "grown up" when it came to running a big company. But he also retained his incredible passion and creativity for products that mattered to customers and mattered to Apple.

Employees embraced that passion immediately. They didn't mind when projects they'd been toiling on were canceled because they were given new products to work on that made sense—that connected with Apple's culture. And Jobs understood how marketing was an expression of that culture. As he put it, "Nike doesn't talk about the product [in its marketing]. They honor great athletes and athletics. Customers want to know who Apple is, what do we stand for, and where do we fit in this world. Apple is not about making boxes, though we do that well, but at its core value, we believe that people with passion can change the world for the better."

He launched the "think different" campaign to rekindle Apple's spark and announce its values to the world, describing it as a message that "touches the soul of this company."

How many twentieth-century companies talk about their soul when they talk about their culture? How many nimble, focused, and feisty companies would even blink at such a notion?

It's hard to believe, but Apple is an old company now. And with its founder gone, and its success unprecedented, it would be incredibly easy for Apple to rest on its laurels and see its culture of innovation, adaptation, design, and its drive for category-maker leadership go stale. But Tim Cook, as CEO, has done an extraordinary job keeping Apple Apple. He talks eloquently about Jobs' attention to culture and how that keeps him focused on the same concerns.

"Steve's greatest contribution and gift is the company and its culture," Cook said. "He cared deeply about that." Elaborating, Cook described how Jobs did so. "It was his selection of people that helped propel the culture. You hear these stories of him walking down a hallway and going crazy over something he sees, and yeah, those things happened. But extending that story to imagine that he did everything at Apple is selling him way short. What he did more than anything was build a culture and pick a great team, that would then pick another great team, that would then pick another team, and so on."

Instead of letting that culture go stale, Apple continues to nurture it, and it does so intimately but also at scale. That approach went into the design of the new Apple campus. According to Cook, "Steve wanted people to love Apple, not just work for Apple, but really love Apple, and really understand at a deep level what Apple was about, about the values of the company. He didn't write them on the walls and make posters out of them anymore, but he wanted people to understand them. He wanted people to work for a greater cause."

And to keep that culture alive for generations of employees to come, Jobs initiated the development of Apple University. According to Cook, "[Jobs] wanted to use it to grow the next generation of leaders at Apple, and to make sure the lessons of the past weren't forgotten."

On the curriculum: how to communicate, examining past decisions to find flaws and better answers, and culture.

If Apple, one of the largest companies in the world, can become nimble, focused, and feisty, so can any business at any stage.

2

A DIFFERENT MINDSET

IN SPRING 2004, a few months before the company's IPO, Google released an 80,000-word prospectus to its current and potential investors. The document opened with a letter from co-founders Larry Page and Sergey Brin.

"Google is not a conventional company," they began. "We do not intend to become one. Throughout Google's evolution as a privately held company, we have managed Google differently. We have also emphasized an atmosphere of creativity and challenge."

And so began a long and carefully constructed statement as to exactly what kind of publicly traded company Google intended to be.

Though the letter was inspired by Warren Buffett's own approach to talking to his investors, Wall Street had never seen anything quite like it before. Buffett is a legend, and investors hang onto his words like groupies. In contrast, here was a young startup—albeit a very promising one with an exciting IPO in the offing—dictating to investors in no uncertain terms how differently it would think and behave as a shareholder-owned entity.

Bold and refreshing to some, the Google founders' letter to others was an expression of arrogant immaturity. The phrase "Don't be evil" struck many in particular as a simplistic take on the way conventional companies generate capital and shareholder value. Yet the "founder's letter" has become a rite of passage in Silicon Valley in the years since, imitated by other startup CEOs, such as Groupon's Andrew Mason and Facebook's

Mark Zuckerberg, before their own ceremonial IPO. This is despite sniffs of disdain and outright pushback from the establishment. One commentator in 2012, for example, noted that Zuckerberg in his letter used the word "people" forty-one times in eighty-three sentences and the word "business" only seven times, then proclaimed that reality would soon overcome such idealism. "Whether thrust defiantly into the faces of would-be shareholders or proffered delicately as a corporate heirloom of inestimable value, such epistles are doomed to enter into a slow, painful strangulation as market forces have their way."[1]

Why would a company's founders—on the verge of becoming incredibly rich through the good faith of the investment community—bother to articulate and share thoughts and beliefs that go well beyond—or even contradict—the traditional concerns of business?

For the most part, a prospectus is a dry and technical document, heavy on whatever numbers and calculations support a firm's approach to a particular way of doing business. The prospectus is written in this way because that is what investors look for when they are trying to assess the firm's capacity to generate profit, gain market share, execute strategy, and earn shareholder returns. The founders of Google, Groupon, and Facebook, on the other hand, feel that something else—something beyond the numbers— has made them successful to this point and will help them continue to be great destinations for investment capital long into the future.

Note that those founders are not describing their vision or culture but something even deeper and more intrinsic to their purpose. I call this nebulous thing their mindset.

PART CANNON SHOT, PART WEDDING VOW

What is a mindset? The simplest explanation is that a mindset guides the way an organization acts and operates, but that's almost a throwaway description that does not fully capture the power of the concept. In my view, an organizational mindset is the most intangible and yet critical belief to define because it is intrinsic to the organization's culture, vision, purpose, values, strategy, and way of acting in the world.

Typically, you can see mindset most clearly in action. Yet, in many organizations mindset can be very confusing because it is not concretely articulated. Indeed, mindset can be particularly difficult to divine in organizations run by traditional CEOs who are not very open about what they actually think and feel. Holding a mindset "close to the vest" may protect a CEO from getting "caught out" whenever the realities of the market trump an ideal or view. If the company is forced to act in a way that's contradictory to its mindset in a particular circumstance, then no one can call it out on that hypocrisy if the mindset is not clear. Yet, this ambiguity also forces the people in the organization to make guesses about the mindset, which leads to inconsistencies in decision-making and approach. On one day, in one division, the organization may be innovative and willing to bend over backwards for the customer. On another day, and under the purview of a different manager, the organization might be risk-averse or inclined to do as little for the customer as possible to avoid hurting the bottom line. What does the organization really think? Who honestly knows? But chances are you'd better be right when you make a decision or choose a path, or you will be in trouble, even though what is right can be different depending on the situation.

Fortunately for employees, customers, and investors alike, this kind of emotional hostage-taking is becoming less common. Founders like Larry Page, Sergey Brin, Andrew Mason, and Mark Zuckerberg are leading in a very different way by being incredibly clear, upfront, and open about the mindset they value, follow, and wish to instill or drive within their organizations.

I think the impulse to do so formally through a founders' letter comes from a worry that what made their organization special so far is suddenly vulnerable to outside forces. An IPO, after all, is a transformative event. Other than a merger, I can think of no bigger "natural" threat to the values and culture of an organization. As we saw with Apple in Chapter 1, things can change dramatically when new decision-makers—read "shareholders"—become a de facto part of the leadership of the company. Indeed, those shareholders traditionally have very different priorities and desires that can be at odds with or even hostile to the most cherished aims or cold-blooded strategies of the founders or the management of an organization.

Articulating a mindset in such a public and definitive way is part cannon shot, part personally written wedding vow. It says "Back off!" to those who would challenge the core beliefs of the organization or try to change them. And it says "Let's go!" to those eager to jump on board.

And while a founders' letter is written to prospective investors, that cannon shot/wedding vow is aimed as much at people inside the company as outside. In fact, founders like Page and Brin intended the message to hit home not only with the 800 or so employees of Google in 2004, or the 53,000 in 2015, but also the employees of Google who are not even born yet. Page and Brin articulated the Google mindset in such a formal and provocative way because it showed their commitment to those principles forever.

A clearly articulated mindset is characteristic of organizations that understand the critical importance of culture. They do this because, as Google Chairman Eric Schmidt and senior executive Jonathan Rosenberg put it, "culture and success go hand in hand."[2]

But the genesis of a culture is the mindset that the founders and leaders bring to the organization. The culture is built, in other words, around the way the organization intends to act and operate, which in turn shapes the organization's strategy, operating model, and business practices, and drives the decisions that get made.

Nimble, focused, and feisty companies like Google don't become that way by chance. In this chapter, we're going to focus on the three mindsets that NFF companies have in common. Specifically, they believe that:

1. Fast is better than big,
2. Possibility is more important than profitability, and
3. Being hungry and "outrospective" is critical.

MINDSET #1: FAST IS BETTER THAN BIG

Companies that are nimble are strikingly different from traditional companies. They believe that being agile, flexible, and flat is essential for success in today's dynamic world.

In contrast, most organizations in operation today retain the mindset that size, efficiency, and momentum are the formula for long-term competitive advantage. Chances are you work for or lead such an organization. We looked at this archaic belief a bit in chapter one with the Blockbuster story, but there are a thousand more lumbering Blockbusters for every nimble rival—although that's changing as more dinosaurs find themselves stuck in tar pits.

Companies that believe big is better than fast have organized themselves to maximize efficiency and scale to deliver standardized products and processes to mass markets. This formula for success has largely shaped the world we grew up in. I remember seeing McDonald's signs change over the years. In the early '70s, they proudly announced that 5 million people had been served. Today, it's billions upon billions. And each of those customers has eaten the same food across restaurants that look identical, all over the world. Henry Ford, the father of mass industrialization, was incredibly innovative in so many ways, but his defining difference came from grasping the power of being big in a world of millions of consumers longing for the same product. He built his factories to produce that product cheaply and efficiently—and was so focused on that mindset that he refused to alter his design or even the color of his automobile to meet variations in taste.

How do companies like McDonald's, Ford, and Blockbuster deliver their products to a mass market effectively? First of all, they learn how to break down the work of the organization into the smallest specific tasks that are so simple that errors and variations have been almost eliminated, then they give individuals those tasks, which they call jobs, and get them to do their jobs in the same fashion, over and over again. They also need a hierarchy in place to assure those tasks are being done correctly. Supervisors oversee workers doing the same task. Silos form around tasks that are similar. Managers oversee workers who are collectively doing a variety of tasks. As the number of different jobs increases, the layers of management expand and grow. The flow of information between those silos and layers is strictly controlled, and everyone must do exactly what he or she is supposed to do for the system to function efficiently. When that happens, scale pays off—literally. Margins do not need to be high in order to accrue tremendous profit in such a system.

Is the work engaging? Probably not, or at least not until you reach a level in the hierarchy that gives you a different kind of challenge—managing people instead of processes or overseeing processes that are more complex and strategic. Does the work require creativity, innovation, or passion? Again, not much until you get to higher levels. Creative impulses on the shop floor could throw a wrench into the works and bring the efficient machine to a screeching halt. On the other hand, in these big-is-better companies there is a lot of creativity needed in the marketing department.

It's necessary, after all, to artfully convince consumers that the same product they can get anywhere—one that is not very different from a product they can get from a competitor—actually is meaningful and desirable enough to buy. Why else would you drink Pepsi and not Coke, drive a Chevy and not a Ford, or fill your tank with one particular brand of gasoline over another? The subtle differences between these products must be branded as loudly and brashly as possible.

Naturally, companies that believe big is better than fast have a bias for unbridled growth. What's better than a store, gas station, or dealership in every city? Answer: a store, gas station, or dealership on every corner. All growth is good because it leverages efficiencies of process, resources, production, delivery, marketing, etc. Revenues and profits grow incrementally at scale as a result.

In a VUCA world, however, the dynamics of markets, competition, capital, employees, and technology have radically changed the rules of the game. As we discussed in chapter one, a company built to make the same product over and over again will not be able to meet diverse needs, or adapt quickly to changes in the market, or respond with agility to the disruptive innovations of new competitors, or engage younger generations of employees and customers who have different priorities and values. Meanwhile, capital and consumers will be drawn quickly to upstart companies that design better processes or fulfill different needs or bring new technologies to bear. Blockbuster, meet Netflix.

Does it sound strange to hear that Google—the behemoth of the internet—prizes being fast over being big? In fact, Google has gone to great lengths to design a work environment that enables agility and fluidity in all its processes and decisions, and actively encourages informal collaboration over formal organization. Most pointedly, it is fanatical in its resistance to the natural and insidious takeover of the company's culture by conventional rules of management (which are the default mode for responding to almost any confusion, complexity, challenge, or need, as Netflix noted) and the growth of hierarchical chains of command. Why? Because it believes those forces are responsible for slowing down big organizations and making them more cumbersome, inflexible, and unresponsive while killing innovation, passion, and engagement. These are not ideological or ethical arguments to Google but practical ones. Google believes that a culture built on the mindset that fast is better than big serves its strategic aims and will continue to drive the success of the company for the foreseeable future.

There's good logic behind that mindset. Google creates products that are highly valued by users and customers, but those products can also be duplicated by rivals and new upstarts. So Google works to sustain product excellence through constant improvement and innovation as a way of fending off the competition. In other words, the same product can't be produced in the same way over and over again at scale and still be successful. Note that Google relies very little on marketing or advertising to make its case with customers and users. It lets the product speak for itself.

Google encourages people to come up with ideas, innovations, and improvements beyond the task at hand because it believes those unplanned outcomes could potentially be bigger and more profitable than anything Google is devoted to doing currently.

Google also understands, better than most companies, that markets can change overnight. Accordingly, it maintains a looseness around assigned responsibilities that allows employees to do work beyond their job description. Instead of forcing people to keep their heads down and "stick to their knitting," Google encourages people to come up with ideas, innovations, and improvements beyond the task at hand because it believes those unplanned outcomes could potentially be bigger and more profitable than anything Google is devoted to doing currently.

Fundamentally, this mindset is rooted in a profound understanding of the modern dynamics of markets, of what organizations are capable of doing well versus what they don't do well, and of how employees are best motivated and empowered to contribute to organizational goals. Google's founders, Page and Brin, did not come from management or business backgrounds and they saw this as a virtue, not a defect. As creative engineers themselves, they knew what conditions fostered good work from such people. In fact, they looked to academia and the college campus, of all things, as ideal models for the type of organizational looseness they wanted to instill in Google. They believed that Google would only thrive and grow if they were able to "hire as many talented software engineers as possible and give them freedom."[3] So they set out to make Google an attractive center for world-class thinkers who then had the time and space to collaborate in an appealing environment, where interactions could occur frequently and in unplanned ways.

To make this possible, they believed it necessary to "reinvent the rules of management"[4] and remove the barriers of hierarchy, budgeting, and industrial-era management and oversight. They were contemptuous of formal planning because they believed it does not promote high-quality outcomes but a kind of stubborn, institutional adherence to an inflexible path. They also abhorred the status that gives workers with seniority and tenure more say than others. In their new hires, Google looked for people who were smarter and more capable than current employees and leaders. Anyone could win an argument as long as the reasoning was persuasive. Management levels were flattened. Top executives were never pandered to, and did not get the distinctively better office with the great view. Instead, space was used in a pragmatic way according to the needs of various projects or teams. Meetings were kept small, spontaneous, and fun. Leaders made as few decisions and exercised as little power as possible. Information was allowed to be free-flowing rather than restricted and directed up the food chain.

Brin and Page wanted a culture of *Yes* at Google, and they disrupted any force within the company inclined to say *No*. For example, many of us in corporate America have experienced disappointment when bold ideas and inspiring plans get thwarted, watered down, or made pointless by another division or level of management within the organization. The guiltiest department is typically legal, with finance trailing in a close second. Google saw the typical legal department as too risk-averse and negative to fit within the Google culture, so it hired lawyers who were willing to be creative contributors on business and product teams rather than gatekeepers blocking great ideas.[5]

The results have been extraordinary. Google has experienced unprecedented growth in a short time. But that growth arc does not resemble the slow and methodical approach of traditional companies. Rather Google is able to embrace a "grow big fast" strategy by identifying and seizing opportunities quickly, mobilizing with agility to take advantage, and achieving scale rapidly. This approach to innovation and growth occurs in an atmosphere characterized by a certain degree of chaos, disorganization, and spontaneity—a complaint or criticism that Schmidt and Rosenberg respond to by quoting race-car driver Mario Andretti: "If everything seems under control, you're just not going fast enough."[6]

MINDSET #2: POSSIBILITY OVER PROFITABILITY

"As a private company," Brin and Page continued in their founders' letter, "we have concentrated on the long term, and this has served us well. As a public company, we will do the same. In our opinion, outside pressures too often tempt companies to sacrifice long-term opportunities to meet quarterly and market expectations…If opportunities arise that might cause us to sacrifice short term results but are in the best long term interest of our shareholders, we will take those opportunities. We will have the fortitude to do this. We would request that our shareholders take the long term view."

I'd like to think the world is full of CEOs who wish they could act this way, if only Wall Street would let them. But part of me fears that, by the time they've scaled the heights of a Fortune 500 organization to become CEO, the pressure to meet quarterly expectations has already thoroughly beaten this spirit out of them. Perhaps that's why new-economy startup founders, with a touch of naïveté in their tone and bolstered with capital from eager investors, are still plucky enough to think that they will be rewarded and not crushed when they voice such a possibility-over-profitability mindset out loud.

There's a lingering suspicion about such an attitude. It's probably inherent in any skeptic from Wall Street or from the managerial profession, but it was certainly exacerbated by the excess idealism of the dot-com boom. Remember when Pets.com was said to be worth more than something like GE and GM combined? Despite generating no revenues, having few customers, and offering little more than an idea, pioneering e-commerce companies were valued many multiples over traditional product and manufacturing companies. No one could really explain why—except to point to the vast untapped potential such companies represented. But no one looked too closely below the surface, either, to see if a viable company existed beneath the hype.

A sickening stock-market collapse provided a correction to such think-ing but obscured an important point as a result. The pursuit of possibility over profitability provides distinct advantages when it comes to building an enduring and successful enterprise today. This mindset is key to the focused culture of organizations that are now clearly outpacing traditional companies in terms of real growth.

It is not to say that new-era companies abhor profits. They believe in profitability. But they do not pander to the common shareholder mindset of eking all possible gains in the short term at the expense of long-term growth while in the process short-changing and alienating customers. Instead, companies that believe in possibility over profitability trust that if they make customers extremely happy—indeed, if they exceed their expectations, and not just please them but delight them—this will result in far greater returns in the long run. Accordingly, instead of disbursing short-term profits to shareholders, they reinvest in their own business to foster the incremental and disruptive innovations that will tighten the bond with customers for the long haul. As Mark Zuckerberg wrote in his own founder's letter: "We don't build services to make money; we make money to build better services."[7]

Companies that believe in possibility over profitability trust that if they make customers extremely happy—indeed, if they exceed their expectations, and not just please them but delight them—this will result in far greater returns in the long run.

Amazon is another powerful example of this mindset. Founder and CEO Jeff Bezos is known as the Prophet of No Profits for his obsessive focus on growth over earnings. This has made Amazon a remarkable suc-cess story in the history of American capitalism, amusingly described by Matthew Yglesias in Slate.com as "a charitable organization being run by elements of the investment community for the benefit of consumers."[8] In 2013, Amazon's net income was a paltry $274 million on sales of $74.5 billion, or less than half of 1 percent. It's hard to imagine investors of any traditional company tolerating such razor-thin margins. Where are the corners that can be cut, the fat that can trimmed, the unrealistic schemes that can be put off to make Amazon more profitable in the short term? Bezos will have none of it and insists that Amazon's reinvestment in products and services that delight customers is the best way to go.

As Bezos put it in a letter to shareholders, "Our heavy investments in Prime, AWS, Kindle, digital media, and customer experience in general strike some as too generous, shareholder indifferent, or even at odds with being a for-profit company... To me, trying to dole out improvements in a just-in-time fashion would be too clever by half. It would be risky in a world as fast moving as the one we all live in. More fundamentally, I think long-term thinking squares the circle. Proactively delighting customers earns trust, which earns more business from those customers, even in new business arenas. Take a long-term view, and the interests of customers and shareholders align."[9]

This mindset leads to a strategy that Yglesias sees as truly formidable. "Amazon sells things to people at prices that seem impossible because it actually is impossible to make money that way. And the competitive pressure of needing to square off against Amazon cuts profit margins at other companies, thus benefiting people who don't even buy anything from Amazon... if you own a competing firm, you should be terrified. Competition is always scary, but competition against a juggernaut that seems to have permission from its shareholders to not turn any profits is really frightening."[10]

For companies like Amazon, customers are always top of mind. Products and services are created with a laser-like focus on customers' needs and what they value. Such companies not only try to keep lock-step with their customers as needs evolve, but actually try to stay a step ahead. They're continually solving for customer problems and opportunities rather than starting with the question of how they might open a new revenue stream. They're infinitely curious about the consumer and what makes her tick. Their decisions never veer far from those desires or potential desires. They know that they need to move quickly to fulfill those needs because the customer can easily find a better solution or a better supplier if the business can't deliver.

From a long-term growth perspective, Wall Street ought to be very interested in such a mindset and the strategies that result. Companies like Facebook, Amazon, and especially Google are actively transforming the economy. They're organized embodiments of creative destruction. They're category killers and category makers. They destroy products, services, and whole sectors that do not effectively identify and deliver value to consumers, and they reshape or invent sectors that do. Of course, they want to make money from their innovations and performance excellence, but they believe that making money and generating shareholder returns is the cart that follows the horse, not the other way around as traditional companies believe. The horse is the innovation and value. The money is in the cart. And the cart is very, very big.

Google has integrated this mindset into its purpose, operations, strategy, and workflow. According to Schmidt and Rosenberg, Brin and Page began Google with a few simple principles, "first and foremost of which was to focus on the user. They believed that if they created great services, they could figure out the money stuff later."[11] Or as Brin and Page put it themselves in their founders' letter, "Serving our end users is at the heart of what we do and remains our number one priority." But as Schmidt and Rosenberg add, this is because they believe that if they focus on the user, "all else will follow."[12]

Google makes a great distinction between the user and the customer that's worth noting. The customer—the entity that gives Google money—is predominantly advertisers, at least in the case of their search-engine services. The user is us—or everyone who uses those services. Google doesn't believe in pandering to the customer, because it thinks this will deflect from the primacy of the user. The user is the target for value that makes the user Google's true customer. What will the user want? What will the user value? What will the user be blown away by?

If Google focused only on what its advertising customers wanted, those answers would likely be very prosaic and small. Advertising customers want results in the short term and don't really care about long-term implications. User customers, however, have a different kind of investment in Google innovation. They want constant improvement and big leaps. They want to do the stuff they do now even better and be delighted by what's next.

That's why Google very deliberately divides its innovation efforts along a scale that runs from incremental to big bets. Google openly focuses 70 percent of its work, attention, and resources on continuous improvement of products and services in existence. It knows that it must continue to meet and exceed expectations to fulfill the trust that customers and users have in Google, and satisfy their needs. Then, it devotes 20 percent of its work, attention, and resources to emerging products that are showing some signs of becoming successful offerings. This keeps innovations flowing in the pipeline and getting closer to release. And it devotes the remaining 10 percent of the resources, brainpower, and creativity of Google to long shots, or what Google calls "moon shots"—stuff that's completely new, very risky, and highly likely to fail.[13]

How many companies ever do that? Today, innovation is a buzzword and many organizations have enlisted innovation-expert leaders to "drive innovation in the organization" or developed venture-capital wings to seed innovative startups that might strike it rich someday. But that kind of innovation, while welcome, seems divorced or separate from the inherent operations of the company. It may be the worst form of window dressing—the high-tech equivalent of diversity initiatives that don't truly address diversity needs.

Is 10 percent really enough if Google truly believes in the possibility that moon-shot innovations could change its business and transform markets? Well, Google, as I've said, is not averse to using money smartly. It has no desire to throw money wastefully against the wall like a handful of wet spaghetti to see what sticks. It believes that the "cost of experimentation and failure has dropped significantly"[14] but also that smaller bets combined with deliberately limited resources forces ingenuity because "creativity loves constraints."[15]

At the same time, however, the Google mindset, strongly reinforced by Page and Brin at every opportunity, is always to think big. And not just big, but BIG. Google people talk routinely about "10Xing" their jobs and projects—considering how the project, idea, or launch can produce not just incremental results but results that are ten times what is currently happening. Possibility first. Profitability follows. And in a way, this mindset inures Google to the risk of failure. Because the moon shots are not enormous bets, and because they are aligned with thinking big, there is always limited harm and some good to come out of them. As Page puts it, "If you are thinking big enough, it is very hard to fail completely. There is usually something very valuable left over." And Google makes sure that everyone knows failure is not an executable offense; failure is to be rewarded and reinforced because it is the only way that gold can be discovered.

This way of thinking is drastically different from the way organizations have traditionally operated. For decades, big companies have had a sharp focus on the bottom line. They strive to maximize quarterly profits, bump up shareholder value, exploit earnings potential, and hit targets and bonuses. Profit maximization has become so entrenched in our way of thinking that we rarely question it, let alone strive to change it. This approach sets up a debilitating construct that can cripple a culture. After all, companies reward and promote those who deliver the best results—executors who can maximize earnings and cut costs—leading to a senior team with a financial-first focus.

In contrast, an orientation toward possibility, or what Carol Dweck, a professor of psychology at Stanford University, calls a "growth" mindset, leads to a very different kind of culture, one that embraces employee empowerment and customer focus. Cultures that embody a "fixed" mindset in which potential is seen as limited are more typical of traditional twentieth-century organizations.

In her research, Dweck and her colleagues asked a diverse set of employees at seven different Fortune 1000 companies whether they agreed with a number of questions. For example, "When it comes to being successful, this company seems to believe that people have a certain amount of talent, and they really can't do much to change it." High levels of agreement indicated the company had a relatively fixed mindset, while low levels indicated a growth mindset. Dweck and her team then sought to understand how the organizational mindset influenced employees' beliefs and behaviors, things such as workers' satisfaction, perceptions of the organizational culture, levels of collaboration, and innovation.

The results proved that the organizational mindset had a dramatic impact on employee perception. Employees at fixed-mindset companies often expressed less commitment to their companies, thought their companies didn't "have their back," and indicated that a handful of "star" workers were highly valued at the organization. These employees were less innovative and collaborative, worried more about failing, and often kept secrets and cut corners.

Growth-minded companies had a more optimistic outlook. Supervisors took a more positive view of their employees, rating them as being more innovative, collaborative, and committed to learning and growing. They saw more management potential in their employees.[16]

Employees at fixed-mindset companies often expressed less commitment to their companies, thought their companies didn't "have their back," and indicated that a handful of "star" workers were highly valued at the organization. These employees were less innovative and collaborative, worried more about failing, and often kept secrets and cut corners.

My point is that inculcating a strong organizational way of thinking around possibility (growth) over profitability (fixed) is critically important to organizational success. It not only affects your strategy and approach, but it actually determines the way your people view your company and one another.

Coming from a fixed view—that what we do as an organization leads to a certain range of profitability and must be pursued in order to drive incremental levels of growth—is exactly the wrong approach. NFF companies come from a different starting point. They ask, "What can I make that my customer/user really wants or needs?" By leveraging that growth orientation they create cultures that are positive, engaging, innovative, and supportive. And the money follows.

MINDSET #3: HUNGRY AND "OUTROSPECTIVE"

That imperative to focus on customers and users is actually the driver for the third mindset of NFF companies. Organizations with feisty cultures are "hungry and outrospective" by nature.

What does it mean to be outrospective? Well, I made up the word, but I think you can guess the definition. The perspective of an outrospective company is outwardly directed rather than inwardly focused. What's outside your company worth looking at? Why, your customers and users, of course. Unlike your employees or, to some degree, your partners and suppliers, customers and users are largely free to buy your services or not. (Unless they're locked into service agreements—hello, wireless carrier!) So it helps to know what they are interested in, or value, desire, like, don't like, need, or don't need.

The other thing that's outside your company is the world. Interesting things happen there sometimes, occasionally having an impact on what you do and how successfully you do it.

Most companies are inwardly focused. This means that they are predominantly worried about meeting their own internal needs, not the needs of customers, and they are more curious about their own internal processes than they are about what's going on in the world. How do we know this? Listen in on a meeting. Even if someone brings up a customer concern—let's say the product doesn't do everything the customer needs it to do—the response of the company is to filter that complaint through the capabilities the company already has in place, which can be incrementally improved upon as a way of "doing something" to solve that challenge. And if—minutes before the meeting—everyone just learned that the world has fallen apart or aliens have landed in spacecraft, the only relevant question that will get raised during the meeting is likely to be: How do we find a way to continue business as usual?

Often leaders of such companies talk about having a customer focus and an "inside-out" approach. But again, those companies view customers as a means of meeting the company's needs, not the other way around. And having an inside-out approach means you're starting from inside and are likely to view everything outside through a very particular (and often peculiar) lens. You gaze at what's going on in the world and think, how can we get more efficient about our processes or how can we increase our margins?

This mode of thinking, very aligned with the notion of profitability over possibility, is not only inward looking, but it's also upward looking and backward looking. It's upward looking because changes to existing processes are likely to be decided by someone above you in the hierarchy. And it's backward looking because the company is obsessed with an understanding of what it did well in the past, what got it to where it is today, and how to propagate or continue that success in a linear fashion going forward—not with what's staring you in the face, what's around the next corner, or what's out there in some distant region of the world.

In other words, instead of being eager and curious about customers and the world, inward-focused companies have a tendency to be passive about the world, and to see customers in a fixed or monolithic way. Ironically, such companies are often very active, aggressive, and busy in dealing with their internal needs and processes. They are not lazy, just not very aware.

By way of example, imagine a meeting between Google and the Detroit automakers. Actually, this meeting has already occurred, and it went nowhere—at least initially. Google made the overture. It had been thinking about getting into the car business. Why? Well, it spent a lot of time and effort developing the best mapping system in the world, so why not figure out how to incorporate that knowledge—which users value very highly—into a new business? Google had been developing self-driving car technology but decided it would prefer to collaborate with existing automakers than become an automaker itself. According to someone present, "In one meeting, both sides were enthusiastic about the futuristic technology, yet it soon became clear that they would not be working together. The Internet search company and the automaker disagreed on almost every point, from car capabilities and time needed to get it to market to extent of collaboration. It was as if the two were 'talking a different language.'"[17]

As Slate.com writer Will Oremus put it, "Detroit automakers speak the language of established industry leaders, trafficking in terms like profit margins, brand image, and liability. Google, despite its size, still deals in the conceptual vocabulary of a tech startup: blank slates, prototypes, moon shots—and, yes, disruption."[18] Google is focused on setting and address-ing evolving consumer demand, while Detroit automakers still seek to meet existing consumer demand. These vastly different philosophies show up in every facet of their organizations, particularly culture.

Given the decades-long doldrums of the US auto industry, it's hard to remember that Detroit was once a hub of stimulating innovation, capi-tal, and energy. A century ago, it was the Silicon Valley of its day. Smart inventors, engineers, entrepreneurs, and business leaders—not to men-tion capital—flocked to Detroit in the early 1900s to engage in a flurry of activity and build something new, something compelling, something very different: a functioning automobile.

The fact that automobiles were on these creative types' minds in the first place was radical. As Henry Ford said, "If I asked people what they wanted, they would have said faster horses." And indeed, horses were everywhere—even pulling trolley cars—while steam-engine trains were taking passengers the longer distances they needed to go. So there was no compelling apparent need at that time to develop an automobile, just a curiosity and hunger to do so and a vision of potential consumer demand based on the value those inventors and business people thought was latent in an emerging market.

Ford, in particular, was curious enough to perceive needs that went deeper than the surface. When he invented an automobile, he didn't say, "Well, now I have the perfect mousetrap, let the world beat a path to my door." Instead, he considered the customers or users and determined their perception of value. Price was a big concern. By making his Model T affordable (and by paying his own employees a wage that turned them into automobile consumers), Ford stimulated demand. It's telling that he later faltered because he didn't see to other things consumers valued, such as color, style, or variations in model.

Google has this kind of user orientation today. As we've discussed, it is very fast, collaborative, and vigorous (Mindset #1). And it is laser-focused on the value-perspective of the customer or user (Mindset #2) over any incremental concerns about profitability. But it is an insatiably curious and outwardly directed company, too. (Mindset #3.)

Companies that are hungry and outrospective do not discover their path by following a limited or narrow understanding of the customer or even the market they are in. They are as curious about that customer as they are about the projects they are focused on, and they are hungry both for insight and for discoveries that will genuinely affect the world, not merely push the needle in the direction it has already been pointing.

Market research does not play a strong role in this process because that approach to understanding the customer is inherently biased toward confirming what the organization already knows or wants to do. In fact, many of Google's innovations come from combining ideas or innovations in new ways. This sort of genre-mixing is common among artists and pure scientists; it is exceedingly rare in business. Most organizations suppress the curiosity and outward focus that lead to insights arising from seeing patterns or connecting disparate forces or ideas. They would rather focus on the narrow band of problems the company grapples with every day.

This is where the importance of diversity also comes into play. The notion of diversity as a form of political correctness has done a grave disservice to the development of new strategic capabilities in most organizations. How can a company be innovative, discover new things, or possibly understand how the customer perceives value, if everyone in the company thinks the same, and not enough people are representative of the variety of customers? Without a mix of voices, experiences, perspectives, and outlooks, it's impossible for a company to be sufficiently outrospective in today's global economy.

Companies need to ask themselves constantly, "What business are we in?" and "How might we continue to best serve our customers or potential customers?" Hungry and outrospective companies disrupt themselves constantly. They don't stop asking questions—even when there's no evidence that questions need to be asked. They don't sit on their own success, navel-gazing on recent achievements and quarterly earnings. They act upon their possibility mindset. They focus on the market and the customer. And they encourage and expect their people to play a major part in the direction of the company, regardless of role or tenure.

BUILDING AND CHANGING MINDSET

Companies that are culture-based and nimble, focused, and feisty are clear about their mindsets and do everything they can to inculcate them in the organization. The leaders drive those mindsets home constantly. It is the singular area in which they correct the thinking of others and do not allow for latitude. They know that if they get mindset locked in, then people will act appropriately within those constraints to deliver better innovations and higher levels of performance.

Those companies also make sure that they bring the right people on board in the first place. Mindsets can be taught and are definitely reinforced by culture, leadership, rewards, etc., but it's far easier to win those battles if you have mindset alignment from the get-go.

Mindset is the underlying operating system that drives the actions, behaviors, and business practices of the organization. Like rewriting code, it can be difficult to change because whatever mindset is already in place—whether it is explicit or implicit—can be an insidious deterrent to a fundamentally new way of thinking. Nevertheless, mindsets can be shifted even radically. That's what Satya Nadella, CEO of Microsoft, is trying to do.

Microsoft is now more than forty years old. It's the second- or third-largest technology company in the world, flipping places with Google depending on the quarter. It made $22 billion in profits in 2014. But a lot has changed since regulators found the company so dominating and threatening that they wanted to break it up. It's been a long time since a Microsoft product drew much interest, much less killed or made a category. The brightest young engineers do not flock to Redmond the way they once did. Microsoft is seen as a comfortable, corporate environment more than a creative hub of innovation and entrepreneurship. This is in spite of the fact that Microsoft has the biggest research and development engine in the industry, Microsoft Research, with a budget of $11.4 billion in 2014.

Nadella is trying to "end the factional strife inside Microsoft, making the 118,000-strong work force nimbler. He has rallied them around mantras, like making personal computing more personal through wearables and other devices. To better translate Microsoft's innovation into products people want to buy, he has directed the company's research group, the biggest in the technology industry, to work more closely with product engineers."[19]

Eliminating internal fiefdoms. Flattening out middle management. Making it easier to communicate and collaborate across the organization. Bringing engineers and creative innovators together. Pushing product excellence. Making smaller bets with potentially bigger payoffs. And allowing failure to be part of the process. It's all starting to have an effect. As an outside member of the technical advisory board says, "There's an eagerness in the business units to pick up ideas that are going to make a significant difference."[20]

Companies that wish to thrive today and over the long term must reinforce or adopt mindsets that work with rather than resist the dynamic forces at play in our fundamentally changed world. In the next section of this book I'll show you how they do that.

PART 1

ORGANIZATIONS THAT WIN: HOW THEY'RE NIMBLE, FOCUSED, AND FEISTY

3

THEY POSITION TO PIVOT

NOKIA, the Finnish telecommunications company, was originally founded in 1865 in Tampere, Finland, as a ground-wood pulp mill. Over the years, the company periodically added a number of other business areas to its portfolio, including forestry, cable, rubber, tires, footwear, plastics, chemicals, power generation, and eventually electronic devices. However, it was Nokia's entrance into the mobile-phone market that changed everything and made Nokia the brand we know today.

In 1992, new CEO Jorma Ollila was so convinced that Nokia's future was in telecommunications, he made the strategic decision to divest the company of all of its non-telecommunications enterprises. So, during the course of the 1990s, Nokia sold off its legacy cable, consumer electronics, and rubber divisions and put its focus squarely on mobile telecommunications. By 1998, Nokia had surpassed its rivals in this fast-growing industry and became the largest mobile-phone manufacturer in the world. Revenue grew from 6.5 billion euros in 1996 to 31 billion euros in 2001, and the company could seemingly do no wrong.

Then, in 2007, Apple introduced the iPhone.

Apple's vaunted capability for innovation and new product development made Apple the winner and Nokia the loser. Apple disrupted the industry. Nokia was late to the game. The iPhone ate up mobile-phone market share and forced other manufacturers to play catch-up. Nokia wasn't able to do so successfully and announced its intention to sell off its mobile-phone division to Microsoft in 2013.

Or so the story goes.

The problem with this narrative—much like the story of Blockbuster in chapter one—is that Nokia was actually ahead of Apple in the smartphone market. A few years before Apple introduced the iPhone, Nokia research engineers unveiled a prototype of an internet-ready, touchscreen mobile-phone handset with a large display that they thought would give the company a significant advantage in the fast-growing smartphone market. In 2004, at its headquarters in Finland, the company demonstrated it to customers as an example of what was in the company's pipeline; it was greeted with much excitement and anticipation.

What happened then? A stunning series of cultural flops led to complete and total reversal.

Management at Nokia worried that the product would be costly and risky. A former employee, Ari Hakkarainen—a manager responsible for marketing on the development team for the Nokia Series 60, then the company's premium line of smartphones—explained in a *New York Times* interview why the company did not pursue development.

"It was very early days, and no one really knew anything about the touchscreen's potential," Mr. Hakkarainen explained. "And it was an expensive device to produce, so there was more risk involved for Nokia. So management did the usual. They killed it."[1] For a large and prosperous organization, there simply wasn't a taste for pursuing possibility over profitability. Hakkarainen went on to say that the biggest obstacle for the company was without a doubt its stifling bureaucratic culture. In subsequent interviews with a *Times* reporter, Hakkarainen and other former employees depicted an organization so swollen by its early success that it grew complacent, slow, and removed from consumer desires. As a result, they said, Nokia lost the lead in several crucial areas by failing to fast-track its designs for touchscreens, software applications, and 3-D interfaces.

In other words, it's not that Nokia lacked the innovation capabilities or the talent to come up with new, breakthrough products. Rather, it lacked an organizational culture to support these ideas. According to Adam Greenfield, a former Nokia employee, Nokia's problem is not, and never has been, that it lacks creative, thoughtful, talented people, or the resources to turn their ideas into a shipped product. The problem with Nokia is that the company is fundamentally, and has always been, organized to trade in commodities. Think back to Nokia's roots. Whether those commodities were stands of timber, pallets of paper, reels of cable, pairs of boots, or cheap televisions for deployment in hotel chains, much the same basic logic applied: acquire, or manufacture, great quantities of a physical product for the lowest achievable cost, and sell for whatever the market will bear. This worked with mobile phones up until the point when customers considered them as so much more than communication devices.

Nokia fought back and tried a variety of different strategies to stem the tide, including entering into an alliance with Microsoft to produce Windows phones, but the decline continued and the company was forced to announce several rounds of layoffs. On April 25, 2014, Nokia sold its mobile-phone business to Microsoft for 5.44 billion euros.[2]

Behind the story, the rise of Nokia and the subsequent demise of the company we knew rested on its ability and failure to pivot.

ESTABLISHING A TRIPLE THREAT

Nimble organizations have a distinct ability to innovate. They do so by deliberately structuring and positioning themselves either to pivot toward new opportunities or to counter forces that might otherwise diminish their competitiveness. This first mode of innovation is a way of going on offense—organizations pivot to create new products, services, or markets. The second mode is a form of defense—organizations hold off competitors or preserve the value of their offerings by improving performance or otherwise shoring up their market position.

Leading a sizable and established organization today is a daunting task, given the critical need for flexibility, innovation, and rapid reaction to sudden changes in the market or the competitive or technological environment. It seems appreciably easier for an organization to be fast and adaptive when its culture is young, its market is immature, its founders and people are entrepreneurial, and its customers are fickle and demanding. Indeed, I have found that many (but importantly not all) NFF organizations are new-economy companies in their first or second generation of leadership.

And yet, in truth, it is difficult for any organization, large or small, upstart or market-leader, to pivot.

The modern concept of the "pivot" was actually coined by a venture capitalist and author of *The Lean Startup*, Eric Ries, in 2009. Ries was talking about the challenges that startups face in deviating from their original vision to seize new and better opportunities. Focused relentlessly on that vision or the process of building and directing their organization, the founders or leaders avoid distractions that might impede momentum or energy, even turning aside customer feedback that can get in the way.

"So how do you know it's time to change direction?" Ries asks. "And how do you pick a new direction?"[3]

Ries observes that unsuccessful startups either avoid such discussions and decisions entirely and fail to change, or they jump too completely or unthinkingly from one vision to another. The latter kinds of changes are just as risky because they "don't leverage the validated learning about customers that came before."[4]

As an alternative, Ries introduces the concept of the pivot, "the idea that successful startups change directions but stay grounded in what they've learned. They keep one foot in the past and place one foot in a new possible future. Over time, this pivoting may lead them far afield from their original vision, but if you look carefully, you'll be able to detect common threads that link each iteration."[5]

A pivot, then, is neither a wholesale change nor a blind leap into the unknown, but a flexible and calculated shift that straddles what has worked in the past and what will work in the future. I think of it as being like a basketball player who gets the ball in the Triple Threat position and has the opportunity to seek an open lane through dribbling, pass to a teammate, or take a shot. In other words, when an organization makes such a move, it is not coming to a full stop or becoming paralyzed, nor is it losing its grip on what it knows how to do well. Rather, it's leveraging its agility to alter direction, bolt forward, and seize opportunity quickly and decisively.

Although Ries was talking about startups, his concept is even more critical for established businesses. An organization's ability to pivot—to quickly change direction, and to just as quickly move people, finances, and other resources into place to support this shift—is absolutely essential to success in today's fast-moving VUCA world.

A couple of decades ago, five-year plans were the norm for businesses in nearly every industry, and these plans worked quite effectively if their leaders picked the right strategy and stayed on a steady and solid course of executing. Today, due to the constantly shifting nature of businesses and industries, three-to-five-year strategies do little more than set up organizations for failure. To meet this challenge head-on, organizations need to make fast decisions, pivot toward opportunities quickly, and rally the workforce to engage on new challenges.

Most twentieth-century organizations, however, were never designed to proactively change. The very best ecosystem they could build for themselves, in the pursuit of operating efficiently at scale, was based on rigid hierarchy and reinforced by a "stick-to-the-knitting" approach to process and strategy. As Gary Hamel, a leading business thinker and author, has observed, "There's a great mismatch between the pace of change in the external environment [today] and the fastest possible pace of change at most organizations. If it were otherwise, we wouldn't see so many incumbents struggling."[6]

Fundamentally, new-era organizations—the ones that are nimble today—have no expectation that they will always be doing what they are currently doing. This is because they know that what they are doing today may not carry them to where they ultimately want to go. Their core mindset is that "fast is better than big" because they believe that they must be incredibly responsive to the changes of their external ecosystem in order to survive and be successful in the long term. Primarily, they are driven by their understanding of the customer, and what value they can deliver or provide. They base that value on what they do well, but they are willing and eager to discover new sources of value through innovation on every front.

Fundamentally, new-era organizations—the ones that are nimble today—have no expectation that they will always be doing what they are currently doing. This is because they know that what they are doing today may not carry them to where they ultimately want to go.

After all, the current value proposition of their goods and services can be eroded as successful strategies and approaches get copied or improved upon. Companies that are positioned to pivot structure their organization and employees so that these decisions to turn toward new opportunities are made quickly, innovation comes more easily, and leaders and employees take risks and play bold. They have the environment and infrastructure in place (including the company structure, processes, systems, resources, and people) to enable quick moves and experiments that may not pan out—while not breaking business operations. Their "How" enables them to have a quick and effective process to refine and change their "What."

In this chapter let's look at three strategies that large organizations have used to position themselves to pivot: learning from startups, spotting opportunities, and simultaneously exploring and exploiting.

THEY GO TO STARTUP BOOT CAMP

John Chambers led Cisco Systems from 1995 to 2015—a period of enormous disruptive change across every market and platform in the information-technology sector. Unlike so many other IT companies, Cisco has managed to stay on the forward edge of change and often leads its market as the disruptive innovator rather than the business struggling to catch up. As Chambers puts it, "I've watched iconic companies disappear—Compaq, Sun Microsystems, Wang, Digital Equipment—as they failed to anticipate where the market was headed…When you're a large company with significant market share, it's tempting to view market disruptions as a threat, but we view them as an opportunity."[7]

To manage this, Cisco works to actively nurture a startup mentality. One of its most successful strategies for doing so, Cisco calls a "Spin-in." A team of engineers and developers is formed to work on a specific project. But instead of keeping that team within the confines of the organization, it is actually moved outside the organization and "launched" as if it were a startup. One team that Chambers describes has 280 employees focused on a multi-billion-dollar business. The team members are incentivized with financial rewards just like the founders and early employees at a startup. They work long hours closely together, recruit the talent they need, and foster the cultural norms and processes necessary to make decisions and change direction quickly.

Cisco's approach differs from a Skunk Works project (an innovation endeavor that is set off from the rest of an organization) in some fundamental ways. Rather than establishing a permanent off-site head-quarters for a renegade culture devoted to mad-scientist projects, a Cisco Spin-in is a very deliberate, strategic approach to developing a specific project that is believed to be critical to the growth opportunities of the company. Even more important, Cisco's team of engineers and developers are subsequently brought back into the organization proper, and the startup itself is absorbed into the business.

No doubt, Cisco could do just as well financially, and motivate talented employees to develop a startup mentality, if it assigned and spun-out its projects into stand-alone businesses. However, Cisco's own culture would not receive the long-lasting benefit of that experience and learning. It would be a motivational tool to encourage talent to leave the organization, not lead it.

Instead, by spinning-in the startup project team once that project has become viable, Cisco gains immeasurably from the startup mindset and skills that have been learned. If you work for a large company, can you imagine going off-site to work in a startup for an intense eighteen months, tasting the glory, and then coming back to your old company? You would be a changed person, and you would find your company's stifling processes and approaches intolerable. How many endless meetings or stale performance reviews could you sit through? How much dithering over decisions could you stand? In other words, once you've tasted what a startup is like, and experienced the exhilaration of a nimble culture, you are going to be driven to bring that energy back to your old place of work—and change it for the better. And that's what John Chambers counted on when developing the muscles to pivot at Cisco.

GE takes a similar approach with its own twist. CEO Jeff Immelt says, "If the only common thread you have as an industrial company is that you're well managed, you can still be a pretty good company, but you're not going to be a dominant company, a competitive company over time."[8]

Immelt took over GE four days before 9/11 and subsequently experienced the rocky markets that accompanied the downfall of many once high-flying internet startups. Even before the Great Recession of 2007 that brought the global economy into another nosedive, Immelt anticipated that industrial giants like GE would enter a period of tepid growth. He believed that GE's relentless focus on operational excellence, market dominance, and the constant improvement of existing processes, while still critical, was no longer sufficient to ensure that the organization would continue to thrive in the future. A business-as-usual approach, even if it successfully protected GE against new competitors, would not position the company to take advantage of explosive growth opportunities going forward.

So Immelt, from his first days as CEO, began to institute a massive pivot in the company's culture and focus: GE would continue to be exceptional at operational excellence, but it would also learn to seize opportunities for organic growth through innovation. The aim of the efforts would be, as Immelt put it in his shareholder letter of 2007, "to embed growth into the DNA of our company."[9]

This began with a challenge to GE leaders to develop at least three "Imagination Breakthroughs" per year, designed to bring in at least $100 million in new business. These ideas would be put to review and receive billions in investment if deemed worthy bets, and the results were tied closely to bonuses. The essential message, however, was that making bets, being creative, and staying growth-focused was now critical for success at GE. This way of thinking about the business of GE was a developmental stretch for managers long steeped in Six Sigma, but in the new GE, as Immelt put it, "you're not going to stick around this place and not take bets."[10]

In support of this, GE developed a new curriculum for leadership development called "Leadership, Innovation, and Growth" (LIG). Participants visited Crotonville, the company's management-training center north of New York City, to learn how to identify and overcome barriers to change, develop a better balance between short-term priorities and long-term opportunities, think about their businesses differently, and communicate in the language of change, growth, and innovation. Most important, they were guided in how to build an action plan for a concrete change agenda for their business. Then, these leaders were returned to their business units and set to work, their learnings, skills, and values reinforced by new measures in the performance-review system.

The value of this is enormous. Not only is GE developing new leaders, but it is also putting them to work on practical plans that will drive new growth for the company; and then it is seeding those leaders back into the organization and reinforcing their changed mindset with performance measures and rewards.

THEY SPOT OPPORTUNITIES FAST
AND CHASE THEM CHEAP

As Ranjay Gulati of Harvard Business School notes, "The problem these companies face is, as they get bigger, as they scale, things slow down. They lose speed because they have so many systems and structures and processes, and they lose the ability to take risks. GE's a smart company. They understand the pathology of bigness, and this allows them to be responsive."

GE did not stop with its LIG program and its focus on Imagination Breakthroughs; it wanted to create a culture of pivoting throughout the organization. So the company turned to Eric Ries, the source of the concept of the pivot, and asked him to help inculcate that lean twenty-first century startup mentality in a $150 billion enterprise. The result was FastWorks, a program designed to create a culture, according to Beth Comstock, GE's chief marketing officer and FastWorks sponsor, "where we operate faster while delivering better outcomes. At the heart of it is the discipline of testing and learning that permeates the entire the organization."[11]

Ries helped GE build an approach and develop a playbook based on those practices, and my team and I worked with GE's nearly 300 FastWorks coaches scattered across all the businesses to navigate and influence the existing culture, knowing that those practices would promptly fall flat if they were to hit a resistant or ill-equipped organization. This program has had a profound effect on GE's ability to become growth-oriented and innovation-focused at all levels.

As an example, in one of GE Healthcare's groups, a small team of engineers, marketers, and product designers is plotting the future of medical devices. With hopes of disrupting the market, the group is using a limited budget to streamline the development of a new PET/CT scanner while addressing customer concerns over price, performance, and ease of use. Similar to what all other GE businesses now have, Healthcare has a growth board that approves or rejects potential FastWorks projects. Wei Shen, whose team is developing the PET/CT scanner, felt as if she were on the TV show *Shark Tank* when she pitched the idea, which was initially rejected early in 2015 because it involved building a prototype that would cost a few million dollars. She secured approval after nixing the full prototype and cutting the projected cost by more than half.

If Shen's team followed tradition, it would have spent two to four years building a new product based mostly on basic market-research surveys. Under FastWorks, the group constantly takes its ideas to customers throughout the development process to learn what will sell and what won't, redesigning the scanner before devoting the time and money to creating a final product. The first two iterations cost a total of less than $300,000. Shen aims to have a product out in about half the normal time. The customer feedback is invaluable, Shen says. "I can build a product to have the best image quality, but it may not be at the right price point. Or I can build a product that's so fast it can accommodate thirty to fifty patients a day. I can have a system that's 50 percent lower-cost."[12]

In this way, a corporation once so focused on execution and operational excellence is now developing a culture in which there is room for failing, learning, and seizing opportunities—all at an accelerated pace. Recently Immelt even launched a "Power of the Pivot" award to recognize those in the organization who will speak up, call a spade a spade, and lead others to change. The goal is to have an organization in which thousands of small changes can take place every day, even as larger "imagination breakthroughs" are also happening.

One of my close collaborators at GE, Simeon Sessley, whom you may recall from the foreword, believes that GE's Six Sigma heritage has allowed it to become a company capable of thousands of pivots, large and small. Six Sigma, after all, is a discipline for making many small incremental improvements in processes. However, the innovation, growth, and customer-focus framework that has been culturally ingrained in the company changes the way people think, communicate, and work. In the past, Simeon says, GE, like most companies, was focused on answering financial-first questions such as, "Where are we in meeting our revenue goals, our profit margins, and our execution objectives?" Now, people are starting to focus increasingly on secondary questions that challenge beliefs and the status quo, such as, "Are we really meeting our customer needs with this path? Are we innovating enough? How will we disrupt our own businesses?"

These questions lead GE to think more about continual transformation and long-term opportunities rather than on the meeting of quarterly results.

THEY BALANCE EXPLORATION
AND EXPLOITATION CONSTANTLY

What does an organization look like when it is positioned to pivot at any level and toward large or small opportunities? Maybe a lot like Toyota.

According to Matthew May in *The Elegant Solution: Toyota's Formula for Mastering Innovation*, Toyota implements a million new ideas a year, many of which stem from their employees. These ideas are often small and easy to implement, but cumulatively they snowball to create a major impact.[13] In a *Harvard Business Review* interview, Katsuaki Watanabe, the former CEO of Toyota, said, "There is no genius in our company. We just do whatever we believe is right, trying every day to improve every little bit and piece. But when seventy years of very small improvements accumulate, they become a revolution."[14]

Toyota's innovation in how cars are made enabled it to make cars more quickly and cheaply with less labor than American companies. In other words, by focusing on "How"—the culture and work processes of the organization—Toyota was able to achieve a faster and more effective "What"—the production and sale of vehicles.[15]

Incremental and disruptive innovation are commonly discussed as diametrically opposing philosophies, when really they should work in concert within an organization. Being able to make small incremental changes actually positions an organization for innovations that are more disruptive and that have a greater impact. This positioning occurs because once change and innovation are normalized in the way organizations operate, it becomes easier to surface, accept, and enact more disruptive or non-linear innovations. A culture of innovation gives employees and leaders the muscles and agility they need to make quick changes, develop breakthrough ideas, and diminish the common fear of failure and risk.

Toyota understands this. While it continually refines and produces some of the most reliable, affordable, and best-selling vehicles on the market, like the Corolla, which passed the 40-million threshold in 2013, it is also capable of seeking out and exploring new industry-shaking innovations, like the Prius, the first vehicle since the Stanley Steamer to offer a viable alternative to the internal-combustion engine.

Despite some doubts and hiccups in developing a new technology, the company fought through adversity to unveil the Prius in Japan in October

1997, two months ahead of schedule.[16] The first Prius came to North America in July 2000, when national gas prices averaged about $1.50 a gallon. Some questioned whether the new technology would be appealing given low gas prices, so the company set modest sales goals of 12,000 units per year.[17] Customers, however, thought differently. By the end of 2013 Toyota announced that it had sold more than 6 million hybrid vehicles throughout the globe, generating 41 million fewer tons of CO_2.[18] The Prius has become not just the best-selling hybrid, but also one of the world's top-selling cars. Toyota managed this pivot because it was good at making continual improvements to existing processes, while also being culturally oriented toward making small and large bets.

Companies that are nimble—even giant companies like Toyota and GE—believe that being fast is more important than being big. They refuse to rely on the comforting view that "scale never fails." Instead, they consciously architect an organizational culture that embraces risk and change; and they structure their organizations and processes to eliminate bureaucracy, improve communication, and speed up decisions. They avoid becoming stuck in the product-lifecycle loop, and make sure that experimentation and the surfacing of new ideas is always on the agenda. Most important, they focus those innovations, changes, and investments on a keen and curious understanding of the changing customer.

QUANTUM LAWS OF BUSINESS

According to quantum mechanics' Heisenberg Uncertainty Principle—something I still struggle to get my head around—atoms can be in two places at once.[19] Sometimes, when I talk to leaders at new-era companies, I sense that they believe they need to be two companies at once.

To which I say, Yes, you do.

If we could formulate a new Uncertainty Principle for business, it would help us understand why winning today is so challenging. At one point companies could do one thing exceptionally well—build a computer like Dell, master execution through Six Sigma like GE, dominate a market like McDonald's, deliver a catalogue like Sears—and that capability would create a channel for growth and prosperity. At one point markets were similarly static and manageable. Today, organizations must be capable of meeting challenges on multiple fronts in order to deal with splintered and dispersed markets, and even—gulp—multiple realities.

By learning how to position to pivot, they gain the adroitness, agility, awareness, and decisiveness needed to be more than one company at any one time.

Accordingly, they can stay lean by constantly making improvements to existing processes or solutions; seizing new technologies that might help them solve problems better or meet needs in better ways; changing existing products to meet new needs in the same markets, repositioning products for new markets, or entering new markets with new products.

And, at the same time, they can be vigilant about innovation because it leads to disruptive growth and helps reshape markets in ways that give them advantage.

They are able to make these shifts successfully because their *how*—the culture, mindsets, and philosophy of the organization—is more important than their *what*. By keeping one foot firmly stable in the "How" they can pivot toward any "What" and shoot for any measure of success.

In most organizations, as Gary Hamel notes, change is regarded as an episodic interruption of the status quo; something initiated and managed from the top. The power to initiate strategic change is concentrated there, and every change program must be endorsed, scripted, and piloted before launch. Transformational change, when it does happen, is typically too late and convulsive—and often begins only after a "regime change."

What's needed is a real-time, socially constructed approach to change in which the leader's job isn't to design a change program but to build a change platform—one that allows anyone to initiate change, recruit confederates, suggest solutions, and launch experiments. A pivot, in other words, doesn't have to be an earth-shattering move, nor does it need to be a complete reinvention of the organization. Instead, companies that are nimble pivot by making thousands of changes every day—from strategic decisions to small tweaks—rather than by relying on a few big, multiyear initiatives. They are, in Nilofer Merchant's words, not 800-pound gorillas but a cohesive group of 800 gazelles that can move quickly and lightly across the landscape, changing direction at a moment's notice and in unison.[20]

Make no mistake, these companies also have big and bold initiatives. But they don't rely on them as their sole driver of change and growth. They constantly experiment, and they constantly make small bets—believing that some will eventually lead to business opportunities even bigger than their current one. They're attuned to their markets. They use social media to interact with and listen to customers—not to broadcast or promote. They rely on data, but they don't obsess about risk parameters or consequences, nor do they navel-gaze and gerrymander decisions to meet the needs of the organization over the needs of customers or markets. They empower their people to make adjustments. They leverage their intuition as a guide and apply agile development processes to bring concepts into action. They don't view change management as a set of processes for moving from point A to point B, but as a workplace philosophy that encompasses real-time collaboration, participation, alignment, and awareness.

How can you position your organization to pivot?

Too often, I run into organizations that try to become more innovative or customer-focused by adopting the processes and models of more successful organizations without making deeper changes. I've seen the leaders of retail organizations come back from the Disney Institute and say, "Let's start calling all of our store sales people 'cast members!'" As if that label will turn a slightly wary and perhaps cynical twenty-something into a more engaged, customer-focused, crowd-pleaser in the store. How many organizations successfully Zappos their customer service, or GE their way to flawless execution?

It's not about processes and operating models. Those can be adopted, but they won't stick or make a meaningful impact unless they are embedded in your culture. The way you structure and position your company must be a conduit for the beliefs and mindsets you have in place.

So, when contemplating the attributes I've described above for companies like Cisco Systems, GE, or Toyota, recognize that whatever approach you take must be right for your culture. At the same time, the approach you take—if you push it hard enough—is going to change and develop your culture, so be sure that this is where you want to go and what you want to become. GE is the master at this—using initiatives that drive innovation and growth to deliberately change culture and give the company the *how* it needs to tackle the *what* it wants to pursue.

QUESTIONS FOR YOU TO CONSIDER:

* Does your company focus more on exploration or exploitation, or is there an equal emphasis on both?

* On a scale of one to ten (ten being most likely), how likely is your leadership to recognize the need to pivot?

* What processes, structures, and beliefs may be preventing your company from making necessary pivots?

4

THEY STRUCTURE FOR SPEED

HCL TECHNOLOGIES is a US $6 billion business and information-services technology company headquartered near New Delhi, India, with operations in more than thirty countries. The company had been growing rapidly since the mid-1980s until that trajectory began to stall in 2000, even relative to HCL's competitors. By 2005, Vineet Nayar, who had worked for HCL his entire career, was asked to take over as CEO. His only condition to the board was that he be allowed to take an unconventional approach to managing the business.

Nayar knew that the company had become bogged down by its own processes and bureaucracy, and he believed that it was heading toward an inevitable decline unless something radical was done. This conviction was reinforced shortly after he assumed his role as CEO when he visited a key customer who had canceled a long-standing HCL contract. When Nayar asked what HCL could have done better, the client said, "Your employees did nothing wrong as individuals. But your organization did not support them."[1]

To Nayar, this criticism defined the crux of the problem. Customers gain most of their value from a company through their interactions with customer-facing employees, but companies are typically oriented in the other direction—on the needs, perspectives, priorities, and directives of the hierarchy. Nayar's key insight was to reimagine the interface between customers and customer-facing employees as actually composing the "value zone" of an enterprise. He then set out to reorganize HCL Technologies to maximize that value.

His initiative was called Employees First, Customers Second (EFCS). The cliché of business is that the customer comes first. But to Nayar, if customer-facing employees were not supported in the right way, those customers would never receive "first-class" service. So the organization actually needs to operate in service of those employees in the value zone who, in turn, work to serve the customer. Every role other than those in the value zone, including the CEO, should serve as "enabling functions." In other words, the hierarchy needs to work to support value-zone employees, not the other way around.

Nayar's philosophy changed the way HCL Technologies operated. Instead of supervising, assessing, sanctioning, and rewarding employees, managers had a new role—encouraging and empowering employees to create value with customers. HCL Technologies set up a number of practices to drive this transformation. It implemented a Smart Service Desk—a ticket-based online system that allowed employees to submit a ticket to enable functions to solve their problems and help support their role. They created a voluntary 360-degree feedback system so that managers could be assessed by employees and that feedback was posted on the HCL intranet. Indeed, Nayar got the ball rolling by posting his own 360-degree process online. HCL also started opinion polls to keep employees engaged while surfacing their feedback and ideas. It launched "Directions" as an annual company-wide event to take strategic discussions out of closed-door meetings and share them with all employees while allowing them to ask questions about vision, strategy, and daily practices. Recognizing the importance of that, Nayar spent seven hours a week replying to employee queries.

What happened as a result? Nayar's new approach helped make HCL Technologies more "nimble, focused, and feisty." Thousands of employees were empowered to make daily improvements to processes that created more value for customers. HCL Technologies became better at responding quickly and effectively to customer needs, and its market share began to grow. During the eight years of Nayar's tenure, HCL expanded operations to thirty-two countries and increased its revenues by six times.[2]

THE IMPACT OF HIERARCHY ON TRUST, DECISIONS, AND SPEED

Why are so many organizations hierarchical by design and nature? Is the basic pyramid structure of most org charts an effective way of directing employees, allocating resources, and pursuing strategic objectives or an elegant means of imposing power and control while stifling individual initiative?

I'm sure the motives behind hierarchical structures are complex and diverse, but I don't think they were or are all bad.

Research out of Stanford by Larissa Tiedens and Emily Zitek on the value of hierarchical relationships supports this view. According to the research paper "The Fluency of Social Hierarchy: The Ease With Which Hierarchical Relationships Are Seen, Remembered, Learned, and Liked," people appreciate hierarchy because it makes tasks, relationships, and thinking easier, whereas a truly flat or egalitarian model can be stressful, difficult, or unproductive for an individual to navigate or manage. As Tiedens puts it, "there are things that are good about hierarchy, and things that are good about equality. When you're creating an organization it's important to think about what structure will serve your goals best."[3]

One fascinating organizational psychologist, Elliott Jaques, conducted a life-long study of human behavior and how we organize around tasks. He carefully examined the nature of the tasks involved with various jobs and developed structures for managing their complexity and time horizon. Under his guidance, the Oakland Police Department changed its approach to community policing by organizing its team structure with four levels of hierarchy—from a beat police officer in the field to the ultimate supervisor. This was, in Jaques' analysis, the right amount of hierarchy for the tasks assigned to the "customer-facing" beat officer. Any more levels of hierarchy and the problems of the community would have been poorly understood by those in management. However, any less hierarchy and the beat police officer would have felt under-supported by the police department.[4]

You can measure the right amount of hierarchy in an organization, according to Jaques, by the level of trust that exists and the degree to which people at all levels feel supported and cared for in their roles. In other words, a certain number of levels is ideal depending on the size of the organization and the complexity of its work. In the largest and most complex organizations, for example, there should be a maximum of eight levels. In smaller, more intimate teams, two or three levels may be sufficient. This sounds right to me, on the basis of my experience working with various types of organizations, as long as the hierarchy and its chains of management are supporting and serving their people versus stifling or creating bureaucracy. Google or Facebook may have very empowered engineers who are given great latitude in determining how to spend their time or allocate resources, but they do have some degree of oversight and support within a hierarchy that is flatter than in a company like GE or Wells Fargo. Other organizations, as I will discuss, are even flatter.

I don't pretend to know the magic formula for how much or how little hierarchy is ideal in an organization. However, I think there is no question that traditional "tall" hierarchical structures make organizations move more slowly. They change slowly, execute slowly, allocate resources slowly, disseminate information slowly, and—most important—make decisions slowly.

Today, that last output—the ability to make decisions quickly and responsively—is becoming a critical factor in the success or failure of an enterprise. According to Forrester Consulting, "one-third of all products are delivered late or incomplete due to an inability or delay in decision-making,"[5] while product teams spend three-and-a-half hours waiting for decisions for every eight-hour workday, even as, because of competition, customer expectations, globalization, and a 24/7 mindset, the decision-making window is shrinking quickly. According to Kerem Tomak, vice president of analytics for Macys.com: "In the dot-com space, we have in general seven seconds or less to entice the customer; otherwise they will be going to our competitors. That means we need a laser focus on how we deliver products and services the minute the customer comes to the site."[6]

Indeed, employees of companies with traditional hierarchies find that a lack of focus on the customer and a lack of speed in decision-making are frustrating. Responsibility, authority, and decision-making in such organizations generally sit with a few leaders at the very top. Employees who are doing the fundamental work of the organization—managing customers, making products, selling services—are forced to drive information and process decisions through layers of bureaucracy in order to obtain permission or direction to get things done. Often, it can seem as though each additional step on that ladder encumbers an obvious decision with unrelated internal concerns or priorities at the expense of truly addressing the issue at hand. Burdened with the results of that "sausage-making" exercise, employees do not always like or appreciate the position it puts them in. Indeed, I've found this particularly true of those employees who must go back—after great delay—to face the actual customer in question.

Not only does this hierarchical orientation slow down the organization, but it also hurts its agility. In other words, it's the antithesis of nimble. Managers higher in the hierarchy, wrestling with their own priorities or the priorities of their superiors, are separated or detached from the problems of employees; accordingly, they are less likely to have the urgency or awareness needed to spur any organizational change that could better meet or solve those challenges. The organization is inherently conservative as a result and stays whatever course it has been on toward whatever goals it has determined are important. Employees in turn stop trying quite as hard since they see no reward in the responsiveness of managers. Eventually they disengage from the priorities of the organization with their sense of motivation and their passion and creativity stifled or thwarted. This is especially true among younger employees who feel a close connection with customers and markets and don't see increased flexibility in decision-making as a responsibility but as more of a right. As Vineet Nayar has observed, Millennials "have little interest in hierarchy and are not particularly impressed by the titles and positions within the traditional pyramid structure." Naturally, they will take their brains, hearts, and talents elsewhere if they are frustrated by hierarchical bureaucracy for too long.

So what's an organization to do? In this chapter, I want to look at how NFF companies balance their needs for efficiency, control, and coordinated execution with their need for responsiveness, customer sensitivity, and market awareness.

THEY PUSH DECISIONS TO THE FLAT-EDGE OF THE PYRAMID

An NFF company structures itself so that decisions can be made quickly and the organization can be more agile, flexible, and adaptable in pursuit of its vision. Fundamentally, it distributes authority throughout the organization so that decisions can be made closest to the source of the problem, challenge, or task in question. In this sense, it flattens the hierarchy of the organization to maximize its contact with primary business' needs. In other words, instead of focusing decision-making at the top of the pyramid, NFF companies orient toward the bottom edge.

Vineet Nayar focused his organization on customer-facing employees working in what he called the value zone. Nordstrom, the upscale clothing retailer founded in the late 1800s, does something similar, which it calls "Inverting the Pyramid." It's a powerful example of how a concept around decision-making can transform and drive an organization's success.

When employees join Nordstrom, they take a simple one-day orientation course and are given a gray card. This card is Nordstrom's entire employee handbook. It reads: "Welcome to Nordstrom. We're glad to have you with our Company. Our number one goal is to provide outstanding customer service. Set both your personal and professional goals high. We have great faith in your ability to achieve them." To guide the conduct of those employees Nordstrom has one rule: "Use good judgment in all situations. There will be no additional rules. Please feel free to ask your department manager, store manager, or division general manager any question at any time."

Nordstrom structures itself so that employees are empowered to treat customers as they themselves would like to be treated. Employees are encouraged to exercise good judgment to do whatever is necessary to satisfy the customer. Meanwhile, the hierarchy of the organization is structured to support those front-line employees in that task. Why? Because Nordstrom believes that the relationship between customer and employee is critical to capturing that customer long-term. After working with some of the world's largest retailers throughout the years, I can't express how differentiated an approach this truly is. Most retailers I've seen hinge on processes that rely on manager approval, limiting critical thinking, and shrinking the employee-empowered decision spectrum rather than expanding it.

Other organizations that distribute decision-making flatten their authority closest to the user, research, product, or market because this is where the best solutions will be recognized and can be responded to most quickly. This is a fundamental rethink of the direction of hierarchical empowerment. As Steve Jobs said, "It doesn't make sense to hire smart people and then tell them what to do; we hire smart people so they can tell us what to do."

As Steve Jobs said, "It doesn't make sense to hire smart people and then tell them what to do; we hire smart people so they can tell us what to do."

THEY RELY ON VALUES, NOT RULES, TO GUIDE DECISIONS

If hierarchy is not telling employees at NFF companies what to do, then how are they guided or led? Primarily, such organizations rely on shared values, information, mindset, and vision to steer employees in making independent decisions.

Recently I had contrasting hotel experiences that taught me a lot about the power of letting values guide customer service. In one experience, I had plans to meet a group of girlfriends in Las Vegas for a weekend get-together. Unfortunately, I came down ill. Rather than subject my friends and others to a highly contagious virus, I decided to cancel my plans. It was less than twenty-four hours before my planned visit, and I knew that my hotel reservation could not be changed on less than two days' notice, but I decided to try anyway.

I called the hotel, told the person on the phone my situation, and asked if she could do something for me. I didn't even want my money back, but I thought she might transfer my reservation to a different day. The person I talked to could not truly believe what I was asking. With a belligerent tone, she told me to wait and put me on hold to consult a manager. Twenty minutes went by—I was curious about what would ultimately happen, so I stayed on the line. She finally returned to the call and did not remember who I was or what I was calling about. I explained again. She went for the manager again and another twenty minutes went by. The manager eventually came to the phone, but he did not know what I was calling about, so I needed to tell the story again. The manager could barely control his anger and derision that I would even ask for a change in my reservation and told me the policy was clear and there was nothing he could do for me. He then hung up. It was clear to me that this hotel's internal policies and regulations were clearly understood and highly prioritized. It was also clear that, as an individual customer, I was neither valued nor considered in the formula for whatever drove success in that organization.

A month later, I visited a nearby Ritz-Carlton to have a leisurely lunch with a friend. We enjoyed each other, the food, the setting, and the easy conversation we had with the waitress who served us. I mentioned how much I liked the salad dressing and the waitress returned before our lunch was over with a gift box she had put together. Inside was a bottle of the salad dressing. I was touched and surprised and offered to pay for it. She insisted that it was her gift to me because she knew how much I had enjoyed the dressing. This interaction felt completely authentic and meaningful, and I was touched and delighted.

Reading up on Ritz-Carlton, I learned that its motto is "Ladies and gentlemen serving ladies and gentlemen." I also learned that each Ritz-Carlton employee is authorized to spend up to $2,000 per incident on a customer at the employee's discretion to ensure that the highest standard of customer service is met. As CEO Simon Cooper puts it, "The concept is to do something, to create an absolutely wonderful stay for a guest. Significantly, there is no assumption that it's because there is a problem. It could be that someone finds out it's a guest's birthday, and the next thing you know there's champagne and cake in the room. A lot of the stuff that crosses my desk is not that they overcame a problem but that they used their $2,000 to create an outstanding experience."[7]

Ritz-Carlton trains its employees carefully so that they know what that kind of freedom means according to the values and mission of the organization. But, because of that training and the quality of the employees it hires, it is able to give all employees total trust with the customer. This latitude allows Ritz-Carlton employees to deal with customer concerns immediately with a very authentic response to needs rather than fighting upstream through a bureaucracy focused on processes and policies.

Not only does such latitude give Ritz-Carlton more responsiveness and agility, but it also reinforces the quality of its people. Which employee would you rather have in your organization—one who is angry at a customer for getting ill, or one who independently offers a customer a better experience as a gesture of human connection?

Just to show you that this approach to empowerment is not limited to organizations that aim to delight customers, consider the US military.

Gen. Stanley McChrystal ran Joint Special Operations Command in Iraq and Afghanistan for nearly five years, and later commanded all US and international forces in Afghanistan. He talks about the challenge of Al Qaeda's emergence and how the military needed to rethink its assumptions.

"We grew up in the military with this classic hierarchy: one person at the top, with two to seven subordinates below that, and two to seven below that, and so on. That's what organizational theory says works," he explains. Against Al Qaeda, however, "we had to change our structure, to become a network. We were required to react quickly. Instead of decisions being made by people who were more senior—the assumption that senior meant wiser—we found that the wisest decisions were usually made by those closest to the problem."

In order to get to the best ideas and decisions, he tried to create a "shared consciousness." He wanted everyone to understand the organization's goals and strategies. "My command team and I guided our values, strategy, and priorities," he says. "The leaders lower in the organization made tactical and operational decisions in line with those principles."[8]

In a rules-based culture people are forced to ask, "Can I?" and many times don't have the opportunity, flexibility, or confidence to make empowered decisions. In a values-based culture, individuals are empowered with clear decision-making criteria (the values) that actually empower them within a given framework. They have a deep understanding of the strategy and values of the organization and can make their decisions in support of this direction.

THEY RELY ON SELF-ORGANIZED TEAMS AND INDIVIDUALS TO RUN THE SHOW

W.L. Gore is an example of a company that has been very intentional and thoughtful in structuring its teams to encourage quick decision-making and innovation. Founder Bill Gore left a flourishing career at DuPont because he thought its corporate practices stifled innovation and agility. He imagined his ideal company structure not as a pyramid but as a "lattice" connecting every individual in the organization to one another, with no layers of management. Gore believed information would flow freely in all directions in such a structure, and that individuals and self-managed teams would be able to go directly to anyone in the organization to get what they needed to be successful.

As Gore has grown, it has imposed some structure: the CEO, four major divisions, a number of product-focused business units, and the usual business-support functions, each with a recognized leader. But it remains flat, with self-managed teams as the basic building blocks, and no management layers. How can that possibly work with an organization of 9,000 employees located in thirty countries worldwide? Part of the formula is the company's commitment to keeping its operations small and informal. It generally doesn't allow a facility to grow to more than 150 people. This is reflective of Bill's belief that once a unit reaches a certain size, "we decided" becomes "they decided." It also reflects the science of the evolutionary psychologist Robin Dunbar, who discovered, while studying the world's remaining hunter-gatherer societies, that clans tend to have 150 members. The key finding is that, cognitively, humans aren't built for maintaining meaningful relationships when groups are larger than that. At Gore, once a branch exceeds 150 employees, the company breaks it into two and builds a new office to maintain that connectivity.

The ability for people closest to the research and product to make independent decisions was illustrated by the invention of an improved guitar string. An associate in Gore's medical products group named Dave Myers came up with the idea of coating guitar strings with the company's ubiquitous polytetrafluoroethylene or PTFE because he thought it would make guitar strings easier to play. Myers, on his own initiative, persuaded John Spencer, another Gore associate, to conduct market research on the idea. It wasn't the first time a company had tried coating metal guitar strings with plastic, including nylon and polyurethane, but previous efforts had underperformed and failed in the marketplace. Undaunted, Myers and Spencer pushed their idea forward, eventually field-testing samples of their PTFE-coated strings with more than 15,000 guitarists. As it turned out, the guitarists reported that the primary benefit of Gore's strings wasn't comfort—they were marginally better in that department—but that their tone held up better than other brands. Guitar strings, which are made of metal, are notoriously short-lasting—they have to stand up to hours of exposure to human sweat during the course of a gig, which quickly corrodes them and dulls their tone.

The input received from these guitarists was used to develop prototypes of the very first Gore guitar strings, given the brand name Elixir. These prototypes were sent out to 5,000 working musicians for testing in real-world conditions. After a few tweaks, Elixir strings were put into production and introduced with a big splash—quickly gaining the number-one position for acoustic-guitar strings sales, and pivoting the company into an entirely new market.[9]

Whole Foods has self-directed teams that meet regularly to discuss issues, solve problems, and appreciate others' contributions. The company organizes its stores into a variety of interlocking teams, which range from six to one hundred members, with larger teams subdivided into sub-teams. Teams—and only teams—have the power to approve new hires for full-time jobs. It takes a two-thirds vote of the team for a candidate to become a full-time employee. Teams compete against their own goals for sales, growth, and productivity; they also compete against different teams in their store and against similar teams in different stores and regions.[10]

"We aren't interested in hierarchy; we just don't feel it's effective in any way," co-founder John Mackey explained. "We like to think of ourselves as a democracy, a structured and disciplined democracy. Energy and ideas work their way up, rather than the other way around. When it comes to rules, I believe that less is more."[11]

GitHub, a company that functions as a collaboration platform for software developers, uses an open-allocation approach to allow programmers to determine what they want to do and how they want to go about doing it. "Unlike traditional companies where projects are assigned top-down," previous CEO Tom Preston-Warner says, "GitHubbers tackle whatever projects they want, without any formal requests or managerial interference."

As Preston-Warner elaborates: "You know, these huge companies complain all the time about not being able to innovate, and yet they put these very strict, controlling hierarchies in place, and they're mystified by why they can't innovate. Well, if you tell people what to do every single day, and they get in trouble if they do something that's not on their list, then how could you possibly innovate?"

Is this approach applicable to a more traditional company? Preston-Warner thinks so and believes that in such a company "your main job as the manager...is to communicate strategy, and then let other people determine what's important in order to accomplish that strategy."[12]

Red Hat, the distributor of Linux and OpenStack cloud software, has a similar approach. CEO Jim Whitehurst, who came from Delta Airlines and had a background in management consulting, fully intended to hold Red Hat teams more accountable and to impose a more clearly delineated chain of command. He soon discovered, however, that the company's culture already did a better job monitoring and assessing projects and driving innovation than anything he could design through a system of reporting and oversight. In fact, formalizing processes already baked into the culture would have actually impeded the ability of the business to make decisions about product quality quickly. So instead of reversing that openness, Whitehurst embraced it.

In FY 2015, Red Hat saw a 17 percent increase in revenues.

FASTER, NOT HARDER

"The beauty of an open organization," Whitehurst claims, "is that it is not about pedaling harder, but about tapping into new sources of power."[13]

In my view, NFF companies that work to their full capacity at speed do so by being pragmatic about hierarchy. They "structure" their organization not according to idealistic notions of egalitarianism or traditional notions of authority and rank but to support people closest to business needs.

At Red Hat, for example, managers are relied upon not to supervise employees but to be creative about directing or facilitating them to do their best, most value-rich work. Chipotle, the popular restaurant chain, upended its hierarchy to have managers focus on developing people under them while also creating fantastic restaurant experiences for customers. This creates a culture of empowerment from the bottom-up, while also providing significant opportunities for growth and development for all.

Hierarchy, in that sense, is the platform for personal growth, organizational agility, customer service, and market focus. Too much or too little hierarchy presents problems in those areas. I'm as big a fan of Zappos' customer-service approach as anyone, which you'll hear about a bit later, and I'm in awe of the revolutionary way it empowers employees to see to customer needs. But I'm skeptical or at least agnostic about its drive to become a Holacracy™ with zero hierarchy. If indeed CEO Tony Hsieh actually sees it all the way through, I worry that a complete lack of oversight would hamper employees' ability to do the right thing at the right time in the right time frame.

And it's not because I think employees will be too lazy or indifferent if they are not being watched like hawks. In the past few years, starting with Netflix, a number of companies have loosened their vacation policy from hierarchical oversight by giving employees the freedom to take as much vacation as they would like. This was a shock to many people who quickly fantasized about the long trips they would take with their paid freedom away from the office. The reality, however, at least for one organization, is that the opposite result has occurred. Triggertrap, the British photo-equipment company, has found that employees take too little rather than too much time off. They felt guilt, apparently, about being away and very responsible for their duties. Yet, the lack of time off was contributing to employee burnout and slowing the organization down. Now, instead of letting employees decide how much time they should or shouldn't take off, Triggertrap is publicly tracking vacation days, making teams responsible for ensuring people don't burn out, and offering bonuses to those who take off at least fourteen days every six months.[14]

Ultimately, NFF companies are not in the game of trying to control or impede their people. Rather, they want to support their people to give their all and help make the company better. Such organizations build programs, processes, and practices that enable employees to make decisions in their areas of concern. They construct well-defined guidelines for their employees, giving them clear direction and expectations, but they also afford them the maximum possible flexibility and the power to act autonomously. They firmly believe that employees steeped in the culture and closest to the value zone are best positioned to understand the critical needs of the organization. In a sense, those employees actually drive the organization forward, operationally, strategically, and culturally.

Most important, they give the organization more speed, agility, and customer smarts than it would have otherwise.

QUESTIONS FOR YOU TO CONSIDER:

* Do you know where your "value zone" is?

* Does your company rely more on values or rules to guide your employees' and teams' actions?

5

THEY SOLVE PROBLEMS BY CO-CREATING AND COLLABORATING

ON A WARM FLORIDA AFTERNOON in April 1970 three men left for work together. They weren't headed for their corporate offices and they didn't have any meetings or sales calls on the agenda that day. These men had a loftier goal in mind: They were going to the moon.

Jim Lovell, John "Jack" Swigert, and Fred Haise formed the crew of Apollo 13, the third mission in the American Apollo space program intended to land on the moon. The crew launched from the Kennedy Space Center at the planned time of 2:13 P.M. EST on April 11 in the Apollo spacecraft. Apollo 13 was actually made of two independent spacecraft joined by a tunnel—the orbiter Odyssey, the craft in which the crew would live during the journey to the moon, and the lander Aquarius, which would be activated when the crew prepared for the moon landing.

On the evening of April 13, the Apollo crew wrapped up a television segment explaining its mission and discussing life aboard the ship. Jim, Jack, and Fred were more than 200,000 miles from Earth and very close to the moon at this point. Mission Control saw a low-pressure warning signal on a hydrogen tank in Odyssey. This signal might have indicated that the hydrogen inside the tank needed to be resettled by heating and fanning the gas, or it might have been a hint of a more serious problem. Mission Control asked Apollo 13 to take a look. Jack Swigert flipped a switch for a routine procedure, and moments later the entire spacecraft shuddered. Alarm lights lit up, oxygen pressure fell, and the main power supplies dropped rapidly. Swigert updated Mission Control back in Texas with the now-famous phrase, "Houston, we've had a problem."[1]

The crew was not aware of the full extent or particular nature of the problem at that moment, but later studies revealed that a series of sparks from exposed wires had caused a fire, destroying two oxygen tanks. This ended any hopes of a successful moon landing.[2] Instead, the space crew and ground crew were left scrambling to figure out how to get the astronauts home safely. Rapidly losing power and breathable air, the ship threatened to become unlivable and unbearably cold very quickly.

Ground Control decided that the Apollo 13 crew should power down the Odyssey entirely, then scramble down the tunnel and find refuge in the Aquarius, something it had not been designed to provide. So the three men piled into the Aquarius as they had been instructed, and hoped that the spaceship would serve as their lifeboat in space.

The situation was frightening to all involved. It also presented a series of complex, urgent, and dangerous problems with incredibly tight restraints and limitations, and a very rapid shift in priorities. The new mission was to return the ship to Earth along the fastest route possible while conserving sufficient power, oxygen, and water for a safe journey. This challenge was made even more complicated by the fact that Aquarius had actually been designed to contain two men for a short time but would now have to accommodate three men for a longer distance and duration. The ground team was sent into a flurry to solve those challenges while providing instructions to a space crew that was effectively blind and practically helpless.

In meeting problem after problem, the NASA team found solutions together under extreme pressure. Not one single person could have pulled this off. It required each and every one to play a role. For example, to sift dangerous levels of carbon dioxide from the air, the ground crew instructed the space crew in how to build a makeshift air filter using only parts available on Aquarius. To preserve power, the crew was told how to correctly sequence the shutdown of every nonessential system, even as cabin pressure fell and temperatures dropped to near freezing. It was so dire that water intake had to be minimized to ensure that the Aquarius had enough liquid to cool its hardware; all the while their food supply was becoming inedible. There was no rest for anyone involved. The intensity of the collaboration, innovation, teamwork, and problem-solving required is difficult to imagine. Yet, what could have been the most spectacular failure of the space age became one of NASA's finest hours when Aquarius splashed safely into the Pacific Ocean on April 17.

PREPARING FOR GRACE UNDER PRESSURE

How were the astronauts on Apollo 13 and the engineers at Mission Control able to overcome each successive problem during a period of incredible life-and-death stress?

No team can adequately prepare for every crisis, but the team at the Kennedy Space Center was probably more prepared than most. If it had not already been capable of achieving such a high level of collaboration, I doubt it could have manufactured that capacity during the heat of the moment. Instead, the team needed the right people, the right environment, and the right processes in place not only to put astronauts on the moon, but also to find solutions and anticipate problems to resolve unforeseeable crises.

Reviewing old interviews and accounts of those events, it's incredibly interesting to learn about NASA Flight Director Gene Kranz, and the culture of collaboration he fostered. Kranz was the man in charge of the team back on Earth that rescued the Apollo 13 astronauts. When some of his associates were interviewed later, they described how Kranz was always very confident in the team's ability to make good decisions even during a stressful crisis. They also emphasized how closely his team listened to his guidance and how much the members trusted him. Impressively, at a time when most organizations and corporations were driven by a buttoned-down, command-and-control philosophy, Kranz was lauded for being a leader who empowered others, listened carefully to them, and fostered an atmosphere of trust and collaboration while building his team's capacity to problem-solve and innovate.

One story in particular stands out for me. When the disaster first struck Apollo 13 and the astronauts were forced to abandon the Odyssey, debate ensued within the Ground Control team as to whether the astronauts should then be force-marched through a long power-down procedure or should be allowed to rest. Kranz listened to three experts discuss the issue, saying very little throughout. Then he made the decision to power down and directed the team members to act. Everyone—even those who had held divergent views—coalesced immediately around a very complicated and intense procedure that required many contributions and total commitment.

Like the best leader, when Kranz was confronted with an ambiguous problem, he encouraged open debate about the best step forward; then he made a decision. Everyone got on board, acted, and drove toward a solution. In the movie, this is dramatic because Kranz kept his composure under significant pressure. In reality, it was only possible because Kranz had a special relationship with his team. He did not have a "Don't question me, I'm in charge" persona, so his team knew it could offer challenging views. And he respected his team members' knowledge and insight. He was also decisive when he needed to be. He could have dithered and remained paralyzed and had the decision get made for him by the rush of events flying by. Instead, he took in all the data and then made a timely choice based on his own experience, insight, and gut feeling. His team, in turn, respected his decisions and acted on them without hesitation, putting aside any differing opinions. This atmosphere of trust and respect fortified the team's ability to do a few essential things exceptionally well:

1. confront challenges
2. collect data
3. assemble points of view
4. make timely decisions
5. act in unison

WHAT IS COLLABORATION?

The ability to become or stay nimble—in order to better serve customers, and to drive disruptive innovation rather than be disrupted—is highly dependent upon a workforce that is encouraged, able, and positioned to react and pursue solutions just like the team at NASA. This success requires a culture that is rooted in trust, with the systems and processes in place to support effective collaboration, and with people who are willing and driven to work together. It takes a deep-seated commitment from the organization to make that happen. Highly collaborative organizations have clear guardrails and understandings of how and when to properly collaborate. They also encourage the destruction of silos within their company walls, and leverage the power and brilliance of their people to come up with the best strategies and execute. These companies truly rely on their people and culture to co-create the future.

In my experience, too many leaders and their organizations believe they are highly collaborative but fail to understand what collaboration really means, what it takes, what impact it should have, and when it should be applied (as well as when it should not).

Some leaders fear that collaboration is slower than the "go it alone" path. There's a saying in Africa, "If you want to go far, go together. If you want to go fast, go alone," which probably rings true for many of us when assigned to a team project. Most of us think: instead of pooling responsibility and discussing everything to death, just let me go back to my office, close the door, and get something done. But in nimble organizations, the opposite is true. You can both go far and go fast together, if you're doing it well.

One of the biggest and most common flaws I've seen is that organizations that mistakenly believe they are collaborating are actually spending their energies on consensus-building. Consensus-building exists to drive toward unanimous or nearly unanimous agreement, ensuring head nods around the room, or to force-fit a decision that everyone can agree on. Good collaboration is not this.

Consensus-building is not only incredibly slow—often stymieing teams for months—but it can also promote passive-aggressive behavior. The dark underbelly of consensus is that it makes it possible for people to agree to support something that is so broad that their specific role and contribution isn't really necessary to the idea, project, or strategy's success.

Jim Collins, author of *Good to Great*, said that in his years of research, "No major decision we've studied was ever taken at a point of unanimous agreement."[3] Collins observes that there was always healthy debate and lingering disagreement when decisions in these great companies were made. Yet, the people in these organizations would quickly switch from debate mode to unify behind the decision in order to move forward.

It's also important to understand when you need collaboration. I once read a report by the *Economist* about collaboration and trust. In studying numerous organizations and interviewing more than 400 people, the researchers found that in many instances "collaboration" wasn't actually the optimal approach given the particular circumstances. Instead, what was needed at that moment was something closer to cooperation or coordination.[4]

Cooperation is best applied when the organization is focused on a broad but mandated goal—something that the organization needs to come together on. Think of your most recent human-resources or process-improvement initiative. Cooperation can work even if the commitment levels of those participating in the work are uneven. Some can pull the weight of others and it still nudges the organization forward. In these situations, there's less need for trust than there is for politeness and mutual consideration. Nor does information necessarily have to be completely transparent or shared. The overall value of the initiative may bring desired change but will not produce a dramatic transformation or burst of innovation. There's not enough energy in cooperation for earthshaking results.

Coordination, by comparison, is narrower in scope and focused on getting something done. Think execution of a strategy or plan. Coordination is often catalyzed by directive—"Take care of this and make it happen"—but while the process is improved by healthy teamwork, exceptional teamwork is not necessary for coordination goals to be achieved. Often, tasks can be handled almost as well by individuals as by the team because roles are not truly differentiated and everyone involved does not have to be contributing at peak levels to produce the best outputs.

Collaboration, however, is needed when the desired results must be exceptional and can't be achieved by one person alone, or even by a group of people who are not all passionate about and committed to a common cause. In other words, the goals of a collaborative effort are mutually shared and imbued with a sense of possibility and represent an exceptional achievement. Collaborative efforts can make the world a better place. Inside an organization they are best reserved for moon shots and solving big, hairy problems because the creative energy that results can lead to potential game-changing or even life-saving strategies or approaches, as with Apollo 13.

Clear distinctions between cooperation, coordination, and collaboration are so important today because the need for speed and agility demands that the organization apply the right approach at the right time. To do otherwise would be to waste time and opportunity. Nimble organizations know when to cooperate, when to coordinate, and when to collaborate. They also are very aware that through collaboration the richest veins of gold will be found. Accordingly, nimble organizations put great emphasis on the character and personality of their people, on creating a trust-rich environment, on deepening relationships, and on building the capacity of their teams to come together and be extraordinary. To that end, I've found that companies that leverage collaboration effectively share a few distinct attributes.

THEY KEEP ROLES VERY CLEAR AND LEAVE TASKS OPEN

The myth is that the best way to ensure collaboration is to bring together team members with overlapping roles and responsibilities so that this dynamic will encourage them to share their ideas and contributions across multiple areas. My colleague Tamara Erickson has studied and written on collaboration for many years. In her *Harvard Business Review* article "Eight Ways to Build Collaborative Teams," co-written with Lynda Gratton, her research shows that collaboration dramatically improves when the roles of individual team members are clearly defined and well understood—in fact, when individuals feel their role is bounded in ways that allow them to complete a significant portion of their work independently, they thrive. Without such clarity, team members are likely to waste energy and spend many a meeting negotiating roles or protecting turf, rather than focusing on tasks.

Interestingly, Erickson's and Gratton's study provides another truly compelling insight: "Team members are more likely to want to collaborate if the path to achieving the team's goal is left somewhat ambiguous. If a team perceives the task as one that requires creativity, where the approach is not yet well known or predefined, its members are more likely to invest time and energy in collaboration."[5]

This role clarity, coupled with open tasks, helps collaboration naturally flow throughout an organization and within teams. Take a hospital emergency room, for example. Before the next patient or ambulance arrives, the doctors and nurses have no idea of the nature of the task ahead. Will the patient require surgery, heart resuscitation, medications? The condition of the patient is unknown, and what will be required of the team is ambiguous. But you'd better believe the team of medical experts doesn't waste time negotiating roles when the patient arrives. Everyone is clear. The team is able to quickly move into action to get the instruments ready, prep the patient, and address the problem.

Or consider the way a team of cyclists competes in the Tour de France. Many individuals in the peloton, the main pack of riders, are capable of winning a single stage through an extraordinary act of courage, strength, and stamina. But the goal of the tour is to see each team's overall leader win. This necessitates a sound strategy, but mostly it requires that each member of the team have defined roles, even as the tactics or circumstances of the race invariably change in dramatic and unexpected ways. Those who are meant to pace the team leader up a steep climb must throw themselves into that task without consideration for their own position in the race. Similarly, those who have the "domestique" role must race back and forth between the team car and the race leaders to keep the team supplied with water bottles and food. Without that kind of collaboration, no team could even finish the grueling three-week-long race.

In turbulent and ambiguous times, collaboration is a thrill rather than a bureaucratic burden. This is why the challenge of a crisis can bring teams together and create a special level of performance and accomplishment.

Anyone who has fully engaged herself in the efforts of a sports team or a creative project team knows how exhilarating the unexpected paths toward success can be. In turbulent and ambiguous times, collaboration is a thrill rather than a bureaucratic burden. This is why the challenge of a crisis can bring teams together and create a special level of performance and accomplishment.

THEY BRING A VARIETY OF CONTRIBUTORS TOGETHER TO GET TO THE BEST SOLUTION

How can an organization create a collaborative atmosphere in which silos are naturally broken down and people collaborate on a daily basis? Perhaps Pixar has more to show us than just great movies. The animated film company recognizes the critical value of collaboration and deliberately designs and leverages collaborative processes through its teams on a daily rather than an extraordinary basis. Indeed, it is because of effective collaboration that Pixar consistently creates box-office hits that are deeply cherished by passionate fans.

I expect that it's not easy to perform under that kind of pressure. Every time Pixar releases a film, audiences expect to see a new iconic movie that will make them laugh, cry, and see the world differently. To meet those exacting expectations, Pixar has turned its creative process into a quality machine.

Pixar had already turned out several great films when it ran headlong into that pressure to replicate its outstanding level of performance. While attempting to develop *Toy Story 2,* the sequel to its most iconic hit, Pixar discovered that the early drafts of the film were not coming close to meeting its standards. This second-rate quality would have been OK for Disney, the company financing the sequel, because Disney was only expecting Pixar to produce a "straight-to-video" movie that could extract more value from the cherished characters featured in the first film. To the leaders at Pixar, however, this wasn't good enough, so they decided to turn their full attention to the creative process at work in producing the sequel.

They quickly realized that the problem had a lot to do with the quality of the talent at work. Essentially, Pixar had put its "B-team" on the job and was seeing the inevitable consequences. When the "A-team" was brought in, a much better film—indeed one of the greatest animated films ever made—was produced in an aggressive eighteen-month time frame.

Pixar learned a couple of valuable lessons. First, culturally speaking, it could not tolerate producing sub-par quality. So it needed to figure out how to produce top quality while still meeting the business needs of the film industry by keeping a number of different projects in development at the same time. It solved this second problem by reconceiving the creative process from a solo act to a collaborative one.

As Ed Catmull, one of Pixar's founders, puts it, "People tend to think of creativity as a mysterious solo act, and they typically reduce products to a single idea." But a movie, Catmull says convincingly, is actually made up tens of thousands of ideas, impossible for the output of one person alone. Instead, hundreds of people are intrinsically involved. "Creativity," Catmull continues, "must be present at every level of every artistic and technical part of the organization. The leaders sort through a mass of ideas to find the ones that fit into a coherent whole."

After *Toy Story 2*, Pixar changed its approach. Rather than have its development department come up with ideas for new movies (which was the role such a department normally fills in the industry), it was now assigned to assemble small incubation teams to bring ideas to a point when they could be convincingly "sold" to the top leaders of the organization. The most important priority for management at that stage is to make sure the incubation team functions well together.

When the green light is given, the production team is formed and co-led by the producer and the director. This team, in turn, is supported by the "Brain Trust," which is composed of the senior and most experienced leaders of the organization. The production team can convene the Brain Trust at any point to receive candid feedback and ideas; though the product team isn't forced to follow any of the feedback or ideas. The Brain Trust is just there to be supportive and helpful.

In addition, Pixar, like every film company, uses its "dailies," or the film that has been shot that day, to check in and assess its progress. However, unlike other film companies, Pixar opens its dailies to the entire organization rather than just the Brain Trust and encourages creative feedback from all, accelerating the process by which problems are identified and creative solutions are found. Finally, group post mortems are also conducted not just to heap praise on successes or scorn on failures, but also to balance the positive and negative to constantly improve processes and outputs.

I think it's important to note that there must be some pretty fundamental underpinnings in place at Pixar, or anywhere, for that matter, to produce this magical elixir. For teams to collaborate effectively, team members must be carefully chosen. They're brought together because they have specialized skills, exceptional talent, and high passion to achieve results. This dynamic makes everyone on the team essential. But for such a team to work together collaboratively, there must also be a strong foundation of trust—the kind that allows for argument, dissent, candid feedback, and excellent chemistry. This trust is necessary for the team to make quick leaps from data or input to solutions, and take big jumps forward into areas that would otherwise be considered risky. As for that risk, failure is OK during collaboration because participants know (and trust each other to understand) that great success is not achievable without the strong possibility of failure; and in a trust-rich environment, everyone is willing to try again knowing that failure, at the very least, provides important data that contributes to success later. To do it right, Catmull says, all must feel they have the ability to communicate openly with anyone else, and that it is safe to offer ideas and candid feedback. And when that success does come, it leads to new and often disruptive sources of value, not derivative value or incremental improvements.

THEY SURFACE AND TAP THE WISDOM OF THEIR CROWDS

Collaboration is a kind of collective wisdom that produces higher-quality insight than anything individuals could manage on their own. Francis Galton, an English anthropologist and psychologist, discovered this more than 100 years ago. He was at a fair in 1906 when a weight-guessing contest caught his attention. The goal was to guess the weight of a butchered ox. Around 800 people entered their guesses; the person closest to the weight would win a prize. After the contest, Galton ran a statistical analysis on the guesses. He found that the average guess of all the entrants was only one pound away from the actual weight of 1,198 pounds. This collective guess was better than both the actual winner's and better than the guesses made by the "cattle experts" at the fair. Galton's findings became known as "Vox Populi" or "Wisdom of Crowds," and show the true power of the collective.[6]

More recently, we've seen this in "Who Wants to Be a Millionaire," the popular game show originally hosted by Regis Philbin in the US. If you remember, contestants are given three different lifelines to help them answer increasingly demanding questions. They can use each lifeline only once per game. These lifelines include the "50:50," in which the computer eliminates two of the four potential answers; "Phone-a-Friend," which allows contestants to make a short phone call to one of their friends who may be an expert or particularly knowledgeable in that category; and "Ask the Audience," in which studio-audience members use touchpads to vote, and the percentages of the audience answers are displayed to the contestant in a bar graph for the contestant to choose from. While the "Phone-a-Friend" experts answer the question correctly 65 percent of the time, the studio audience predicts the correct answer at a rate of 91 percent.[7] That's right, a group of random people with completely different expertise, backgrounds, and knowledge is able to pinpoint the right answer at an extremely successful rate, significantly better than an individual expert. Now, I don't know about you, but if I have a million dollars on the line, or a decision that will dictate the future success of my company, I'm giving serious consideration to picking the crowd rather than asking the expert. And if our organizations are truly committed to selecting, developing, and empowering the best "crowd" possible, that percentage should creep toward perfection.

Organizations, and their most senior leaders, commonly undervalue the power of the collective to make decisions. They empower the few—those who have climbed the company ranks with their expertise, influence, and, most important, results—to set the wide-reaching strategies and make the most important company decisions.

Thomson Reuters is an example of a company that has deliberately expanded the search for wisdom throughout the organization. According to Mona Vernon, the VP of Reuters' Data Innovation Lab, the media and information company has struck upon a pretty interesting way to home in on its best engineering talent.[8] Reuters has figured out a way to crowdsource for problem-solvers—from behind its firewall.

We all know that silos exist in most companies. One of the key problems with leveraging engineering talent, or any talent, in those organizations is that these people get tethered to a single department, locking up much-needed skillsets, which locks down skillsets and contributions that could be valuable in other areas of the organization. Vernon cautions that employee crowdsourcing competitions are not easy to set up, especially at a large company. Thomson Reuters has 55,000 employees spread all across the globe and 17,000 of them are technologists, but regardless of the size, they've been able to successfully find problem-solvers from across the ranks. In one example involving text extraction, the employee who came up with the winning solution was sitting two or three cubicles away from the team, effectively hiding in plain sight.

Vernon offers some advice as well on how to successfully orchestrate something like this. After her team works with the organization's respective businesses to identify a problem, define the outcome, and get buy-in, team members translate the idea into a technical problem statement. "That's actually quite a challenge in itself," she said. Translating a business problem into a data problem requires setting up clear boundaries and defining the success criteria for a minimum viable product. Also, she went on to say it's important to understand that not everything is crowdsource-worthy. Vernon said she's turned down problems that were more strategy-oriented, recommending that one should avoid system-level problems and challenges that require highly specialized domain expertise. For example, if you need to be an expert in how you manage mutual funds in order to participate, that effectively minimizes the number of people who can contribute, basically contradicting the reason for running the challenge in the first place.

I think that example and many like it are interesting, as they help us to quickly find the best talent in our organizations. In essence, we're finding the best man or woman—or men or women—to solve for a certain situation. It's finding your needle in the haystack but in an accelerated way. More broadly though, many companies are also using other tools to really tap into the wisdom of many or all of their voices at the same time, as similarly shown in Francis Galton's work.

This brings me to prediction markets. Prediction markets work like the stock market. "Investors"—or you could think of them as "players," since this is a gamified approach to research and decision-making—are given a bank of play money or points to invest in answers to questions.[9]

Underneath prediction markets is the fascinating phenomenon that when you ask a diverse group of people not "What are you going to do?" but rather, "What is going to happen?" the results tend to be far more accurate. Internally at companies like HP, Motorola, Intel, Google, and others, prediction markets are being used for everything from anticipating the likely success of an idea or a product, all the way to predicting when a product might ship. Basically this technique is helping these companies make the appropriate moves and potential pivots every day based on the collective thinking of their people.

According to Julie Wittes Schlack, senior vice president for innovation and design at Communispace,[10] it works like this. These companies ask their people questions such as "Will this product appeal to four- to six-year-old girls?" or "Will Product A outsell Product B?" Sometimes they ask more multivariate questions, such as, "Which of these products will be most successful among four-to-six-year-old girls?" The interesting nuance is that participants answer only the questions on which they have a strong opinion. They can invest in the likely failure of an idea as well as in the likely success of one. And they can invest as few or as many points as they want, depending on their confidence in their own predictions. When they invest, they explain why they're doing it, providing some texture and qualitative insight behind the numbers. Gaming elements such as net-worth scores offer participants recognition, reward, and status, as well as an opportunity to compete to increase the value of their prediction port-folios. As with a stock market, the theory is that if you enable people to put their (play) money where their mouths are, you'll get a truer picture of what is likely to have value in the real market. Originally developed as an alternative to traditional political polling, this methodology generated interest and credibility as a means for companies to tap into the cross-functional and front-line knowledge of their employees.

It's particularly astounding to me how impressive the results have been. For example, HP's employee-prediction markets were generally more accurate than official company forecasts, and Intel's market for predicting product demand has been as much as 20 percent more accurate than official forecasts. This practice has radically changed the way these companies create and execute strategy and engage their team members who are closest to their customers.

AMPLIFY FOR IMPACT

In our evolutionary development as a species, we learned that the safest and most effective way to search for food required teamwork. There was strength in numbers when there was also commitment to a common cause, and a clear understanding of the specialized roles each individual had to play. Some were "herders," others "flankers," and others "spearsmen." By developing a clear strategy in advance, and giving people the "training" needed to perform effectively in their defined roles, while also allowing them the freedom to adjust and develop new plans on the fly, the clan was able to be successful at bringing down dangerous game and survive.[11]

We may have evolved significantly in the hundreds of thousands of years since, but surely our formal organizational settings still have a way to go to be better at collaboration. The way our organizations were built in the twentieth century certainly contributed to any collaborative endeavor dying on the vine. Traditional organizational structures hinge on hierarchy, where decisions come from the top and planning processes are designed to handle issues in the most straightforward way possible, without balancing much complexity or ambiguity. Three-year planning processes, for example, don't require effective co-creation and collaboration; in fact they work better with workforces that understand it is their job to deliver, not question or contribute to strategy. But our increasingly complex and connected world requires something different.

One advantage we have today over our ancestors is information technology. By using daily practices, such as at Pixar, in combination with technology, the collaborative process can be dramatically sped up. According to Don Tapscott, organizations regularly fail in this game because they don't have collaborative-conducive environments that can leverage new technologies meaningfully. When technologies are applied as a panacea to collaboration woes, they will surely fail, just as an overloaded email inbox fails to inform the recipient in any insightful way. Rather, information technologies need to draw in users to treat virtual collaboration as a place to ideate, converse, debate, and stir up solutions. Reddit, the community-created news website, provides a better model for such collaboration. Users are drawn toward topics and areas that interest them. They contribute freely and engage in active dialogue. In a business organization, they would also share goals, co-create strategy, trade feedback and perspectives candidly, surface the wisdom of their crowds, and discover previously unexpected areas of wisdom and value to exploit.

From increased employee engagement, to a reduction of inefficiencies and silos within a company, to more rapid and powerful innovation, the impact of better collaboration is enormous. Breakthrough social technologies are only deepening the potential as social and collaboration tools are beginning to be used in a sophisticated fashion. Large, global companies with far-flung workforces and partners are learning how to leverage these platforms to do a better job of surfacing problems and collaborating on innovative solutions—all at speed and scale.

But as I advise my clients, more important than any technology are the culture, people, processes, and leadership driving collaboration. The structure of the organization must support real collaboration, not impede it or make it a heroic act that only occurs in a crisis. The process of collaboration must be clearly understood: there is a time for ideation and surfacing options, there is a time for decisiveness, and there is a time to unify around that decision to execute—each stage requires people willing to commit and engage. And ultimately, it is up to leaders to identify, nurture, and develop real collaboration within their teams.

Touching back for a minute on the example that Pixar shows us. Undoubtedly the success of its very collaborative approach is evident for its organization, but it also, very possibly, led to the greatest era of success at Apple. Recall that Steve Jobs was the owner of Pixar during his exile from Apple. His latest biographer, Rick Tetzeli, notes in his book, *Becoming Steve Jobs: The Evolution of a Reckless Upstart into a Visionary Leader*: "For much of its first decade, Apple was riven by internal conflicts, many of them initiated or exacerbated by Steve. After getting fired, however, he had the good luck to experience, at Pixar, a strong collaborative culture. It had been molded by Ed Catmull, a would-be animator who had developed into a great manager over the years. As he steered Pixar through the many difficult periods that preceded the creation of *Toy Story*, he nurtured an intelligent, respectful, and effective culture. Catmull was so firmly in charge of the place that he was able to keep Steve from getting too involved in the production, so Jobs watched from a distance as writers and animators worked their way through failed plotlines, poorly conceived characters, and interference from Disney's then-chief of animation, Jeffrey Katzenberg. After *Toy Story*, he got to see the team do it again, with *A Bug's Life*, and then again and again and again. 'Watching our collaboration, where we were making ourselves better by working together, I think that fueled Steve,' says John Lasseter, who now heads Disney Animation and Pixar with Catmull. 'That was one of the key changes when he went back to Apple. He was willing to be open to the talent of others, to be inspired by and challenged by that talent, but also to inspire them to do amazing things he knew he couldn't do himself.'"[12]

That extra gear of creativity, productivity, and innovation Jobs employed in his second round at Apple was precisely what has built the successful Apple of today. And notably we have Pixar to thank for that.

QUESTIONS FOR YOU TO CONSIDER:

* Do you have a clear and well-adopted process for effective collaboration in your organization?

* Think of an example where effective collaboration occurred at your organization. What were the factors that contributed to that success?

* How well do you tap into the wisdom of your workforce on a consistent basis?

6

THEY LEAD WITH PURPOSE

SIDNEY GARFIELD graduated from the University of Iowa medical school in 1928 and went on to complete his residency in general surgery in Los Angeles County. He hoped to set up his own fee-for-service practice, the standard route for sole practitioners at the time, but the Great Depression and the difficult financial strain it put on patients forced him to look for other options.

In 1932, the Colorado River Aqueduct project was begun to bring water from the Colorado River to the Los Angeles basin. The construction project required 5,000 workers spread throughout the desert, and the health-care options available to them were spare. So Garfield took a loan from his father and formed an agreement with the water district to launch Contractors General Hospital, a small, twelve-bed facility in Desert Center, California. He started with one nurse, a cook, and a handyman who doubled as an ambulance driver while Garfield took care of the administrative work himself. The plan was to offer fee-for-service medical care to workers who got sick or injured on the job, and to receive reimbursement through Workers' Compensation insurance.

Garfield began treating patients, but he found it difficult to make money. Many patients couldn't afford to pay for any illnesses or injuries incurred off the job, and the insurance companies discounted most of the payments on Garfield's claims. Adding to his financial woes, Garfield refused to turn away any sick or injured patient, often leaving him with no payment at all. As a result, Contractors General Hospital was on the brink of bankruptcy seven months into operations.

The largest insurance company on the Colorado River Aqueduct project was Industrial Indemnity Exchange, partially owned by a man named Henry J. Kaiser. Harold Hatch, one of the company's insurance agents, and Dr. Garfield struck up a conversation about the problems the doctor was facing. No one wanted to lose medical care and coverage for the aqueduct workers, but it was impossible to stay in business under the current system. After much discussion, the men came away with a plan. The insurance companies would pay Dr. Garfield an up-front, fixed amount per day for every worker, about five cents a day for each person. This would alleviate the hospital's financial squeeze and encourage Garfield to focus on providing preventive care while also tending to injuries and illnesses. Nearly all 5,000 workers enrolled, leaving Dr. Garfield with around $500 a day to run the hospital, and the "prepayment" system was born.

When the aqueduct project began to wind down in 1938, Dr. Garfield planned to start a private practice in the Los Angeles area. But again, another opportunity presented itself. A group of contractors, headed by Henry Kaiser as general chairman and his son Edgar as executive-in-charge, won the contract to build the upper portion of the Grand Coulee Dam on the Columbia River—the largest construction project in history at the time.

When Garfield visited the Coulee construction site, he was inspired by the possibilities. He saw a company town of more than 15,000 people, an obvious need for medical care, and a run-down, thirty-five-bed hospital that could easily be improved. Garfield agreed to set up a prepaid practice similar to what he'd done in the desert. This time, given the greater scale and need, he was able to hire top-of-the-line physicians and staff while refurbishing the hospital into a state-of-the-art treatment facility. He also expanded operations by hiring general practitioners, a surgeon, a pediatrician, and various administrative and operational support staff.

At the time, prepaid coverage was not offered to wives and children, just workers. This lack caused families to either delay or avoid treatment whenever possible, which actually led to higher costs and more serious health problems down the line. Garfield and Kaiser struck a deal to provide prepaid care to families for an additional fifty cents per week for adults, and twenty-five cents per week for children. As a result, the group provided care to 15,000 workers and dependents, becoming the first comprehensive, prepaid, hospital-based group practice in the country to do so.

When the Grand Coulee Dam was completed in 1941, the Garfield group dissolved its practice. Garfield joined an Army medical reserve unit after the attack on Pearl Harbor and remained a medical resident and teacher at Los Angeles County General Hospital and the USC School of Medicine. This experience only deepened Garfield's belief in providing high-quality medical care for underserved communities.

Once again, a situation of great need—and a man named Henry Kaiser—intervened in Garfield's career. Henry Kaiser set up Kaiser Shipyards in Richmond, California, to help supply the Army with Liberty ships, tankers, small aircraft carriers, and a variety of other ships. Within a month of the US entry into World War II, Kaiser Shipyards had 30,000 workers, many of whom had been rejected by local draft boards for health reasons. Kaiser faced a major health problem, and Dr. Garfield was his answer. Kaiser requested President Franklin D. Roosevelt to release Dr. Garfield from his military obligation in order to run a prepaid group practice. The request was granted and Kaiser and Garfield set out to bring an innovative health care system to a group of people in dire need.[1]

Today, Kaiser Permanente is one of the nation's largest not-for-profit health plans, serving more than 10 million members. Over the past 100 years, it has had some up-and-down moments. One down phase, some KP patients might point out, occurred during the decades when the HMO approach was the norm, which brought a focus on cost containment over patient care. But in the past twenty years, Kaiser's trajectory has become more closely aligned with the model established by Garfield and Kaiser. Those pioneers of health care recognized that the fee-for-service, volume-based system was fundamentally broken because it did not give care providers an economically viable way to provide patients with the best care possible. To counter this, Kaiser and Garfield believed in providing coordinated care with a heavy emphasis on preventive measures through salaried group practice clinicians.[2]

Kaiser Permanente baked that purpose into its business model, and its success was validated time and again. Today, Kaiser Permanente operates under a care delivery and reimbursement model that is distinctly at odds with most health systems and health insurers. Its clinicians are salaried and embedded in a group-practice approach, not affiliated freelancers, and patients are not able to go outside the network. Those patients have "prepaid" for their care in the sense that they are Kaiser Permanente plan customers and that their costs are "capped." This arrangement, in turn, forces Kaiser to focus on quality, prevention, wellness, and care coordination to keep its own costs down.

It's a virtuous cycle that leads to continuous improvement, innovation, and value delivery. Meanwhile, Kaiser Permanente, aligned with its purpose, has clarity around its direction, whether the decision in question is one about overall strategic vision, or a "smaller" moment between a clinician and a patient.

THE RENEWAL OF PURPOSE

If there's a trending topic among the thought leaders and companies I follow closely, it's purpose. Increasingly, the business landscape is shifting from an emphasis on "how" to an appreciation of "why," as leaders and employees alike ask "what it's all about" for themselves as individuals and for their organizations. Though Kaiser is less explicit about articulating its purpose than some organizations, I think it serves as a great example of the power of purpose. Lots of health-care organizations aim to provide high-quality, affordable care that improves lives, but few are able to deliver on that because "how" they do things has little alignment with "why" they are doing it. Kaiser has done a great job of aligning *how* with *why*.

While the question of purpose has been long-simmering in the zeitgeist, and perhaps lurking below the surface for many of us, I think widespread social acceptance for openly discussing purpose was made possible by the success of purpose-driven leaders like Jeff Bezos, Steve Jobs, and Howard Schultz, among others. Many before them had shown that it was deeply satisfying to make a difference in the world by striving to achieve higher-order objectives outside of business; but few so clearly and effectively married a sense of purpose with the direction and success of the business itself. These leaders see that alignment as critical for their competitive advantage. As Howard Schultz, the much-admired CEO of Starbucks, put it poignantly, "We have no patent on anything we do and anything we do can be copied by anyone else. But you can't copy the heart and soul and the conscience of the company."

In the years since I've been in the corporate world, I've had countless discussions with leaders at Fortune 500 companies about how they are trying to shift their organizations away from a focus on profit above all else and toward a crisper sense of purpose. In many ways, this new consciousness makes perfect sense. Whereas companies in the mid-twentieth century by and large had an ethos of "win at all costs," successful new-era companies often have young, idealistic founders, and are more dependent on the strength of their relationships with employees and customers. If those relationships are merely transactional (i.e., based on money), the bonds can be easily broken and loyalty can be readily given to other companies offering better pay or better deals. If professional executives aren't always inclined to see social good or higher purpose as important to business success, their customers and employees are often willing to remind them of this—whether overtly, through voiced insistence, or passively, by leaving them.

If professional executives aren't always inclined to see social good or higher purpose as important to business success, their customers and employees are often willing to remind them of this—whether overtly, through voiced insistence, or passively, by leaving them.

Sometimes, when I'm trying to help a particularly hard-nosed executive see the light on this, I like to play an interesting game called the "Random Corporate Serial Killer." It works like this: Suppose you could sell your company to someone who would pay a price that everyone inside and outside the company agrees is more than fair (even with a very generous set of assumptions about the expected future cash flows of the company). Suppose further that this buyer would guarantee stable employment for all employees at the same pay scale after the purchase, but no guarantee that those jobs would be in the same industry. Finally, suppose the buyer plans to kill the company after the purchase—its products or services would be discontinued, its operations would be shut down, its brand names would be shelved forever, and so on. The company would utterly and completely cease to exist. Would you accept the offer? Why or why not? What would be lost if the company ceased to exist? Answering that can crack the shell of the hardest executive, I've found, and force him or her to reflect on his or her deeper purpose and reason for existence.[3]

Purpose, or an organization's "why," is the fundamental reason why you do what you do as a company. It serves as your "North Star," an aspirational and inspirational guide that allows your enterprise to stand securely on its foundation while constantly striving to create more impact. It is a unique differentiator because it has the power to provide focus throughout an organization, from the C-suite to the front line. No profit, product, strategy, or pivot can create this level of alignment in your organization and across your people.

If there's any other source of resistance to thinking in these terms, I find it comes from a sense that asking "why" feels childlike compared to delivering on "how." If you have a child or remember your childhood, you will likely recall that string of perplexing questions around "why." For a phase of our emotional and psychological development as a species, it's a constant fixation. Yet, somewhere along the way we stop asking. Maybe we believe we have the answer, or maybe we are too ashamed to ask the question, thinking no one else worries about such things or everyone already knows. Saddest of all, perhaps we can easily feel too busy or overwhelmed to care enough to explore the answer. But exploring "why" is critical to connecting ourselves with what matters and aligning us with what we want to do or accomplish and how we want to act in the world. It's part of our core as human beings and part of the reason we come together in societies or groups.

> Exploring "why" is critical to connecting ourselves with what matters and aligning us with what we want to do or accomplish and how we want to act in the world. It's part of our core as human beings and part of the reason we come together in societies or groups.

Resistance to the "why" question is not as strong during a company's early stages. Like children, organizations in their infancy are constantly asking why—why are we doing this, why us, why does the world need what we're doing? But as organizations become bigger, older, and more mature, the "why" often falls out of the conversation. However, in order to be effective at "how," we must understand, clarify, and leverage our "why."

What does it take to become a purpose-led organization? It takes knowing that purpose can't be relegated to a marketing campaign, or used as an ode to a past that no longer translates to current strategies, leadership, people, and practices. Purpose also must go beyond Corporate Social Responsibility efforts, as too often such approaches are divorced from the real beliefs, interests, and behaviors of an organization. Leveraging purpose requires creating a constant level of awareness and action that anchors or connects an organization to what it is doing for its stakeholders. The ideology of the organization's purpose must be rooted deeply within the culture to guide all actions and beliefs. It must be a pivot point whenever people meet to discuss strategies or solutions, make decisions, or build and implement programs and practices. Ultimately, that purpose becomes the reason that employees join the organization and customers buy from it. Products, working conditions, and other circumstances are secondary because they come from purpose rather than the other way around.

Perhaps the greatest shift that must take place for an organization to become purpose-led is the change in one specific mindset. Fundamentally, an organization that focuses on profitability as its purpose undercuts anything else it might say it holds true. This is where a lot of top leaders fall down. When I ask them—especially at Fortune 500 companies—why they want to become purpose-driven, they quickly mention the contribution such an orientation makes in terms of generating higher profits. Now, while I firmly believe that purpose and profit are not in any way exclusive, and that a "both/and" rather than "either/or" paradigm is critical for success, organizations and individuals must prioritize one over the other. If they don't, then reality will do it for them. Leaders committed to leading with purpose should be willing in a crunch to sacrifice short-term profits for long-term adherence to what matters. In contrast, leaders who value profitability first and foremost will rarely hesitate to sacrifice purpose for short-term gain if it gets in the way of making money. It takes care and discipline, not to mention dedication and faith, to commit to the larger possibilities that are generated through purpose. The pressures of Wall Street and life conspire against that adherence.

New-era companies are typically overt and strong in their beliefs. They derive great energy from their purpose, but that energy is not just, only, or even primarily inwardly focused. Rather, it provides the organization with a clear way of seeing the world outside its walls, and it helps connect the organization to customers, users, investors, stakeholders, and culture mavens. As a result, such organizations have more access to and awareness of the way others think and feel about the products and services the business is striving to offer, and more insight into evolving needs and interests in the market. This knowledge helps employees at all levels of the organization constantly evaluate and identify what value means for customers. In turn, it gives the business a significant advantage over competitors.

THE DIFFERENCE BETWEEN PURPOSE AND MISSION

Many organizations with mission statements use purpose and mission interchangeably, but that overlap can often lead to confusion. Generally, your mission statement is a declaration of the business you are in, and provides clarification of your company's goals, objectives, and even the values you hold near and dear. Mission statements vary, but they are often focused on "what" you do and "how" you do it. The operative word, "you," is what makes it much more for internal alignment rather than making it some sort of existential declaration. This is because mission statements can change with strategy and new opportunities.

Purpose, on the other hand, does not change. It is timeless. The reason a company existed ten years ago is—in all likelihood—the reason it will exist ten years from now. Purpose transcends mission. It focuses an organization on the constant pursuit of possibility, which is different from the pursuit of profit. Jim Collins, author of *Built to Last*, puts it this way: "While purpose does not change, it does inspire change. The very fact that purpose can never be fully realized means that an organization can never stop stimulating change and progress in order to more fully live its purpose." When an organization elevates purpose beyond words on a page and drives it deep within the processes and practices of the business, it helps guide decisions and actions that are more clear, aligned, and intentional, even as it directs strategy and helps uncover opportunities for innovation.

The best organizations use their sense of purpose to guide their change and evolution, while growing closer to the needs of customers.

Purpose transcends mission. It focuses an organization on the constant pursuit of possibility, which is different from the pursuit of profit.

It is through purpose that companies focus on the customer most effectively. Indeed, purpose and customer-focus are intertwined, and it is rare to be exceptional at one without also being keen on the other. Consider some leading companies and their purpose statements:

- Nintendo—"Put smiles on the faces of everyone we touch"
- Nike—"To bring inspiration and innovation to every athlete in the world"
- Johnson & Johnson—"Caring for the world, one person at a time"
- Kellogg's—"Nourishing families so they can flourish and thrive"
- ING—"Empowering people to stay a step ahead in life and in business"
- Southwest—"We exist to connect people to what's important in their lives through friendly, reliable, and low-cost air travel"

All of these companies have purpose statements that focus on their customers. Athletes. Families. People. They also get to the heart of what they do for their customers. Make them smile, inspire them, nourish them, help them, empower them, connect them. These statements don't address the company's investors or talk about the money they'll make, since this is not the reason that they exist. Profits, revenues, or even strategy cannot align and focus an organization on the customer, but purpose can.

I've talked a bit about Netflix already, so I thought it would be helpful to consider the organization in light of its purpose and that connection to and focus on the customer. Interestingly, Netflix doesn't explicitly communicate its company purpose anywhere, and yet I believe I have a strong sense of that purpose as a customer and observer. I spotted a statement on Netflix's website that I think characterizes that impression precisely:

"We strive to win more of our members' 'moments of truth.' We win those moments of truth when members expect Netflix to be more pleasurable than their other options, based upon their prior experiences. The pleasure comes from easy choosing, total control over when to play/pause/resume a video, and content that suits the taste and mood of everyone in the household."

In my view, Netflix believes that it exists to provide customers with the most pleasurable way to choose, participate in, and enjoy television shows and movies in the comfort of their own homes. If I can sense that purpose clearly, as an outsider, reading its website, and studying its growth and story from a distance, imagine how powerful it must be to people working at that organization and acting on that purpose.

When you juxtapose that purpose with Netflix's mission, "to become the world's best entertainment distribution service," you can understand how there's a distinct difference in the outward focus versus inward nature of those two statements. Netflix's mission has evolved in the years since it was launched. It now also produces content. Perhaps it will become a fully integrated entertainment company in the future. But its purpose to win moments of truth will likely remain at the core of whatever it does or becomes. In pursuit of that purpose Netflix is willing to forgo profits for growth, and has been busy adding new offerings, entering dozens of new geographic markets, and enrolling millions of new subscribers. Interestingly, its share price also more than doubled in 2015, making it one of the best-performing stocks in the S&P 500. As one waggish analyst noted, "apparently red ink is the new black."[4]

Organizations that aim to leverage purpose to guide strategy and innovation must build a cultural infrastructure that makes purpose actionable for everyone. Purpose does not come to life when it is imposed by command-and-control rules and overly engineered processes that direct employees' behaviors and actions. In fact, this approach prevents employees from embracing and fully delivering on purpose, and makes the organization incapable of achieving any altitude. In purpose-led companies, values trump rules. In other words, purpose-led companies are also values-based companies.

In fact, values are the behavioral and decision-making guides that help employees deliver on the purpose. Purpose-led companies use the power of their values to encourage employee freedom and empowerment, thus pivoting to new opportunities quicker. This is how LinkedIn uses its core value of "our members come first" to make it OK for every employee to ask, "Is this good for the free member?" (not just the paying ones) when making key decisions. In this way, instead of worrying whether a decision will make their manager angry or make the company more money, employees are able to bring the customer into every decision they make because that's what matters most. The values help them support, clarify, and deliver on the purpose of the organization.

Prioritizing values over rules is not only empowering, it's freeing. After all, bureaucratic rules must be constantly assessed and adapted as circumstances change, or the organization will stumble. Values allow employees and the organization to be flexible in dealing with change so long as the direction taken remains true to what the organization believes is right. Recall the example of how Ritz-Carlton treated me as a customer—offering a spontaneous gift in line with my particular interests—compared to the hotel in Las Vegas—talking to me disdainfully because my request conflicted with company policy. Guess which company delivered more value to me and perhaps even discovered a new path to value for itself at the same time?

As Mark Bonchek, the founder of SHIFT Academy, which aims to update leaders' thinking for the twenty-first century, puts it, "Sometimes purpose is about values—who you are and what you stand for. Other times it is about value—what you do and how it benefits others. The ultimate goal would seem to be having your values and value; have what you do reflect who you are, have what you stand for guide what you make, and have your value to the community enhance your value to customers and shareholders."[5]

This is the power of purpose—it serves as your guide for constantly identifying value and your glue for affixing your people to the organization's values.Companies that actualize their purpose through disciplined practices soon discover that this value readily proves its worth.

Let's look at some attributes of companies that bring purpose to a higher level.

THEY USE PURPOSE TO GUIDE STRATEGY

On February 5, 2014, CVS Caremark, the country's largest drugstore chain in terms of sales, announced that it would stop selling cigarettes and other tobacco products in its 7,600 stores by October.

By typical Wall Street measures, this was an extraordinary decision expected to hurt the company to the tune of an estimated $2 billion in annual revenues. Yet, the move seemed pretty straightforward to the company's leadership team. "Ending the sale of cigarettes and tobacco products at CVS/pharmacy is the right thing for us to do for our customers and our company to help people on their path to better health," Larry J. Merlo, president and CEO of CVS said. "Put simply, the sale of tobacco products is inconsistent with our purpose."[6]

The company's decision to drop that cash cow from its stores was a way of reconciling a fundamental contradiction between profit and principle. Tobacco products contribute to the deaths of more than 480,000 people in the United States alone each year. A company dedicated to promoting health and well-being could not, in good conscience, sell that product. Abandoning tobacco was an act of clarity that further aligned the company behind its purpose of "helping people on their path to better health." It was a stunning move that had all the more impact because it reinforced or brought to life CVS's purpose; in the process it became an inspirational piece of evidence that CVS lived according to its purpose for everyone to see—employees, customers, stakeholders, observers, and even competitors.

What happened after the decision was announced? CVS met its goal of ending tobacco sales a month early, becoming completely tobacco-free in September 2014. The move was capped by a corporate name change—from CVS Caremark to CVS Health. That shift was a sign of the bigger picture, that the company was using its purpose to pivot its overall direction, strategy, and corporate image. No longer a quick stop to pick up the basic (often unhealthful) necessities and commodity products that any corner store sells, CVS was now a destination for health. The company already had 900 walk-in medical clinics, with more than half of its revenues coming from its pharmacy services—and the transition to CVS Health and away from tobacco was also a move to expand that line of the company.[7] It was a simple yet gutsy move—but it was only easy because of the clarity CVS had around its purpose.

CVS also launched a smoking-cessation program at its pharmacies to further drive its purpose, while also replacing some of its lost tobacco revenues. The company's MinuteClinic® offers patients a chance to get a stop-smoking assessment and an opportunity to speak with pharmacists to help quit smoking. The company also conducted smoking-cessation program research within its employee population, discovering that participants who enrolled in incentive-based programs were nearly three times more likely to quit smoking than those who received care alone. These findings led CVS Health in June 2015 to launch "700 Good Reasons," a new stop-smoking program for its employees and their dependents. Program participants make a $50 deposit but can earn up to $700 and a refund of their full deposit if they are successful in living up to their commitment to quit. Payments are made to participants who test tobacco-free at six and twelve months.[8]

Those programs allow the company not only to increase the health and wealth of their employees, but also to provide opportunities for its workforce to serve as a reflection of the company purpose. CVS made a number of other major moves in its year of health, including announcing plans to open a technology-development center in Boston with a focus on "building customer-centric experiences in health care." The goal is to create seamless, omni-channel experiences for patients in stores and on the web.[9]

Results were better than the company expected. After tobacco sales stopped in September, the company's third-quarter revenues rose 9.7 percent from 2013. How did this happen? While front-of-store sales shrank, as expected, pharmacy revenue rose 16 percent.[10]

CVS Caremark's corporate courage was also a major brand coup. Even President Obama took note the day the decision was made, saying, "CVS Caremark sets a powerful example, and today's decision will help advance my administration's efforts to reduce tobacco-related deaths, cancer, and heart disease, as well as bring down health care costs—ultimately saving lives and protecting untold numbers of families from pain and heartbreak for years to come."

The CVS decision, and the company's continual commitment to promoting better health, shows the power of purpose when it is owned at the top and permeates throughout the organization. The company did not allow its campaign to stagnate on company posters and office swag; instead, it harnessed the power of purpose to drive major change throughout the organization, clarifying and intensifying it in the process. That purpose now serves as a guide for strategy—changing the company from a ubiquitous corner store to a place for health. It also informs the way the company perceives and delivers value to its customers and employees. It provides a clear path for making decisions and setting priorities. And it continues to serve as an innovation accelerator propelling the company forward.

THEY USE PURPOSE TO DRIVE VISIBLE ACTIONS

I call decisions like the one CVS made "Organizational Iconic Actions." These are major, company-wide decisions that align with a company's purpose and stand out in customers' and employees' hearts. These actions can be one of the most authentic and effective ways to convey what a company stands for. Of course, they vary by company, purpose, timing, and circumstance. Not every company has a clear-cut product or service that vehemently contradicts its purpose; but dedicating time and investment to purposeful actions is a great way to deepen purpose quickly. This is why my new maxim when working with clients around their purpose is to stop and ask, "What's your tobacco?"

CVS is certainly not the only company to "find its tobacco" in recent years. These instances are proliferating in the business landscape. In February 2014, Gap Inc., which also owns Old Navy, Banana Republic, Athleta, and Intermix, announced it would raise its own minimum wage to ten dollars an hour by 2015 to meet its corporate commitment to "do more than sell clothes." The bold move affected around 65,000 US employees who were making less than the ten-dollar threshold.

"To us, this is not a political issue," said then-CEO Glenn Murphy. "Our decision to invest in front line employees will directly support our business, and is one that we expect to deliver a return many times over."

The company firmly believed it was a strategic move to attract and retain talented employees, which would ultimately lead to a better customer experience. Gap's move also received a nod of approval from President Obama: "In my State of the Union address, I asked more businesses to do what they can to raise their employees' wages," he said. "Today, I applaud Gap Inc. for announcing that they intend to raise wages for their employees beginning this year."[11]

Gap's decision propelled it into company with other chains that already had mandated higher wages for their employees, such as Costco, Whole Foods, and In-N-Out Burger. It also helped propel the minimum-wage issue further into the nation's dialogue and focus, with companies such as

Target, Starbucks, T. J. Maxx, McDonald's, and Walmart soon following suit with minimum-wage hikes of their own. Health-insurance company Aetna announced in January 2015 that it would raise its minimum wage to sixteen dollars an hour, a sizeable increase from its previous twelve-dollar rate.[12]

Organizational Iconic Actions take a variety of shapes and sizes—from eliminating products misaligned with a company's purpose and improving working conditions and benefits, to actions that improve society and the environment. They aren't limited to Corporate Social Responsibility but prove an organization's commitment to its purpose and oftentimes contradict a "profit-first" mentality. JPMorgan Chase pledged $100 million over five years to debt-stricken Detroit for economic development, job training, and housing repairs to further the company's purpose to "translate positive financial results into sustainable community and environmental efforts that benefit everyone." Amazon has made a notorious "offer" to employees for up to $5,000 to quit if they don't feel dedicated to propelling the company to become the "Earth's most customer-centric company." General Mills announced that it would stop using artificial colors and flavors in all its cereals.[13] Imagine Lucky Charms without its green clovers and pink hearts. But a company that traces its roots as a food producer back to the 1850s is betting that new awareness of the importance of healthful eating will soon supplant any loyalty to gimmicky cereals. So it's getting ahead of that inevitable change because it's the right thing to do and revitalizes employees and customers.

Such actions transform purpose from a cheap phrase to living proof, from hollow buzzwords to true rallying cry. Identifying and delivering on these promises can have a tremendous positive impact on employee engagement and brand perception—because it definitively shows everyone that you are putting your money (or loss of money) where your mouth is. Yes, taking such a step requires considerable investment and dedication, but it can be one of the most authentic and powerful ways to convey what you stand for.

THEY USE PURPOSE TO DRIVE INNOVATION

At age twelve, Sean Ahrens was diagnosed with Crohn's—a chronic, incurable autoimmune disease that causes inflammation throughout the digestive system. After years of research and suffering he started Crohnology, an online project dedicated to building a patient-centered sharing network to connect people suffering from Crohn's and colitis from all over the world. Crohnology has been a major success, chosen by some of the San Francisco Bay Area's best business accelerators to help propel the idea forward.[14]

A few years ago Sean's journey brought him to Sheila Babnis, the former head of strategic innovation for product development at Roche, one of the largest pharmaceutical companies in the world. Roche was on its own journey—to redesign how it conducted clinical trials, interfaced with and connected with patients, and to improve the value of its medicines. Roche declares that its purpose is "Doing now what patients need next" and the company is committed to delivering the best medical solutions possible in the present while also developing innovations for the future. For Roche, purpose and innovation are strongly connected, a clear declaration that continually striving to find the best possible solutions for patients is its purpose. The implication is powerful: the world's medical needs never stop, and neither does Roche's pursuit of solutions.

But Roche's innovation and product development cycles were out of whack with that purpose. For years, Roche would bring in patients to talk about Roche's drugs and the positive impact they were having on lives. But they were overlooking the power of bringing in patients earlier in the drug-development process. Lost in the process was the opportunity to discover what it was like for a patient to live with a disease and to incorporate those critical insights into the design of clinical trials.

Sean helped Roche align its purpose with its approach to innovation. He did this by serving as the voice of the patient after joining one of Roche's Innovation Advisory Boards, which consist of patients, physicians, drug developers, payers, and customer-centric leaders from a variety of industries. Through Sean's voice, and the involvement of other patients, the company has been able to develop more creative, innovative approaches to data-collection practices, among other things, helping revolutionize the drug-development process. "His advice and guidance have been invaluable to us," says Babnis, "ensuring we are designing patient solutions with the patient front and center in our design process."[15]

This patient-centered approach has led to a deeper level of empathy throughout the innovation process, helping the company create even better solutions for what "patients need next." Roche's purpose, in other words, now helps it to drive and spur innovation, giving it clarity into customers' needs, and providing it with faces, voices, and stories that make the work meaningful. Purpose, as a result, is now the value-diviner behind innovation—not financially, but through the help Roche can offer the patients of tomorrow.

Roche is simply leveraging empathy to prime its innovation engine. Doing so allows the company to use its purpose to spark new solutions rather than letting the chase for profits dictate its next offering. Influential business thinker and London Business School professor Gary Hamel says that this level of empathy is at the heart of innovation. As he puts it, "The best innovations—both socially and economically—come from the pursuit of ideals that are noble and timeless: joy, wisdom, beauty, truth, equality, community, sustainability and, most of all, love. These are the things we live for, and the innovations that really make a difference are the ones that are life-enhancing. And that's why the heart of innovation is a desire to re-enchant the world." Hamel finds that the way most organizations operate and attack innovation is largely disconnected from any sense of humanity and what it will take to inspire true commitment and creativity. "Listen to the speech of a typical CEO," he says, "or scroll through an employee-oriented website, and notice the words that keep cropping up—words like execution, solution, advantage, focus, differentiation, and superiority. There's nothing wrong with these words, but they're not the ones that inspire human hearts. And that's a problem—because if you want to innovate, you need to be inspired, your colleagues need to be inspired, and ultimately, your customers need to be inspired."[16]

Purpose can provide the inspiration needed for innovation to flourish, putting the organization's focus on brilliant, life-affirming, creative outcomes rather than financial or operational outputs. When employees are focused on outcomes that will delight, fulfill, and change the way customers live, they work harder to discover more relevant and compelling solutions that support and extend the company's purpose. This effort provides expansive opportunities for innovation rather than limiting improvements to new derivatives of existing products. Outcome-based innovations come from an empathetic understanding of the customer's world and her needs. It brings us back to the role of culture in driving successful innovation and growth.

Corporate cultures need to embrace the idea of "walking in another's shoes" in order to gain perspective and insight that drives purpose-rich innovation. The first, and hardest, step is helping people remove their own shoes first. That requires a company to offer employees an opportunity to connect to the purpose of the organization, and it necessitates leaders who, from top to bottom, consistently and deliberately guide the organization in a truly empathetic way. With purpose as the lens, awareness of others becomes embedded into cultures and serves as the catalyst for innovation that makes a difference in the world.

THEY USE PURPOSE TO EXTEND AND ALIGN CSR

Unilever, the British-Dutch multinational consumer-goods company, is dedicated to an "authentic purpose" at the core of all of its more than 400 brands, which include Axe, Dove, Lipton, and Knorr. Paul Polman has made purpose one of his core tenets as CEO. "Leadership is not just about giving energy but it's unleashing other people's energy," he says, "which comes from buying into that sense of purpose. But if that purpose isn't strong enough in a company, if the top doesn't walk the talk, then the rest will not last long. The key thing for CEOs is to make that a part of your operating model."[17]

Polman has walked the talk by becoming one of the most influential leaders of the corporate sustainability movement. Through his influence and actions he has used the power of purpose to extend the notion of Corporate Social Responsibility beyond compliance and into the operating model of each of their brands. This has allowed Unilever companies to drive environmental, social, and community issues through its brands while also reaching strong profits.

The impact is consistent through all of Unilever's brands. Dove has set out to strengthen women's self-esteem through its Campaign for Real Beauty, including setting up a Self-Esteem Fund and Project that has reached more than 1.5 million Canadian girls with workshops and online resources. Ben & Jerry's, the quirky ice cream brand, is another Unilever brand that drives social justice and environmental change through its flavors, from Hubby Hubby to promote gay rights to Save our Swirled to combat climate change. Lifebuoy soap, a hand-hygiene product, has kept its focus by preventing the death of about 2 million children before the age of five due to diarrhea and pneumonia by promoting hand-washing.[18]

Unilever is using the power of purpose to transform its brands into forces for good, tackling social and environmental issues through profitable operations. Dove's Campaign for Real Beauty and Ben & Jerry's flavors aren't gimmicks or ploys to gain attention, they are extensions of the very real, authentic brands that Unilever has worked to consciously build and acquire. Like CVS and others, Unilever has elevated the concept and reach of purpose to new heights. "Profit is not a purpose," says Polman, "it's an end product. I always want a deeper result. People assume that if you do something good, it must cost money. I don't know where they get that idea from." Polman has shown that driving purpose doesn't mean you need to compromise; in fact, compromise sacrifices the clarity of purpose.[19]

NFF companies are successful precisely because they connect so strongly with their employees and customers. CSR efforts can buttress and fortify brand, in an age where brand can be everything. And those efforts can lower costs in the long run and create the kind of long-term and out-of-the-box thinking that drives innovation.[20]

Not every company is a Unilever, using purpose to catapult CSR into the business model of the organization. At least not yet. For most companies, elevating CSR into the status of business discipline may be a bit premature and misguided. CSR efforts may or may not deliver better immediate business results, but they most definitely can and should align with and support the organization's purpose. When that happens, stakeholders do not need to see the ROI to back the business case for CSR; they get it at an intuitive level. Indeed, without that alignment with purpose, CSR efforts can be less motivating or powerful because they may seem divorced from the reason that people and customers support the organization in the first place.

Case in point. My team and I were working with one of our clients on a major purpose-led transformation. As part of this process, we worked to align the client's most important programs and practices to its purpose in order to enhance the positive impact on employees, customers, and nearby communities. The range of such programs included everything from communications to performance management to what gets measured in the employee opinion survey. As we got deeper into the organization, however, while conducting an audit to find other areas of alignment, we discovered that the company's community-relations strategy needed to be addressed.

This was a tough problem to point out. The company was involved in some amazing philanthropic endeavors—actively volunteering, donating, and investing in some of the world's greatest causes. But there was a disconnect. The company's most dedicated cause, in which it invested considerable time and millions of dollars, was misaligned with its purpose. That cause didn't have any clear connection to the organization's reason for being; in fact, to an outsider, it only inspired the question "Why?" As we looked at how to shift the organization in various ways so that purpose was aligned everywhere, we knew that something would need to be done with this major CSR endeavor. After all, tens of thousands of employees aligned with one singular purpose were being engaged to support a highly visible altruistic endeavor that was out of joint with that purpose. It wasn't a bad cause, by any means—indeed, it was worthy and needed support—but it was a random rallying cry rather than a focused one.

We had difficult conversations with the CEO and other senior leaders about the issue. We talked about how, if we wanted to drive purpose forward in every program from communications to community giving, the outcome that best served the customer and the communities was the one that should be followed. We looked at other organizations that closely tied their community giving efforts to their purpose, from TOMS Shoes, the "one for one" shoe company that has an annual Shoe Drop Day, where employees travel and donate a variety of goods to children; to Microsoft, which donates software, services, and hundreds of millions of dollars to drive social change through technology.

The leaders understood that they would have to make a difficult decision. What made it even more difficult was the fact that employees really connected with the cause. They looked forward to the fundraising efforts each year, using it as a team- and community-building effort. It was clear that we were going to need to be extremely careful and thoughtful in how we would phase out this cause, and replace it with an equally high-impact cause tied closer to the purpose. This switch was critical for transforming the company to a purpose-led organization.

Indeed, it is very easy for an organization to have poor alignment between its purpose and its CSR strategy because the business and cultural connection often go overlooked. It is not about ROI. It is about permeating the culture with behaviors, experiences, and outlooks that also support the business in a way that makes it possible to do good and make the world a better place while also fortifying the brand, strategy, innovation, and growth trajectory.

IMBUING THE COMPANY WITH AN ENDURING SENSE OF MEANING

Taking the altruistic intent of purpose and driving it throughout an organization to create impact is the move from "talk to walk." We all know that talk is cheap, and relegating purpose to an internal marketing or communications campaign surely does not go far enough to stand out in the heads and hearts of employees and customers. Purpose-led companies are able to take the positive intent of their purpose and use it to create impact that improves the lives of the people they serve. This impact manifests in a multitude of ways, from product and service offerings to better communities. It goes beyond Organizational Iconic Actions, which serve as just one way for organizations to have the impact they intend to have.

Purpose-led organizations are able to fully implement their purpose to serve as a mechanism to drive strategy, innovation, and customer-centric decisions. Purpose is embedded in their people and processes, ultimately creating the collective identity of the company. When this happens, purpose becomes the core of a company's DNA. This is characteristic of all new-era companies. They are keenly focused on the customer, the market, and the world—not just because it is profitable or competitively strategic to do so, though this is also the case—but because that focus is aligned with the purpose that unites everyone involved.

QUESTIONS FOR YOU TO CONSIDER:

* What is your company's purpose (the reason for existing)?

* How aligned is your company's strategy with its purpose?

* In which ways could your purpose provide more focus for your organization?

7

THEY KEEP
THE CUSTOMER CLOSE

WHEN ANGELA AHRENDTS became Burberry's CEO in 2006, "luxury" was one of the fast-growing sectors in the world. The British luxury brand, with its iconic trench coats dating to World War I, should have had a distinct advantage. But even with the booming market, the company was only growing at 2 percent a year. One reason: global expansion had led Burberry to increase its licensees around the world and expand its product lines. They were selling too many products, from dog cover-ups and leashes to kilts, to leverage their brand effectively.

Ahrendts went on a six-month roadshow with her predecessor to get a clearer sense of the company's international presence. In Hong Kong, she found a team that was making polo shirts and woven shirts, but not a single trench coat. In the United States, she discovered that outerwear was being sold for half what it cost in the UK. The inconsistencies were rampant and conflicted with what she knew worked in branding. As she put it, "I admire and respect great brands and helped to build some over the years. From Apple to Starbucks, I love the consistency—knowing that anywhere in the world you can depend on having the same experience in the store or being served a latte with the same taste and in the same cup. That's great branding."

To Ahrendts, Burberry was trying to be something for everybody, which consequently diminished its aura of exclusivity and luxury. She also felt the company had lost focus in other ways. Its emphasis on other segments and multiple products had led it to neglect its core strength—the iconic outerwear that now only represented about 20 percent of its global business. It was clear that the company would need to streamline its offerings and hone its luxury vision. Ahrendts figured it could do that by getting back to its roots, specifically by modernizing its core luxury products, especially the trench coat that was an ode to Burberry's tradition.

Ahrendts named Christopher Bailey, an up-and-coming designer, as official "brand czar" or head designer. She made sure that every decision related to the brand or touching on the consumer would go through Christopher. But efforts certainly didn't stop with branding. She also closed factories, made difficult decisions about layoffs, shifted the company's corporate structure, and led a complete reinvention of the brand. The subsequent marketing efforts narrowed from the broadest possible consumer base to the next generation of luxury customers—specifically, Millennials. This was a gutsy decision at the time because Millennials had a poor grasp of Burberry as a brand. Ahrendts knew, however, that the company's competitors were also largely ignoring that demographic and thus the luxury market for Millennials was wide open.

"We did a lot of studying around the world," Ahrendts recalls, "with all the new markets coming into play. India, Latin America, China. Some of the firms that we worked with said this new luxury consumer will be twenty-five years younger than the traditional Western luxury customer. So we made the decision, very early on, that we were going to target a Millennial consumer."[1]

That decision changed everything. The Millennial consumer helped provide focus for the company's strategic decisions. It moved from just a few basic styles of trench coats to more than 300 SKUs ranging in colors, styles, and accessories. They also began to redesign their marketing efforts to be more attractive to these digital natives. They migrated from several regional websites to a single platform, rich with emotive content such as music, movies, and storytelling. As Ahrendts puts it, "This whole ecosystem was being built and we just knew we had to go digital, but we also knew we didn't have the money to play in traditional media. We knew for every pound we spent digitally, we could potentially get ten times the reach that we could get physically."[2]

Ahrendts is convinced that working in parallel with her design guru to develop the brand, sharpen operations, and ultimately revitalize the culture was critical to success. "Christopher and I talked a lot about how we would do this together," Ahrendts recalls, "because I was insecure. I'd never done this before. He was young and it was going to put him (in) the spotlight. We relied heavily on each other, and said 'OK, together, can we create the kind of brand, the kind of company we always dreamed of working for?' He was very clear on his brand vision. I was very clear on the company vision, not just the business, but the culture and the people." In order to deliver the brand vision, Ahrendts had to foster a culture that was singularly focused.

These efforts mattered and worked only because they were directed at the customer—a segment they identified clearly, targeted precisely, and got to know intimately. The company incorporated that specific customer when thinking about its brand image, business and digital strategy, and the culture it wanted to create. Burberry didn't just give lip service to its ideal customer, it backed up that new focus with substantive actions that had a major impact on operations, marketing, revenues, and market growth.

The results were impressive. By getting back to the company's roots, clearly defining its customer of the present and the future, and transforming its strategy, product offerings, and marketing efforts to focus more squarely on those customers, the company achieved its greatest level of success. At the end of fiscal 2012, Burberry's revenues and operating income had doubled from the previous five years, to $3 billion and $600 million respectively.[3]

WHAT CUSTOMER FOCUS MEANS

Companies with deeply focused cultures know and understand their customers. They drive customer-centricity throughout the organization, keeping the customer top of mind even for employees who are not working with customers directly.

As I discussed earlier about "inverting the pyramid," pushing decisions down the hierarchy of an organization, closer to the customer and into the value zone, is critically important for building a customer-centric culture. It is equally important, however, to permeate that customer-centric focus and frame of mind throughout the entire organization. Companies that do so know exactly who their customer is and is not. They constantly speak with and about that customer, at all levels of the organization. They don't relegate it to a certain function—say, marketing or branding—but rather it's extended to every single employee to guide what that person does on a day-to-day basis. When a company enables and empowers everyone to focus on the customer, versus a certain function or role like sales or marketer "owning the customer," it creates a cultural rather than just an operational impact. This level of customer-centricity contributes to the *how* of a company, not just the *what*.

As described in the previous chapter, a company's purpose and its deliberate emphasis on the customer are deeply linked. Purpose provides focus for an organization, a single why for all the "whats" and "hows" swirling around a company; it is the inspirational and aspirational "North Star" that unites individuals throughout an organization to the larger cause. But purpose is squarely centered on the customer that the organization serves.

This brings up an interesting complexity. While purpose is timeless, customers change. Their growth and evolution—and occasionally their sudden transformation—is what makes the discovery and delivery of customer value so challenging. This is why it is critical for companies to keep the customer of today and tomorrow present—not just in that "value zone" that is occupied by customer-facing associates, but throughout the entire organization.

While purpose helps direct a company's innovation, strategy, CSR efforts, and other major programs, customer awareness deepens, aligns, and granulates this focus. NFF organizations use purpose as their guide, but they use the customer as the target and the reference point. They create ways to enable employees to step into the customer's shoes and develop greater empathy and understanding into the customer's needs and jobs-to-be-done. This understanding then drives the innovation and dedication to creating products and services that serve the customer better, and gives employees the clarity and freedom to engage with the customer unrestrained.

In larger organizations with very corporate environments, the idea of the customer can often become skewed and confused. This is because employees or teams that are not customer-facing come to identify their within-the-company customers as "internal customers." Accordingly, they focus on how they can better serve those internal needs rather than keeping in mind the world outside their office walls. While it is true that customer-centric companies often have an intense focus on supporting their customer-facing employees, they will miss the mark and the point if those efforts don't enhance the organization's ability to deliver value to the customer.

Leadership can also sometimes misalign the organization if it puts too much emphasis on shareholders over customers. I have seen and heard more than a few CEO speeches that gave lip service to the primacy of the customer but then proceeded to lay out plans that seemed more intent on increasing shareholder value than on maximizing customer value. Organizations oriented primarily toward shareholder value make themselves vulnerable in the long term because they undermine their declared sense of purpose and their deep connection to customer needs.

> Organizations oriented primarily toward shareholder value make themselves vulnerable in the long term because they undermine their declared sense of purpose and their deep connection to customer needs.

Companies can also miss the mark when they are confused about the identity of their true customer. Google and LinkedIn, for example, confront this complexity at the core of their business models, and their solutions to that challenge help them further clarify their purposes and hone their drives to customer value. Specifically, the revenue models at Google and LinkedIn are based on advertisers. In a strict, literal sense, this would mean that companies advertising on Google or LinkedIn are in fact their customers. While the needs of those customers are important at both companies, they are not central to the purpose and understanding of customer value. Both organizations recognize that the non-paying user is the true customer. If user needs are not met—indeed, if users are not continually thrilled and delighted by their experience of those services—Google and LinkedIn will falter, and advertisers, in turn, will receive less bang for their buck.

Accordingly, Google and LinkedIn are looking after the ultimate needs of their paying customers by seeing to the needs of their users. Interestingly, this may put them in conflict with their paying customers on occasion. Imagine how easy it would be for a manager or a key account leader to bend to the needs of the paying customer over the non-paying user. Yet, doing so could lead to inherent misalignment between the purpose and customer focus of the organization. LinkedIn is able to maintain a clear-cut focus on the customer by driving the customer into its core values.

Talking to Kate Swanson, a leader in LinkedIn's Global Accounts team, I got a clear sense of the way she relies on the company's culture and values to do her job. As she puts it, "If you have strong values, it's easy to answer, 'What should I do in this case?' That is because you know what everyone up the organizational chain will say because they too adhere to those same values." For example, the most important value at LinkedIn is "members first." As CEO Jeff Weiner says, "We as a company are only as valuable as the value we create for our members."[4]

In her work in corporate sales, Swanson encounters clients who would pay for services that would jeopardize the member experience of LinkedIn. Remember my story about Myspace? The social-network company was willing to do anything to monetize its services, including accepting ads, banners, and more that irritated members and degraded the look and feel of the platform. Not at LinkedIn. Standing at that crossroads between "members first" and easy profit, Swanson knows—and explains to the customer—that doing what it wants would violate the most important value of the organization. Though she realizes this sometimes leads to frustration, she is able to explain to customers that members would go away if LinkedIn didn't stick to what it knows is right, and ultimately that would hurt all stakeholders.

Now, of course, it's not that companies like LinkedIn never slip up or struggle over ambiguous choices. What's special about LinkedIn is that it is both self-aware and reflective. It has the wherewithal to refocus on the right priorities as soon as someone brings attention back to the guidance the culture provides. Once there, it recalibrates to better match the *how*, *why*, and *what*.

Peter Drucker noted in 1973 that the only valid purpose of a firm is to create a customer. Companies, in other words, justify their existence through providing value to customers. Profits and share-price increases are the result, not the goal, of a company's activities.[5] For most traditional companies, this means their focus must shift. Rather than allotting time toward developing the strongest systems and processes possible or serving internal customers, the emphasis must be on how well the organization actually serves customers. A lack of excellence in that area leads ultimately to organizational failure.

There is little doubt that we are in the Age of the Customer. Consumer habits and expectations have changed. There are more choices, quicker feedback loops, and more connective technologies. Customers have more power and say than ever before and will quickly abandon a brand that doesn't meet their needs. Fortunately, any company today can effectively position itself to deepen its understanding of customers by gathering empirical, observational, and real-time feedback from customers.

Many large organizations are taking note of these shifts by devoting attention and resources toward renewed customer experiences. In PwC's 16th Annual Global CEO Survey, nine out of ten US CEOs say they are strengthening their customer- and client-engagement programs, and 82 percent are strengthening engagement programs with social-media users. Eighty-four percent of CEOs also expected changes in their customer growth, retention, or loyalty strategies over the next year.[6]

Shaping a culture built to support the ever-changing customer requires deep intentionality throughout the organization, a level of commitment beyond mere engagement programs. Companies that are actively working to satisfy the customer of today and tomorrow facilitate open conversations that center on the customer while embedding what matters to the customer into important enterprise metrics, and providing opportunities for employees to constantly deepen the tie between their roles and the customer. In this way, companies build their capacity to stay in tune with the changing market and customer ecosystem.

THEY TAKE A BIFOCAL VIEW

In late 2014, Tesla announced that the company had decided to push back the release date of Model X, the company's much-anticipated SUV, to a few months later than previously expected. In the letter, the company declared, "We prefer to forgo revenue rather than bring a product to market that does not delight customers. Doing so negatively affects the short term, but positively affects the long term. There are many other companies that do not follow this philosophy that may be a more attractive home for investor capital. Tesla is not going to change."[7]

This would not be an easy position for most companies to take, and clearly Tesla is advantaged in this regard by its relative lack of legacy stakeholders. GM, in comparison, must keep 200,000 employees and 20,000 dealerships, among other factors, in mind when it makes strategic decisions about product development and release. It tries to navigate those concerns on its own terms for its own best outcomes.[8]

Nevertheless, Tesla's statement was a clear message to shareholders that the company was taking the long view. It formally and forcefully articulated the company's "possibility over profitability" mindset, similar to the way Google declared in its IPO prospectus that "Google is not a conventional company. We do not intend to become one." At its core, Tesla was not comfortable releasing a product that didn't serve the needs and desires of its customers, now and in the future.

Tesla's statement is indicative of something that I call taking a "bifocal view." Bifocals, of course, are eyeglasses with lenses that have two different focal lengths, one for near vision and one for distant vision. Companies that develop bifocal views are able to focus on what's best for the customer now and in the future; it allows them to deliver exceptional products and services, while also staying ahead of the needs of current customers to deliver to the "customer of the future." In the first instance, the relentless focus on current customer needs leads highly effective companies to put extreme, nearsighted focus on helping them deliver the best products and services possible today. In the second instance, their forward, farsighted focus leads them to continuously scan the horizon for new products, new services, and innovations that will move them toward their intended future. Instead of placing all their corporate-resource eggs in one basket, they make numerous small bets—experimenting and rapidly testing possible new initiatives—elevating those that show promise, and quickly discarding those that do not.

Doing well on both of these requires companies' getting to know their customers on a deep level. Sometimes it's about meeting their demands; other times it's about actually setting their demands. Some claim Henry Ford did not actually utter the famous quote, "If I had asked people what they wanted, they would have said faster horses." Regardless, that perspective provides another layer of insight into how best to meet customer needs. Steve Jobs said that he didn't listen to his customers because they didn't know what they wanted yet; but he also said "you've got to start with the customer experience and work backwards to the technology."[9] In other words, Jobs may not have asked customers what they wanted in the moment, but he created products and services with their emerging needs firmly in mind.

Meeting and setting customer demand requires a possibility-over-profitability mindset. Short-term revenues may have to be sacrificed in order to create more effective and innovative solutions for customers in the future. It also requires a careful balancing act to stay two steps ahead of the customer while not getting too far ahead and losing sight of their needs. I liken it to the skill set needed to be a high-performance quarterback. When a quarterback drops back to pass the football, he must be able to fight through defenders, find and anticipate the route of his receiver, and then effectively deliver the football to a target that actually lies in the future. In other words, he does not throw the ball to where the receiver currently is but rather to where the receiver will be. This means the quarterback must know his receivers well and be in sync with them to complete a pass.

It's easy to notice companies that are able to play the quarterback position well. Think about Apple again. The company effectively balances both innovation and execution paradigms to deliver us products and services that feel like the future and fulfill the unanticipated needs of the present. Twenty-three years ago, when Apple introduced the Newton, a clunky predecessor to the iPad, the technology and the customer were not ready and the product failed spectacularly. It is important to stay two steps ahead of the customer and the market, not twenty.

Apple also applies its bifocal view to business operations. Rather than getting completely swept up by the sex appeal of imaginative products that delight customers and culture mavens, Apple simultaneously maintains one of the most complex and effective supply chains on the globe. In fact, Gartner has named Apple number one in supply chain the last five years in a row.[10] It's able to balance its bifocals by delivering the consumer quality products on time, while also offering solutions for what we may want next.

This deliberate attention to the long term and short term is made possible by culture. Imagine if tomorrow the innovators at Apple sat on their laurels and said, "We're good, we're meeting customer demand. Customers are happy with our phones, computers, services, etc., so we just need to continue to deliver on the products and services we're offering." The company would quickly fall behind. But no one expects this to actually happen. Shifting into strict execution mode would go against Apple's culture—an internal ethos focused on the urgency to stay ahead of customers and allow customers to catch up to them. Apple employees expect to continue to drive innovation and find new solutions for their customers. They are pacemakers, not fast-followers. In contrast, too many company cultures actually focus on delivering solutions that meet the needs of yesterday, and barely manage even to consider the needs of today, let alone tomorrow.

It takes a new ethos and sense of urgency to create a bifocal view. But it is possible to make such an ethos take root. Think about Burberry. When Ahrendts took over, she completely redirected the focus of the company to a new generation of consumers who had no knowledge of the company's core product. Burberry pulled this feat off by doing its research, identifying the pivots required to appeal to current customers, and making bold moves that also appealed to the customer of the future. By adopting a bifocal view, companies are able to pivot to new opportunities and predict where customers may be headed—and thereby better position themselves for sustained success.

By adopting a bifocal view, companies are able to pivot to new opportunities and predict where customers may be headed—and thereby better position themselves for sustained success.

Being able to make these predictions is becoming increasingly easier in the age of big data. We have more access to customers' beliefs and behaviors than ever before, and it doesn't need to cost an arm and a leg. The growth of open-source platforms, social media, and analytics technologies has provided an advantage to small and medium-size companies. This helps those who hold the "fast is better than big" mentality. Companies are doing some pretty amazing things to utilize data to better serve their customers. From health care to airlines, companies are leveraging data to get ahead and stay ahead of customers. We have the opportunity today to actually consider what the customer wants in the future. We can then turn meaningful data into customer insight that helps strengthen the products and services we offer at scale. There's an art to this science. Insight and creativity must bolster data and research. But if we start from the customer experience and work backward, we can offer both the faster horse and the automobile, delivering today while innovating for tomorrow.

Perhaps no one does this better than Netflix. The company is powered not only by its effective "freedom and responsibility culture," but also by advanced algorithms that are fed by the immense amount of information the company is constantly collecting on the viewing habits of more than 50 million subscribers.[11] These algorithms are startlingly intuitive, helping the company predict what customers may want to watch and even the actors and directors Netflix should hire to produce shows that delight customer segments.

While these algorithms are critical, they don't always paint the full picture. They can be used to predict content, but offer less insight into customer experiences, conversations, and emotional responses to the content. Because of this, the company knows it must balance those metrics with human judgment and intuition. As Ted Sarandos, the company's chief content officer, puts it, "It is important to know which data to ignore," noting that his decisions are based on 70 percent data and 30 percent judgment.

In order to become even more intelligent about the human, intuitive side of its decisions, the company hired a cultural anthropologist, Grant McCracken, to discover the heart of the customer.[12] McCracken studies Netflix users around the world to better understand consumer trends, and he provides an insightful human perspective on how individuals see themselves, putting a face on the data that drives the company. McCracken's studies include the trend known as binge-watching. Those of us who love good TV shows have practiced this trend for years, guiltily catching up on multiple episodes in short order. Netflix was the first company to buck decades of tradition, common practice, and conventional economics by offering the ability to binge-watch a new show as a key part of its value proposition. This has become the new normal almost overnight. As McCracken observes, "I found that binge watching has really taken off due to a perfect storm of better TV, our current economic climate and the digital explosion of the last few years." Services like Netflix have created more value for customers by giving them control over their TV viewing.[13]

You can imagine how studies like these help the company structure its strategy, making it possible and indeed imperative to release an entire season of a series all at once to satisfy viewers' binge desires. By balancing big data and judgment, and drawing critical insights from each, the company is able to stay closer to the customer and two steps ahead on our journey together.

THEY TALK ABOUT (AND WITH) THE CUSTOMER CONSTANTLY

A few years back my team and I were working with Old Navy to help reimagine its new-hire onboarding. In an early strategy session, a few of the Old Navy team members began talking about someone named Jenny. They openly questioned what she would think and how she would react to some of the possibilities we were discussing. It was clear that she was a person who held tremendous power and influence on the project. I had to ask, "Who is Jenny?" expecting her to be an SVP, sponsor, or executive who would largely influence the direction of the initiative.

But Jenny was not a company leader. She was between twenty-five and thirty-five years old with a couple of kids, a husband named Mike, and a desire for good-quality clothing that fit into her fairly limited budget. Jenny was the company's target customer—a young mother at the sweet-spot of the company's focus. I would come to find that discussing Jenny in meetings was in fact the norm at Old Navy, using "Mike, Jenny, and the kids" as a lens for key decisions and discussions.[14]

One key to driving a strong customer focus in an organization is to embed practices that help create a constant dialogue that centers on the customer. Jeff Bezos is notorious for the empty chair, the seat he insists be left open at meetings to remind attendees that they should be focusing on the most important person in the room, the customer.[15] I've observed and read about this practice being adopted at many companies, both old and new, to help deepen the focus on the customer in conversations. I think it's a practice that becomes even more important as companies grow and increase their distance from the customer.

In other companies this customer focus is not the case. As an outsider, I'm often surprised by how infrequently the customer is brought up. Whether I'm listening in on executive meetings and strategy sessions, or digging into formal corporate communications and executive emails, the emphasis is rarely on the customer. As a result, the "why" behind messaging is often lost, leaving employees unclear on strategic decisions and forcing them to make assumptions about their own decisions that may not be aligned with the organization.

Whatever leaders decide to emphasize or deemphasize reinforces the inherent mindsets, values, and priorities of the organization. When cost-cutting and process improvement takes precedent over the customer, for example, that emphasis drives an internal focus on efficiency and corner-cutting as opposed to an outward lens that's possibility-driven. How and what we communicate helps align or misalign the organization around purpose and customer focus.

In "Combining Purpose with Profits," Julian Birkinshaw, Nicolai J. Foss, and Siegwart Lindenberg touch on the importance of building an organization in which employees are dedicated to goals bigger than themselves. The article talks about "pro-social" goals, which are defined as goals that involve working toward common causes that go beyond just making money and staying in business. Pro-social goals have been proven to create a stronger sense of motivation for employees than goals that emphasize financial gain or personal enjoyment. Indeed, as one of the guidelines for motivating employees to pursue pro-social goals, the authors mention that a company's statements must prioritize pro-social goals ahead of financial goals. "For example, if a medical-products company is seeking to 'put patients first,' then this goal should be center stage in all external and internal communications. Financial goals, in contrast, should be approached in an oblique or indirect way; they should be seen as the natural consequence of achieving the pro-social goals, rather than as ends in themselves. If financial goals are given too much prominence, they will typically displace the pro-social goals."[16]

Genentech is a leading biotech enterprise and a member of the Roche Company we talked about earlier. It's a great example of a company that has focused on promoting pro-social goals. The company has a diverse set of customers, from health-care practitioners to hospitals to medical-device distributors, and it has had debates internally on the ultimate customer. But it has landed on the ultimate customer as the patient, leading Genentech and Roche toward the shared purpose of, as you may recall, "Doing now what patients need next." This level of altruism requires that all employees feel committed and connected to patients. So the company spends considerable effort to make this connection throughout the entire life cycle of an employee, not just during the drug-discovery and innovation process. The company embeds patient-centric messaging and assessments into its recruiting and hiring practices, ensuring it attracts, hires, and retains people who are good cultural fits. As the hiring webpage points out, "When you work at Genentech, you'll come to understand that changing the course of medicine requires the kind of inspiration that can only come from a combined commitment to patients, science, and people." Every day, the company also reinforces these messages to employees and visitors through huge patient posters plastered on buildings across the corporate campus. And many times, real patients and caregivers come to share their stories with employees.

The company's patient-centered emphasis clearly resonates with its employees and new hires, landing the company on the 2015 "best places to work" lists of Fortune, Glassdoor, and *Science Magazine*, among others.[17] Rather than limiting the communications process, the company uses it as a reinforcing mechanism to thread customer-centricity throughout the entire employee life cycle. Communications is not just corporate emails for the company; it is a blend of push and pull with employees to focus on delivering the best patient outcomes possible.

THEY MAKE THE CUSTOMER MATTER IN THEIR METRICS

Last year, I co-facilitated a session at a major retailer alongside the company's VP of strategy. There were thirty or so other senior leaders in the room from all over the company—including HR, talent acquisition, compensation, store operations, and innovation. We were discussing culture and how the company could drive a more customer-centric ethos to better deliver on its purpose. The VP challenged the group by asking, "Who knows our customer metrics?" The room went silent. And then answerless. Not one of the leaders in the room had any idea of what the company's customer metrics were. They were trying to drive an ethos of customer-centricity throughout the company even while the leaders responsible for that change were completely unaware of the metrics the organization was driving toward.

Perhaps this is shocking, but I don't think it is uncommon. Imagine, now, the degree to which conversations between leaders and their teams and business units could be misaligned because of this basic confusion. It's a formula for disaster.

We've all heard the credo, "What gets measured gets done." It's hard to steer an organization toward customer-centricity when the metrics that are emphasized and communicated are in opposition to what's best for the customer. Too often financial metrics are all that are discussed, beaten to death in quarterly meetings, town halls, and store huddles. Too often, the customer is left out of these discussions entirely, or positioned as a mere means to an end.

Yet, if we aren't embedding the customer into our metrics, and understanding how we are defining success accordingly, we will lose sight of our priorities. At the same time, if leaders consistently point their teams toward business metrics that benefit the bottom line and not the customer, that's where people will direct their efforts. To truly drive a culture built to deliver the best customer experience possible, it's critical to embed customer-centric metrics throughout the organization and shift whatever measurements skew that view.

Another client, one of the nation's largest grocery chains, has been able to shift its store metrics over the past couple of years to get closer to the customer. For a long time, it was very much focused on service results. This meant managers clung to their clipboards to apply check-the-box exercises that ensured aisles were clean and employees were meeting limited objectives. Like many other retailers, the company hired and trained secret shoppers to go into stores and look for a checklist of execution points, which ultimately served as the key metrics for how the company measured successful customer service. This approach led the company to focus its attention on this artificial construct, further separating the organization's culture from real customer concerns and needs. As you can imagine, such metrics drove employees' behaviors within the stores, encouraging them to fulfill the activities that arose on the checklist while disregarding those that didn't show up. This not only limited the ability of employees to use critical thinking to best serve the customer, but it also limited actual customer feedback that could have helped the company evolve to meet changing consumer demands.

The company became aware of this growing distance from customers and made the bold move to do away with secret shoppers, while employing direct customer feedback through a receipt-based survey that measured overall customer satisfaction levels. The company followed this up by removing service scores from its bonus structure and performance ratings. Previously, store managers could be promoted only if their service score met a certain level.

As with most major changes that ultimately affect a company culture, these shifts created a bit of confusion at first. Employees had been trained on details that no longer mattered, all the way down to specific words to use when greeting and thanking customers. Now, they were being empowered to use their best judgment to serve customer needs. But over time, the changes have proven to be overwhelmingly positive for stores, creating a deepened level of trust and openness between customers and employees.

Companies embed the customer into their metrics to various degrees and with various levels of success. Amazon doesn't let the imaginary customer just have a seat at its meetings. How could it, when the company's purpose is to become "Earth's most customer-centric company"? The tech giant tracks its overall business performance against approximately 500 measures, with nearly 80 percent of these goals focused on customer objectives. The company also holds its sellers to strict customer metrics, measuring them on the percentage of orders that are perfectly accepted, processed, and fulfilled; on-time shipment; and orders that have received negative feedback. But what the company does exceptionally well is actually utilize the data from shopper recommendations and feedback to build those metrics. In this way, current customers help future customers, and are even likely to see the impact one day. As at other companies, metrics at Amazon drive employees' imperatives and behaviors.

Jeff Bezos' fierce focus on the customer has generated huge benefits for Amazon. The University of Michigan's American Customer Satisfaction Index has ranked Amazon at the top of the online-retailing category for years. For Amazon, it's about building customer-centric metrics that lead to long-term satisfaction rather than short-term company profits. "We don't focus on the optics of the next quarter," says Bezos, "we focus on what is going to be good for customers. I think this aspect of our culture is rare."[18]

THEY FORGE AND REINFORCE LINE OF SIGHT

John Deere's purpose is to "serve those linked to the land, thereby help-ing to improve living standards for people everywhere."[19] In other words, it wants to help farmers do a better job feeding the world. John Deere has tried to do so ever since it opened a small shop in Grand Detour, Illinois, in 1837 to sell small farm tools such as pitchforks and shovels. The company continues to do so today by selling tractors, planting- and seeding-equipment, harvesting machines, sprayers, and other agricultural innovations.

John Deere has a very tangible purpose—it lives in its products and services. But the company doesn't allow this clarity to dissipate as the dis-tance from the product to the hierarchy grows, nor does it allow its credo to become a hollow slogan. It keeps its purpose real and alive by keeping the customer close.

John Deere follows a number of customer-centric practices. For exam-ple, it seeks customer feedback at farms and it develops strategies that are specifically geared to winning customers over generations rather than isolated sales. Indeed, John Deere understands that farmers must make significant investments in farm equipment to achieve long-term viability, so it offers loans for customers to purchase its products. As you can imag-ine, doing this could lead financial leaders in charge of crafting those pro-grams to prioritize company profits over customer needs. To prevent this, the financial services division created the Executive Connection Program, where leaders leave their suits at home and work with their customers on the farm for a day. This process helps leaders build empathy and under-standing of the people they are developing programs to help. In turn, this drives a customer-first approach throughout John Deere's lending programs.[20]

Organizations that build customer-centric cultures understand that it's not enough to talk about what's best for the customer, or to com-municate about purpose, or even to highlight examples of the positive, altruistic endeavors the company is doing to benefit customers and com-munity. While these can strengthen the organization's overall emphasis on customer intimacy, it's critical to give employees, managers, and lead-ers clarity on how their day-to-day roles and responsibilities tie to the customer.

Unfortunately, it's rare for employees sitting at corporate headquarters—whether they're in finance, legal, or IT—to have a visceral understanding of how the work they are doing is affecting the customer. Think about it. It's fairly easy for a customer-facing employee to appreciate the positive or negative effect they have on customers nearly every day. But for those at a distance, it grows increasingly difficult to see that impact and to build empathy and understanding for customers.

Disengaged employees often complain that they feel like a "cog in the wheel" of the organization. I believe that at the heart of that complaint lies a lack of direct contact with work that feels meaningful and important. Often, such employees do not feel connected to their organization's purpose nor to the people the organization is trying to serve. Creating a direct view to what the customers want gives employees a deeper engagement with their work and enables them to solve problems in ways that are fulfilling precisely because those solutions have impact. Recall the story of President John Kennedy touring NASA headquarters in 1961. Coming across a janitor doing his daily cleaning duties, the president introduced himself and asked the man, "So, tell me what are you doing?" The janitor responded, "Well, Mr. President, I'm helping put a man on the moon."[21] This perspective is typical of a unified culture that is able to direct an organization to its North Star.

Disengaged employees often complain that they feel like a "cog in the wheel" of the organization. I believe that at the heart of that complaint lies a lack of direct contact with work that feels meaningful and important.

One of the most effective ways that organizations can drive customer-centricity across the enterprise is to help employees understand how they contribute to the impact on the customer. In an age of employee empowerment, companies need to help employees understand how their roles, practices, and objectives might grow to better serve the customer. When this happens, it nurtures a sense of mutual trust and respect between company and the employee who is being called upon to be a Difference Maker.

For a customer-first economy, micro-level choices are critical because those decisions have macro-level impact.

In "The Aligned Organization," Thierry Nautin, a partner at McKinsey & Company, discusses achieving alignment throughout an organization so that strategy, goals, and purpose reinforce one another. He argues that this process provides a distinct advantage because it allows employees to understand what to do at any moment, with freedom and flexibility, ensuring that the organization moves in the right direction. But Nautin points out that this type of achievement is rare: "More typically, the individual level is where the vision breaks down: employees see only the gap between the aspirational language and their daily work lives and may become cynical rather than motivated. But some organizations make all of the links, so that vision, strategy, and goals come together to become meaningful work. In so doing they instill a sense of achievement that, in turn, enables their people to achieve more and more."[22]

Nautin is talking about creating line of sight for employees that goes beyond aspirational language and breaks down how the purpose and strategy translate to the everyday lives of employees. The best way to do this is to step directly into the customer's shoes, just as John Deere requires of its finance leaders. Some companies bring customers into their meetings and planning sessions to ensure that their voice is heard. Others, like Amazon, leave that aforementioned empty seat open for their customers during important discussions to remind teams of the why. I like to have line-of-sight meetings with teams to help them discover ways they may or may not currently contribute to serving the customer, and expand that discussion to the blue-sky opportunities that would become possible if their roles could grow to meet customer needs even better.

THE FOCUS DIFFERENCE

Organizations that are focused have line of sight to the customer, talk with the customer directly and constantly, align their purpose to the customer's needs, and use appropriate customer-satisfaction metrics to measure progress and success. The difference all this can make is tremendous.

When Dr. David Feinberg became CEO of UCLA Health System in 2007, he discovered that his organization was one of the top-ranked academic medical systems in the country—and renowned for medical advances that transform lives—however, two out of three patients would not recommend the system to others. First and foremost, we must credit Feinberg for caring that this discrepancy existed. For many CEOs, the metrics that matter most are also the most prestigious. The lowly customer—especially the customer we've already "captured"—often gets short shrift. Second, it is instructive that Feinberg did something to understand this discrepancy better. He didn't rely on a consultant or a study to get that information, he did something few executives bother to do. He spent time with customers in person.

In Feinberg's case, this was like doing rounds. He visited patients, introduced himself, and asked what he could do to improve their care experience. In other words, he tried to see the care from the customer's perspective. After a few months, Feinberg and his team had some data. Patients didn't feel they understood who was in charge of their care. Care providers never looked them in the eye or introduced themselves. The food was bad, the rooms were dirty, and there were never enough bedpans or wheelchairs. It could take nine to ten hours to get help in the emergency room.

Feinberg instituted a series of changes large and small to shift that cultural misalignment with the customer. He started with the purpose and values of the organization, and he cascaded it through the way people were hired—borrowing from Ritz-Carlton's Talent-Plus program—to the way teams were formed, and how staff interacted with patients. Doing so, he shifted the perspective of the organization from "You're lucky to see us" to "How can I help you?"

Perhaps most important, Feinberg instructed all executives to do rounds, too, because he wanted to make sure people in functions that were distant from the customer—such as finance or IT—could interact with patients and develop empathy with them, too.

Today, not only is UCLA the number-one academic hospital in the country, but its patient-experience scores are also in the 99th percentile and its financial performance has dramatically improved, as well. On this point, Feinberg says: "I really believe that the reason our financial performance at UCLA has been so outstanding is that we haven't focused on financial performance. But rather we've focused on taking care of patients."[23]

A deeper level of customer-centricity takes a commitment to embedding the customer throughout the organization, into conversations, meetings, programs, and practices. By shifting our organizational focus toward the customer, we can create cultures that are driven by possibility, that can pivot toward new opportunities for value creation, and that give employees more meaning in their lives by enabling them to connect with those who need them and contribute to something bigger than us all.

QUESTIONS FOR YOU TO CONSIDER:

* How would you describe your target customer?

* What practices do you have in place to help your people keep the customer top of mind?

* How do your company metrics reflect what's most important to your customers?

8

THEIR LEADERS ARE COURAGEOUS CONNECTORS

AT THE 2012 DRUCKER FORUM in Vienna, my colleague Tammy Erickson made some comments about how complex and challenging it has become for organizations to do what seems like a simple thing: create new products and services that customers are demanding. According to Tammy, customer-focused innovation is more important than ever, but it requires that organizations learn how to respond quickly to insights they gain through "faint signals." Those faint signals can come from anywhere, of course, but I immediately thought of customers or other voices in the marketplace, and also employees, particularly customer-facing ones. I imagined a customer-service rep, for example, dealing with a customer who has a complaint and expresses a wish or a vague desire for a different product or service. What's the poor customer-service rep supposed to do with that information? In most organizations it goes precisely nowhere, but companies that innovate with the customer in mind, according to Tammy, must "harness the smallest units of knowledge, creating value from bits that in the past would have been ignored or discarded."

To me, that comment shone a light on one of the most pervasive problems I encounter in organizations trying to navigate the world of today via the processes and approaches of yesterday. Traditional organizations struggle in a number of key ways. First, they find it difficult to truly satisfy individual customers. Think of the last time you brought forward a complaint or problem. Maybe your concern arose because of a glitch in the system, but most organizations tend to ignore or discard such complaints by applying a policy-driven, one-size-fits-all solution that serves the organization's need for orderly processes but usually ends up alienating the customer. Second, traditional organizations are cumbersome and slow when it comes to innovation. They focus on large-scale, top-down change initiatives (akin to five-year plans) that too often miss the mark. And third, they don't really know what to do with (or particularly want to manage or leverage) employees who stray from the path, color outside the lines, express doubts, ask questions, offer suggestions, or critique the way things are done. They would rather ignore or discard such people, and in the process they stifle or alienate them, too, further cutting off lines of communication with customers and blocking insights into the market and the world.

I probably don't even need to mention that all this "ignore and discard" behavior is in dramatic contrast to the stated principles of such organizations that so often cite their customer-first, innovation-driven, and employee-centered cultures.

In contrast, "nimble, focused, and feisty" companies work to connect very directly with customers—meeting, anticipating, and even shaping desires—and see complaints, problems, concerns, and bits of data as directions for improving the system and discovering new value. They innovate constantly (in large and small ways) as part of their workflow (leveraging the information they gain from customers and employees) in pursuit of their vision and they don't wait for seismic failures or heroic responses to launch change. And they give employees true freedom and flexibility to make decisions with regard to customer needs and their own work, while encouraging them to initiate and drive solutions.

In past chapters, I've talked a lot about the organizational structures and processes that unleash the capability to be nimble and focused. In this section, we're going to look at how organizations leverage their people and practices to create feisty cultures. Such organizations always seem to be on their toes, are highly (and intelligently) reactive to changing circumstances and changing customer demands, and have the cultural will to align resources or pivot to meet new needs quickly. It sounds great on paper, but as I just suggested above, some organizations pull this off and others don't. So what's the difference?

It starts with a type of leader I call the "Courageous Connector."

THE UNCERTAINTY PRINCIPLE

We've looked at how VUCA (Volatility, Uncertainty, Complexity, Ambiguity) defines the world we're living in today, but I think it would be helpful to review that shift from the past and think about the job of the leader in that context.

Organizations in the twentieth century were designed to optimize processes and quality, bring products and services to scale, and grow market share into unassailable dominance. Success was based on the premise that if the strategy was good, processes were efficient, margins were sufficient, and everyone did the job assigned to him, the organizational engine would create significant momentum.

There's no question that creativity, innovation, and entrepreneurial passion was poured into such ventures, especially at the outset. Who can imagine Henry Ford's automobile, National Semiconductor's computer chip, or Walmart's low-priced consumer goods without people of leadership and even genius behind them? In the best sense, customer demands were being understood, met, exceeded, and shaped. But once the engine of that product or service offering was developed, the organization built to keep it going required something different. Pride was important, and people cared about their organizations and their work, and were zealous about excellence and winning, but being an effective leader meant being decisive and issuing clear commands, while being a "good" employee meant following a straight line without undue questioning, and even the best organizations didn't innovate their existing products or services much until crisis or competition forced a reaction. Leadership was part inspiration, part command, and it cascaded through the organization via the close attention of management.

Today, the number of variables that companies must grapple with (competitors, products, technologies, markets, customer segments) has exponentially increased the complexity of doing business. Meanwhile, business plans and reasonable assumptions about markets and customers quickly become obsolete because linear projections are so frequently disrupted by sudden and often dramatic change. This means that the future is essentially unpredictable. It may never have been actually predictable before, but there used to be a sense that one year would resemble the next. No one really believes that to be true anymore.

Where does this leave the leader? It depends on what kind of leader you mean. The strength of twentieth-century leadership was built on confidence of decision-making, clarity of vision, and depth of understanding. Leaders often knew their business and their markets better than anyone else in the organization, saw where the organization needed to go more clearly, and directed people and resources decisively.

Now, it's widely recognized that leaders can often be less in touch and sensitive to customers and markets than their "lowliest" employees. They may also be technically inept compared to the people they hire to develop their tools, run their operations, and drive their innovations. And the rational ones no longer feel confident about the future. They are, in other words, in a perpetual state of uncertainty about the future, somewhat ignorant about their customers, and largely dependent on those around them. That's not familiar territory, to put it mildly. Given such circumstances, how likely is it that the important decisions a leader makes, the direction he or she sets for others, and the assumptions about reality he or she rely on will actually work out?

The philosopher David Snowden digs into the nuances of control versus complexity in the framework he calls the Four Ontologies. Basically, Snowden categorizes situations according to their degree of simplicity and predictability. "Obvious" situations demonstrate simple cause and effect, so they are easy for leaders to understand, manage, and control. "Complicated" situations require more analysis to determine cause and effect so they require more insight, data, and higher-level decision-making to influence. "Complex" situations really can't be understood clearly until examined in retrospect, when the forces and consequences are more manifest, so managing, controlling, or leveraging them requires a big step into the unknown. "Chaotic" situations demonstrate no relation between cause and effect, forcing the leader to act without data or to be reactive to whatever has just happened.

According to Snowden, leaders need to modulate their leadership approach depending on the level of simplicity or complexity in the situation at hand. As he puts it, "Effective leaders learn to shift their decision-making styles to match changing business environments. Simple, complicated, complex, and chaotic contexts each call for different managerial responses."[1]

With the world becoming increasingly complex, the degree of control, influence, understanding, or analytical thinking a leader can provide the organization is greatly reduced. Insight into the customer, the market, and the needs of the business can no longer come solely or even mainly from the top—it will come from anywhere, primarily through those "faint signals" or "bits that in the past would have been ignored or discarded," according to Tammy Erickson. The drive for excellence and innovation also does not come solely from the top. To be effective, it also has to emerge from the value zone through the employees who are grappling with the problems of their work and struggling to meet the needs of customers.

It's one thing, however, to talk about "inverting the pyramid" or structuring the hierarchy to back up those employees with the resources and support they need. Listening to "faint signals" and "harnessing discarded bits" is an entirely different way of leading, organizing, and engaging in work. For several centuries, during the extended history of the industrial economy, we wanted exactly the opposite from leaders—decisive certainty with no ambiguity—and from employees, an unquestioning obedience and unwavering execution according to dictates that came from on high. As Seth Godin says, "The worker on the assembly line isn't supposed to question the design of the car. The clerk at the insurance agency isn't supposed to suggest improvements in the accounts being pitched. In the post-industrial age, though, the good jobs and the real progress belong only to those with the *confidence* and the background to use the scientific method to question authority and to reimagine a better reality."

This is why the leaders of "nimble, focused, and feisty" organizations are so obsessed with culture. They understand that their best people are Difference Makers, and that culture, rather than command and control, is the guide and the glue for holding those people together and directing them in the right way.

Those leaders are very open about the importance of a strong organizational culture and of talented people who fit that culture. They are incredibly clear, upfront, and open about the mindsets they value because these are the philosophical underpinnings of that culture. They make the customer the target and the purpose of everything the organization does, and they make sure people are aligned with and can fulfill those priorities with energy, focus, commitment, and dedication.

In other words, the job of the new leader is not to have all the answers, set processes in stone, make all the decisions, and command obedient action, but to build the culture in which the freedom, talent, and intelligence of employees can thrive and be harnessed in service of the customer and the organization's purpose.

This doesn't just require a new kind of leadership; it requires an entirely new leadership model. I'm not claiming that the following is the full picture of what makes a great leader or manager, but it is an approach to leadership that is necessary for fostering a "nimble, focused, and feisty" culture.

THE NEW LEADERSHIP MODEL:
COURAGEOUS + CONNECTOR

Effective leadership has always been binary in nature—part leadership, part management. But in the past, successful leadership meant being a "Smart + Commander." Today it is far more important to be a Courageous + Connector. Let me break that two-part model down into its component pieces, starting with courage.

What does it mean for a leader to be courageous? I'm not talking about the courage to lead troops into battle or rescue survivors from a flood but the courage to be vulnerable, confident, and daring even in the midst of uncertainty. Courageous leaders acknowledge doubt, admit they don't have all the answers or even all the data necessary, and still make decisions and lead with confidence. Indeed, many of the most important decisions that executives face today test their courage far more than their intelligence.

By courage, I also don't mean that a leader is brash or devil-may-care about those big decisions. That kind of courage can be found too often in traditional leaders who may seem manic or capricious to the people closest to them, and rarely take into account the ideas or feelings of others. Instead, courageous leaders are bold, daring, and organized. They are not early Steve Jobs—alienating others, favoring secret "revolutionary" project teams over the larger organization—but late Steve Jobs—inspiring new thinking, greatness, and discipline throughout an inclusive and tightly knit organizational culture. They set lofty standards and inspirational goals for themselves, their organizations, and others. Their boldness comes from being hungry and outrospective in mindset—they see problems or opportunities in the world worth attacking, and they go for it because it will have an impact and make a difference. And they are also not afraid of having an organization full of people who share that mindset—they don't need to be the "only" genius or star. In fact, they actively and openly try to establish an expectation for boldness and embed it in the culture. As Beth Comstock of GE says, "I spend a lot of time thinking about how to be bold, aspiring to be bold, fretting over not being bold enough—not just clever, smart or imaginative, but audacious. The tough part is that the world keeps shifting and taking away the firm ground that would allow us to take action. The rise of new technologies, the flood of analytics and data, and the accelerating speed of the global enterprise can complicate decision-making for even the most confident executive. So how do we stay bold?"

Most leaders don't play bold in this way. Some act courageous but actually play it safe by driving single-mindedly toward the long-term plan or making operational or portfolio changes that look good to investors, even as they may be ignoring or avoiding tough calls about the customer or the future that would catalyze very different activities or directions. Other traditional leaders may seem courageous because their hands are all over the company—making decisions in all areas, taking control over the minutiae, maintaining a profile as the face of the organization—even as they eviscerate any inclinations toward daring among others. The courage today's leaders need and admire is courage in service of the customer and the culture of the organization.

Courageous leaders are also very human. They are authentic and real, and personally accountable in the way that people who work hard at relationships must be accountable to others. They try to model that standard and look for such character in others. They are also transparent and straightforward. Many successful leaders in the past seemed to be good at playing mind games. With today's leader, no one has to work hard at guessing or interpreting what the leader truly believes, values, and wants. His or her intentions, motives, and priorities are clear and openly discussed at every opportunity. The leader's beliefs, goals, and mindset become the basis of the culture that the leader is constantly working to shape and architect.

As the researcher John Kotter puts it, leadership "is associated with taking an organization into the future, finding opportunities that are coming at it faster and faster and successfully exploiting those opportunities. Leadership is about vision, about people buying in, about empowerment and, most of all, about producing useful change. Leadership is not about attributes, it's about behavior."[2]

The second part of the binary leadership model is the Connector Manager. Management has always been about helping to execute the vision or strategy of the leader. It still is, but the way in which that is done has changed considerably.

Kotter captures the traditional management role perfectly, but he is missing the mark when it comes to the new requirements for this function. As he writes: "Management is a set of well-known processes, like planning, budgeting, structuring jobs, staffing jobs, measuring performance and problem-solving, which help an organization to predictably do what it knows how to do well. Management helps you to produce products and services as you have promised, of consistent quality, on budget, day after day, week after week."[3] In NFF organizations, though, the best managers are also effective connectors. I don't mean this in the sense that they are good at networking or playing politics. Their organizational insight is wielded in service of a cause. They serve in the role of manager because they are exceptional at helping the people they oversee get the resources, knowledge, and capabilities needed to succeed. They have real relationships with those people, and use their emotional intelligence to be empathetic and caring. They know their strengths and weaknesses and work to support them. They "connect" in other aspects, too. They connect the dots between people's passions, talents, and roles and the company's purpose and objectives. They clarify the link between what the team is doing and what the organization is striving toward. They're good systems thinkers who can see how resources, talents, people, and opportunities could be better aligned, ensuring that the best ideas get surfaced, tactics succeed, and processes are effective and not frustrating. They're also inclusive and collaborative by nature.

MIT's Thomas Malone has come the closest I've seen to describing this role, depicting it as a movement away from "command and control" and toward "coordinating and cultivating." In his book, *The Future of Work*, Malone writes, "To coordinate is to organize work to make good things happen, whether you're in control or not. Coordinating focuses on the activities that need to be done and the relationships among them. Cultivating focuses on the people doing the activities, what they want, what they're good at, and how they can help one another."[4]

If leaders are the guides of the organization, managers are the glue.

THE ATTRIBUTES OF COURAGEOUS LEADERS

In a world of uncertainty, where leaders can no longer be the paragon of the decisive, all-knowing commander anymore, what do courageous leaders provide an organization?

Most critically, courageous leaders establish or reinforce purpose, which is organizational clarity around what is important. They also set the tone and establish or reinforce the beliefs of the culture. They are culture coders who lead in the way they want the organization to behave, inspiring a mindset that hinges on possibility. They also work to build the setting or ecosystem that their people need to feel committed and engaged by the organization's pursuit of its purpose. And in line with that, courageous leaders inspire action within an ethos of innovation and customer service.

They Anchor the Organization to Its Purpose and Values

Courageous leaders take values and purpose very personally. Attack or question those fundamental principles and you are likely to provoke a strong response. When Apple CEO Tim Cook was questioned by a prominent shareholder about the company's focus on environmentalism over pure profit, Cook responded testily: "Get out of our stock."[5] What nerve did that shareholder touch? Cook clearly saw environmental responsibility as a priority and value that superseded the short-term pursuit of profit and he wanted everyone to know. It would be hard not to get the message clearly.

Employees respond to that kind of clarity when it is reinforced. As thought-leader Simon Sinek says, "There are leaders and there are those who lead. Leaders hold a position of power and authority, but the ones who truly lead inspire us. They inspire because they start with 'Why.' And we follow not because we have to, but because we want to, not for them but for us."

This clarity not only provides a road for the organization to follow but it also provides guardrails for the organization to stay within. It is easy in a complex ecosystem when management and supervision are loose to become overwhelmed with choice. As Barry Schwartz puts it in his book, *The Paradox of Choice*, "Choice no longer liberates, it debilitates. It might even be said to tyrannize." By anchoring the organization so solidly to purpose and values, the leader simplifies choice and coheres it around obvious priorities.

Tony Hsieh, CEO of Zappos, is a huge believer in culture providing those guardrails. As he puts it, "Researchers found it actually doesn't matter what your core values are. What matters is that you have them and you align the entire organization around them; and you're willing to hire and fire people based on having nothing to do with their actual job performance."

In other words, adherence to the purpose and values at the heart of culture is a non-negotiable. And if you get that alignment in place, according to Hsieh, "most of the other stuff, like delivering great customer service or building a long-term brand or business, will just be a natural byproduct."

They Set Audacious Goals

How do NFF organizations change the world? By having leaders who rally everyone behind an audacious vision.

A vision is a depiction of a possible future. Will that future come to be? Who can know, but a courageous leader believes in that vision and is committed to seeing it become real. In fact, the leader treats the vision as if it is a reality that will surely happen—and disregards skeptics as those who are simply unaware of that inevitability.

To come up with a vision and state it openly requires some audacity in and of itself. But a truly audacious vision, one that declares a fantastic future and a prominent role for the organization in building it, involves a rare level of boldness. In part, this is because audacious goals can scare people off. Even your own employees may be intimidated by the commitment level necessary. The courageous leader keeps the foot on the pedal regardless of doubts to ensure that everyone understands the goal is serious and will be attained. They also take every opportunity to raise the ante, and are always asking big questions of their people to help them in turn develop a "Why not?" attitude about possibility and opportunity.

This intensity of purpose also helps to shake loose those who are not deeply committed to the vision. If you lose people in the process, that's good, not bad. Zappos has a goal to engineer the ultimate customer experience, and it hires people it believes can help it fulfill that goal. But if those new hires don't feel committed to that vision at the end of their four-week training program, Zappos pays them $2,500 to quit. As Bloomberg News put it, "Zappos is acting on the understanding that the character of a company can be the most powerful yet most difficult competitive advantage to develop and maintain. 'The Offer' suggests a rare company that believes if you really want to amaze your customers, a great way to start is to amaze your employees and inspire them to amaze everyone who comes in contact with your enterprise."[6]

Audacity is easily written off as delusional or naive, especially when the organization in question is a startup and the leaders are young. No doubt, Wall Street would also prefer NFF companies to tone down the rhetoric and focus the conversation on discipline and fundamentals. Yet, without an audacious vision, and a determined commitment to achieving it, nothing bold can ever materialize. Also, a leader would not be courageous if he kept an audacious vision to himself. You can't pull off a Big Hairy Audacious Goal, as Jim Collins used to say, without a workforce unified around making it happen. This is why courageous leaders model openness, boldness, and collaboration. They know they need everyone on board and rowing in the same direction.

No doubt, Wall Street would also prefer NFF companies to tone down the rhetoric and focus the conversation on discipline and fundamentals. Yet, without an audacious vision, and a determined commitment to achieving it, nothing bold can ever materialize.

There's another reason why audacity plays so well today. Because of the complexity and uncertainty of the world, anything is possible. The potential payoff is bigger than ever for organizations willing to roll the dice, take a chance, and play big and bold. Incrementalism, in contrast, is a loser's game because it ensures regression to the mean at the expense of exponential growth and market success.

Audacity gives an organization energy around innovation and growth. Organizations generally become less audacious as they grow larger. In part, this is because Wall Street expects disciplined quarterly results from established darlings to meet its need for predictable forecasting. But the most successful companies are the ones that are always willing to push the chips they've won back into the middle of the table and play big again. As Jack Ma, the founder of Alibaba (which went public with a $25 billion IPO), puts it, "The company will remain a startup no matter how long it has been in existence. Whatever has been stable, I will disrupt that stability. The company needs to innovate and grow."

They Are Honest and Humble Communicators

You might think that a courageous leader who is defiant and audacious would also be a blowhard. This isn't the case. Courageous leaders are transparent, down-to-earth, and straightforward. Howard Schultz, for example, was incredibly forthright and open in interviews he gave after resuming his duties as CEO of Starbucks when the company was in serious trouble. Wall Street pressure to change the business model, reduce benefits to employees, and eliminate philanthropic efforts was intense. Schultz acknowledged that pressure and the dire position Starbucks was in, and then explained over and over why he was sticking with what he believed was the right path. As he said:

"You have to have a 100 percent belief in your core reason for being. There was tremendous pressure in the first three or four months after my return to dramatically change the strategy and the business model of the company. The marketplace was saying, 'Starbucks needs to undo all these company-owned stores and franchise the system.' That would have given us a war chest of cash and significantly increased return on capital. It's a good argument economically. It's a good argument for shareholder value. But it would have fractured the culture of the company. You can't get out of this by trying to navigate with a different road map, one that isn't true to yourself. You have to be authentic, you have to be true, and you have to believe in your heart that this is going to work."[7]

That ability to combine compassion with "telling it like it is" extends into the interpersonal realm, too. Courageous leaders are clear in communicating the rules of the road without mincing words. This isn't done to intimidate or railroad anyone but to clarify expectations, assess performance, and reinforce goals. When candor is communicated with empathy and caring and not arrogance or ego, good things happen. Empathetic communication bolstered by transparency and authenticity improves mutual understanding, respect, and trust. It turns resentment into buy-in. Indeed, studies have shown that the best leaders are humble leaders.[8]

They Are "Stubborn on Vision and Flexible on Details"

Jeff Bezos coined the term "stubborn on vision and flexible on details," and he said this, too: "If you're not stubborn, you'll give up on experiments too soon. And if you're not flexible, you'll pound your head against the wall and you won't see a different solution to a problem you're trying to solve."[9] As a leader, Bezos is able to take the "best truth" at the time, and he refuses to accept the conventional wisdom about the way things are typically done. This makes him a flexible, creative, and relentless driver toward Amazon's vision.

Courageous leaders are locked into their vision but willing and able to continually improvise, innovate, and adapt to ever-changing circumstances in order to achieve it. I mentioned earlier that they are up for pushing their chips into the middle of the table, but this risk-taking is highly disciplined because it is done in service of the vision and with a deep understanding of the circumstances at hand and the resources and tools at the organization's disposal.

As a result, courageous leaders are able to make very tough decisions without excessive agonizing. A balanced reliance on data and instinct helps them to understand when they "know enough" and resist the pressure to wait until they "know it all." This ability reminds me of the concept called "thin slicing" that Malcolm Gladwell talks about in his book *Blink.* Courageous leaders make quick decisions and take calculated risks by finding patterns in events based only on "thin slices" or narrow windows of experience. They are more than willing to make bold moves.

This adaptability and risk orientation helps the leader shift the organization in response to challenges and even disrupt it or the market in order to achieve a better position for future success. As Mark Parker, CEO of

Nike, says, "We're constantly looking for ways to improve. How do you adapt to your environment and really focus on your potential? To really go after that, you have to embrace the reality that it is not going to slow down. And you have to look at that as half full, not half empty."

THE CONNECTOR MANAGER

In the old world of business, the stereotypes were crude but recognizable. Leaders were inspiring commanders, but managers were the drill sergeants. They were the ones who turned vision into execution by pressuring their people relentlessly to meet the numbers and get the job done.

In reality, effective managers have always been good at connecting with their teams to motivate, encourage, and coach them to better performance. That remains true today, but the array of "connection" points has broadened exponentially. Managers must now serve as conduits who facilitate and enable organizational freedom, innovation, and initiative.

The difference is most obvious when it comes to the type of power that managers leverage today. In the past, the source of their power was situational and institutional. Managers got their influence (power measured by stature and title) through their level in the hierarchy, their seniority, the extent of the resources and personnel within their domain, the importance of their business unit or department to the organization's bottom line, and their personal closeness to higher-level decision-makers. Today, managers gain impact (power measured by outcomes) by forming connections to others, solidifying relationships, establishing organizational mindshare, enabling the strengths of the people on their team, aligning with other teams and creating momentum around better ideas, approaches, or solutions for delivering value.

What do Connector Managers provide their organizations? Most concretely, they enable their teams to navigate the organization effectively. They do this by helping to align strengths and passion with purpose, strategy, resources, organizational expertise, and business objectives. The manager has the organizational knowledge to make people more successful, engaged, and smarter in accomplishing their work. The manager is there, essentially, to give employees what they need to be and do their best. Sometimes that means getting the right resources, people, or approvals in place. Sometimes it means giving everyone a clear sense of why the work is so consequential.

More intangibly, managers are also responsible for expanding a sense of possibility. In the past, managers often shut down workers' orientation toward what could be better, bigger, new, or next. They admonished people to keep their heads down, focus on the task at hand, stick to the knitting. Today, execution remains critical, but smart execution requires simultaneously looking up and around, watching the play and not the ball.

While much remains the same, the manager as connector is a fundamentally new and broadly expanded role. Managers are no longer secondary or smaller cogs in the greater machine. They are crucial nodes of insight and expertise that help facilitate innovation, performance improvement, and execution. In the process, they are growing as leaders while also enriching the skills of their people and helping to change and improve the organization.

It is a fantastic time to be a manager. The position has never been more engaging and filled with possibility.

They Connect to the Purpose

It's helpful to think of Connector Managers as shepherds, but rather than safeguarding and directing a flock, they are nurturing the purpose and values of the organization and directing their team accordingly.

Managers are personal embodiments of the leader's vision and sense of purpose. In turn, they help their people unite around ideas and passions, largely by connecting the dots between organizational purpose, vision, and strategy with the objectives of the business unit or team.

In the past, managers focused their people primarily on beating the numbers or outperforming other areas of the company. While competition and score-keeping is a healthy way of inspiring intense performance and teamwork, it's also somewhat missing the point. If the organization truly does have a clear and meaningful purpose, solid values, and an audacious vision, then it behooves a manager to connect his or her team with that larger cause. Indeed, in a recent and poignant study, it was determined that employees who perceived altruistic behavior from their managers also reported being more innovative. They frequently suggested new product ideas and ways of doing work better.[10] You get more out of people—much more—when there's an inherent sense of working for something larger than oneself.

They Connect Their Teams to Drive Results

Despite their primary function as connectors, managers continue to demonstrate strong team leadership. They do this by effectively connecting the strategy of the organization to the execution of priorities and activities of the team.

This is not a simple or rudimentary task. Like most business concepts, it's far easier to write about than it is to implement. The devil is in the details, and the art of the Connector Manager is to create clarity and understanding around how.

Nilofer Merchant calls this the problem of the "air sandwich." As she puts it:

"An Air Sandwich is what happens when a leader in an organization issues orders from 80,000 feet and lobs them to the folks at 20,000 feet, creating a large, empty void. That gap between the top and the bottom is an Air Sandwich, and just like two pieces of bread without the meat or fixings, this sandwich is missing all the stuff that matters: namely, feedback, debates, trade-off discussions. As long as we're eating Air Sandwiches in our organizations, we lack the shared understanding necessary to achieve the kind of results our organizations need."[11]

The manager, in other words, must prompt, guide, and reinforce the conversation around how to make the work of the team effective within the context of the strategy. Managers ensure that collaboration and debate is healthy and not stifled in their teams.

They Connect People and Efforts in the Organization

Connector Managers are also nimble and agile brokers who connect people and ideas across functions, departments, teams, and other divides. In doing so, they are serving as a hub while creating spokes for employees to actively and efficiently co-create and collaborate.

Consultants are sometimes called the bumble bees of the corporate world because, in moving from organization to organization while observing, learning, and teaching, they cross-pollinate their clients with ideas, innovations, and best practices. Connector Managers do this within their own organizations, not by actively moving from one team or business to another, but by making connections between ideas and people that have not been connected before.

This form of cross-pollination has become essential to innovation today. As the *Economist* notes: "Sharing also leads to extra innovation. Ideas overlap. Inventions depend on earlier creative advances. There would be no jazz without blues; no iPhone without touchscreens. The signs are that innovation today is less about entirely novel breakthroughs, and more about the clever combination and extension of existing ideas."[12]

There can be great impact on an organization as a result. Mars Inc. serves as a great example of the power of cross-pollination to spur innovation. A few years back, the Advanced Technologies team in R&D, which was responsible for developing new technologies for the Chocolate Business Unit, was interested in innovating the appearance of the company's products, with inspiration stemming from the "m" printed on M&Ms. The team quickly developed a system to print photos directly on the surface of chocolate bars. Despite this, when they tested the concept with customers they found there wasn't enough demand to bring the product to market.

At the same time, there was another team in Advanced Technologies tasked with printing the faces of the M&M characters onto M&Ms. They did this through lithographic technology, which is traditionally used to print onto confections. This team also tested the products with customers, and this time landed high interest in the product, but the technology and cost prohibited small runs, limiting the scalability of the product.

While both of these teams were co-located, they didn't communicate in a way to connect the dots between the technologies. Luckily, the breakthrough came when a Connector Manager who was familiar with both projects brought the teams together to show how the technology innovation could be applied to printing on M&Ms. This soon launched MyM&Ms, a wildly successful line of personalized M&Ms, which now serve as a focal point of many celebrations—from birthdays to weddings to anniversaries.[13] And without the insight and fortitude of a Connector Manager, the opportunity never would have come to bear.

They Connect Ideas to Resources

Connector Managers do not need to be natural innovators; their role is to quickly spot and elevate ideas that will deliver value and impact. Then, they need to match these opportunities with the resources, talent, and influencers needed to make them happen.

Paul Rogers of GE doesn't mince words when he confirms this premise. "It's bullshit that everyone needs to be an innovator," he says. "The special skill is to spot innovation, make discernible decisions, and provide proper criticism. It needs to be balanced." In other words, managers must have a "Yes" mentality, but they can't say "Yes" to everything. They need to have good insights and instincts about what is worth pursuing, and put those views to the test.

Jonathan Bendor of Stanford University believes that managers must be skilled at applying rigor to promising ideas, or the wrong ideas will inevitably be pursued. The successes and failures of Xerox's PARC provides a great lesson in this regard. While brilliant innovation was the norm at the famed research lab, few of those innovations became viable business concepts for Xerox. Bendor says the people who generated ideas at PARC, specifically the engineers, were not being pushed hard enough to put those ideas to the test. As Bendor puts it, "You guys are brilliant and you're coming up with really neat ideas, but where's the market value?"[14]

In an era when almost everyone has access to the same information, value is discovered by putting ideas together in novel ways and asking smart questions that open up potential that has yet to be tapped. Those ideas then need to be exploited by leveraging the proper resources and business acumen and driving them to market with speed through excellent execution.

THE FEISTY ORGANIZATION

It's become a cliché that the best organizations get the "right people on the bus." Identifying talent that fits the organization's culture is critical; freeing that talent to do the best possible work is obviously the ideal. But how do you get there?

Leaders are not the purveyors of answers anymore, so let's quit pretending they should be all-knowing. The real value they provide is their courage—the courage, specifically, to establish and drive a bold vision while sticking to the values and purpose of the organization even as they make the difficult decisions to be flexible in that pursuit.

The role of the manager is undergoing a rebirth. No longer the drill sergeant of the organization, the Connector Manager is needed to carry the leader's vision by mobilizing people, harnessing their talents, and spotting innovation that will make a difference, while aligning the resources needed in support.

In a feisty organization everyone is engaged in the active pursuit of value discovery, innovation, and customer-focus. Leadership and management make it possible for the real work of the organization to be done by people who are not drones but Difference Makers.

QUESTIONS FOR YOU TO CONSIDER:

* What are the opportunities for your leadership to be more courageous?

* How well do your managers create connections?

9

THEIR PEOPLE ARE DIFFERENCE MAKERS

FEW OF US LOOK BACK on our college days and wish that we'd supported ourselves financially by scrubbing toilets. Student Maid, a cleaning service based in Gainesville, Florida, provides the flip side of that perspective. Kristen Hadeed, who began cleaning houses while a junior at the University of Florida, founded Student Maid in 2008. Hadeed realized there was so much potential for work—especially during busy periods when student dorms and apartments were turning over—that she could start a business. She landed nine contracts, put an ad on Craigslist, hired sixty students, and got started.

Within a few months, forty-five of those students had quit. This attrition wasn't a failure of Hadeed's management or a sign that students couldn't handle housecleaning; it was the industry norm. In the cleaning business, the average tenure of an employee is two-and-a-half months. Hadeed thought she could do better so she changed her approach.

At first, her only requirement for new hires was that they be students with a GPA higher than 3.5. Hadeed was using that arbitrary cut-off to winnow down the large number of applicants, but it turned out that high-achieving students looking for housecleaning work tended to be responsible and dedicated: no matter what was going on in their lives, they showed up on time and got their work done in a timely and conscientious way.

Realizing that her employees were making a difference in the success or failure of her operation, she saw that she could leverage them better if she focused on the culture of Student Maid and made such people the source of the company's competitive advantage.

Hadeed turned Student Maid into something that was less of a job and more of an enrichment experience and a mutual support system. As a student herself, she understood the needs and interests of students intimately. For instance, she knew that they face many pressures on a daily basis—not only the financial pressure to get by but also a great deal of emotional turmoil, ranging from loneliness and anxiety to relationship troubles and problems with self-esteem. On top of that, students are burdened with the complexity of working toward a future they may not be able to envision clearly.

So one of the big things that Student Maid does for its student employees is provide mentorship and counseling. "We do a lot of professional and personal development," Hadeed says. "It's not just, 'Here's your paycheck.'" Hadeed knows that if students have distressing personal problems they can't get off their minds, they're likely to be less happy at work and not do as good a job. She also knows that it helps students stay focused on the big picture if they feel more connected to their dreams: so she hired a DreamLeader with a Ph.D. in counseling to help students map out their lives in accordance with their passions. "The idea," Hadeed says, "is that if they can associate their work with a place that makes them successful outside of work, it's better for everyone—the team members and the company."[1]

To manage workers who are largely on their own, Student Maid relies on a set of ten core values as a guide for taking actions and making decisions. Having core values "ties us together," Hadeed says. "It keeps everyone accountable, not just . . . student cleaners, it also keeps our leadership team and me and everyone accountable. And it's cool because when you have a question or you're not sure how to handle something, all you have to do is look back to the ten values and usually you can find the answer."[2] And her student employees also help guide and build her company. "We really value communication and feedback," Hadeed says, "so when an employee has an idea, it gets heard and sometimes implemented."

Through such measures and others, Hadeed has created a fun and fulfilling place to work for a demographic typically treated as disposable employees with little long-term value. She knows it would be easy for a student employee to quit such a menial and difficult job if she didn't love the culture of the organization and want to be part of it. But in an industry where the average length of employment is a few months, Student Maid has more than 500 employees with an average tenure of two-and-a-half years. And that tenure would be longer if the organization didn't "kick employees out" once they graduated from school to force them to go on to bigger and better things.

THE NEW EMPLOYEE

Leadership author Marshall Goldsmith is fond of saying, "What got you here, won't get you there," as a way of describing the personal and behavioral changes that leaders must make as they assume the top roles in their organizations. In our new era, organizations must realize that "who got us here, won't get us there." A different kind of person is required to enable company success today. Organizations need people who get their "why" and have the agility, drive, and creativity to manage multiple "how"s in pursuit of any "what."

In the past, we hired workers to execute and deliver on narrow goals and objectives. They did not need range or adaptability—in fact, that was probably a net negative. And it was nice but not necessary for them to be aligned with the organization's values and purpose. In contrast, almost every job today, even ones that call for scrubbing toilets, requires engagement, adaptability, and speed, along with self-initiative, flexibility, and creative thinking. As Seth Godin puts it so well, "Judgment, skill, and attitude are the new replacements for obedience."

To leverage those employees, organizations need strong cultures and collaborative work environments that foster initiative and innovation, and they need leaders who, as we discussed in the previous chapter, connect people to purpose, strategy, ideas, resources, and work. NFF organizations have courageous leaders in place who set the tone for the culture and connect and empower their people to fuel the organization. This dose of courage only works, of course, when, once connected, those people provide the horsepower that makes the organization go.

I call these new employees "Difference Makers" for two reasons. First, because they are inherently motivated to create a difference through their work. Such people make the organization better because of who they are, how they strengthen the culture, and how they act on the job. They have an impact on the organization's success not only through the daily performance of their jobs but also through the spirit, energy, and determination they bring. They're not motivated by micro-managers or even particularly by money or rank, but by something inside that drives them to go beyond basic responsibilities and turn what they do into a cause and an opportunity for further growth. They're steeped in confidence and passionate about quality. They expect to be heard and to make a contribution no matter where they stand in the organization. They don't fear losing their jobs; instead, they fear not doing those jobs exceptionally well. They want to transform themselves, their organizations, and the world. It's the organization's responsibility to let this happen. It's oxymoronic to hire passionate people and limit that passion to organizational standards to "toe the party line"; in other words, Difference Makers can only make a difference if they are enabled and positioned to do so.

Second, they are doers who get things done and make things better. Have you heard of the "maker movement"? That's the umbrella term for inventors, designers, and tinkerers who can't stop themselves from hacking, tweaking, building, and creating. In a marvelous way, they combine the revolutionary spirit of the computer hacker and the passionate dedication of the modern artisan who cultivates and improves on traditional crafts. I think that the maker movement taps into a deep capitalist inclination toward self-reliance, initiative, and creativity typical of great inventors and entrepreneurs. I see "maker" types all over now, launching businesses, running food trucks, improving their organizations and communities. They're not waiting for things to happen for them; they're making things happen for others. And companies can leverage these makers by making them "intrapreneurs," to provide ownership and flexibility for them to launch entrepreneurial endeavors within well-established organizations.

It should be no surprise that Difference Makers and Millennials share many traits. According to Deloitte's 3rd Annual Millennial Survey, 78 percent of Millennials are influenced by how innovative a company is when deciding whether they want to work there, and most say their current employer does not encourage them enough to think creatively. They are also looking for purpose-driven, difference-making organizations, even as they believe that too many businesses are focused on their own agendas and indifferent to the greater needs of society. When Millennials step up to be leaders, it's not to climb the corporate ladder or make more money, but to gain an opportunity to influence their organization or world and be the change they seek. They care deeply about doing work that matters, and they want to work at organizations that make the world a better place.

MAKING A DIFFERENCE

Almost every generation is noted for its idealism and passion at some phase. Regardless of whether I'm over-selling Millennials or not, it's important to note that the traits of the Difference Maker employee can be developed and fostered, too. In fact, I believe that more people have these qualities than do not; and that many more people would display them and act on them if they were working in cultures and environments that supported, encouraged, and coached such behavior. Deloitte's 2013 study indicated that only 11 percent of US workers are passionate about their work and possess the attributes needed for extreme, sustained performance improvement, which they defined as: a continuing commitment to accomplishment in a particular domain, a disposition to quest and explore, and an openness to connecting with others.[3] In other words, only one in about ten workers has the passion to see challenges as opportunities to learn new skills and improve performance.

But if you think about yourself and the people you know, does that percentage sit right with you? As the study noted, "many companies today are structured such that they actively discourage passion. In twentieth-century corporations built for scalable efficiency, jobs were well defined and organized to support processes designed to meet plans and forecasts. Workers were trained to protect company information, and any collaboration with those outside of the organization was highly monitored or even discouraged. Most innovation was driven from within the company's four walls, often without feedback or customer interaction." The few Difference Makers Deloitte discovered were concentrated in high-paying leadership roles where a strong sense of personal agency and ample reward and reinforcement was also concentrated, or in organizations where collaboration and input was the norm. In other words, our lack of suitable organizations dampens engagement and passion. There are more Difference Makers out there—or people with Difference Maker potential—than we may believe.

And just to be clear, Difference Makers can come from anywhere within the organization, whether it be the front line or the corporate office. Of course, the "difference making" looks different for various functions, roles, and responsibilities, but organizations should look to expand the number of Difference Makers throughout every facet of the organization to build momentum.

Increasing the percentage of Difference Makers in our organizations has a disproportionate impact on engagement, innovation, and performance. That's why companies like Google, Zappos, Lowe's, Apple, Netflix, GE, and—yes—even Amazon are so upfront and specific about defining the kind of dynamic and revolutionary individuals they want and need. When Netflix announces that it is offering unlimited paternal leave for employees, it is not doing so to win a PR war or pat itself on the back . . . it is flying a flag to the Difference Makers of the world, saying, "This is who we are." They know that more of them means more innovation, growth, and customer focus. Every nudge of the needle toward feisty is gold.

These creative and passionate people don't want to work in organizations where their roles are predetermined, where silos restrict collaboration across units and teams, and where the next day promises to be just like the last one. They want stimulating, dynamic workplaces that promote possibility and potential. As Eric Schmidt and Jonathan Rosenberg wrote in *How Google Works*, "we learned the only way for businesses to succeed is to harness 'smart creatives' and create an environment where they thrive at scale."

So how do we go about identifying and nurturing such people? We need to understand them first.

They Are Altruistic by Nature

Difference Makers are characterized by their deep concern for others. We all know people who are driven to help others—the homeless, the mentally ill, the disadvantaged. When they are inspired by a purpose-driven organization, and pay attention to coworkers and customers, and connect with them in a very deep and present way, they are driven to make decisions and take actions that improve situations, facilitate better experiences, and help everyone involved grow and learn.

Raghu Krishnamoorthy, chief learning officer at GE, says the key difference he sees between Millennials and members of other generations is in the area of giving. For previous generations, giving was a consequence of taking. You get so you give. Millennials, he says, are attracted to giving for its own sake and seek companies that are purpose-driven and devoted to something bigger than profit.[4] I think that we are all similarly motivated at heart, but need supportive environments where those inclinations are rewarded and leveraged.

They Follow Their Values

Difference Makers are rooted by purpose and values. They thrive in organizations with values closely aligned to their own. Indeed, as Student Maid's Kristen Hadeed has observed, working for a purpose- and value-focused organization can instill an understanding of how important values can be in your own life. As she put it, "When you work for us, you realize how important having values [is]. And so, I think a lot of the students adopt personal core values, and create a personal value system after working for us." People judge the rightness or wrongness of a decision or action on the basis of those values, and they speak up or offer better solutions when they encounter something that's out of sync with those values.

They are also quick to speak up about their passions, interests, ideas, and feedback, and will do so in any forum or on any platform, including social media and through other collaborative technologies.

They Create Meaningful Ideas

Difference Makers tend to be insightful, creative, and innovative. I suspect this is precisely because they care so much and are so deeply engaged by what they do. The ideas they seize upon, whether large or small, make a difference for their organizations and the people around them. That's why they're so motivated to pursue such ideas.

As Tim Cook puts it, "You look for people that care enough that they have an idea at eleven at night and they want to call and talk to you about it. Because they're so excited about it, they want to push the idea further. And that they believe that somebody can help them push the idea another step instead of them doing everything themselves."

They Rethink Solutions to Challenging Issues

Because they are driven to make things better, Difference Makers are not only focused on big, breakthrough ideas, but also on rethinking and reconceptualizing existing issues. They are "irritated" by problems that affect their role, team, or organization, much as an oyster is "irritated" by a grain of sand. And like the oyster, they try to create something better as a result.

In other words, they not only notice problems but also feel a strong sense of responsibility for them, and they take action steps to improve things. Schmidt and Rosenberg tell the story of Larry Page printing a page of search results, pinning them to a wall, and saying, "These suck." The people who noticed that message took responsibility for improving the results even though it wasn't "their department." Why? Because they felt compelled to by their own drive to make a difference.

BEING A MAKER

These people are not just motivated by values, ideas, and challenges, they are also doers and makers—people who get things done and make things come to be. Being a maker is rooted in innovation—a compulsion to create, improve, and take action.

We live in a maker era, turbocharged by entrepreneurial energy, an appreciation for disruptive innovation, and an ethic of getting hands dirty and tinkering. Autodesk is a company that has leveraged the maker movement to dramatic impact. It took the company thirty years to grow to 12 million professional users. But the company recently switched its focus and went from B2B to consumers and communities, generating 120 million users in just three years, as tools and resources were opened up to amateurs who then gained the power to be makers.[5] They're creating, designing, and building everything imaginable as a result, harnessing capacity that was once available only to large corporations with massive R&D budgets.

They're Biased toward Action

Makers are not scared of taking action; they're uncomfortable not taking action. They have confidence in themselves as the source of the solutions to the problems or challenges they face. They are not the type to ask permission and fly an idea or suggestion up the corporate flagpole; they are more likely to be the ones who walk in on a Monday with a new solution in hand—an actionable business plan, a prototype, a new model, a better way.

Managers of makers have their hands full just keeping up. That energy must never be squelched or dampened, but only reinforced and carefully directed. Makers won't burn themselves out putting in late nights—they'll burn out going home early, frustrated by problems that managers won't let them solve.

They're Motivated by Results

People who are not makers tend to like processes and procedures. They want guidelines and instructions for the steps they should take. Makers couldn't care less about instructions and are far more interested in outputs and results. They have no fear of failure. They are solution-seekers, not risk-avoiders.

Though they don't like regimented processes, they do like the process of making. For them, the journey is truly part of the reward. And they recognize that mistakes will be made, setbacks will be experienced, and failures may be public. No matter. Those blemishes or missteps are not defeats, but normal bumps and important data on the road to better outcomes.

Makers are also far more interested in the real problems of the world than the invented problems of a bureaucratic group. This external focus drives them to look beyond their own desks and activities to assess whether the customer is truly satisfied with the results. If not, the maker is the type of employee who will corral resources, assets, permissions, and innovative energy to make things better. Difference Makers think nothing of stepping outside their role or beyond their purview to drive needed change.

They Deliver Lots of Important Work at Speed

Makers utilize their formidable skill sets to accomplish large amounts of important work. Not only are they skilled at delivering quality, they are also impressive in terms of the quantity they produce and the speed at which they produce it. They use their passion to fuel their energy to accomplish important outcomes, knowing that meaningful results might require taking on big projects in less time than most would consider healthy or reasonable.

They are not limited by space or time. I don't mean they star on *Doctor Who*. I mean they don't stick to nine-to-five or just work out of their cubicle. As the work world changes, any organization's expectations must shift to embrace working smarter, not harder. When a problem, task, project, or idea seizes them, Difference Makers are on it no matter where they are—office, home, shower, coffee shop, airplane, or on the bike—and no matter what time it is—weekend, after hours, vacation, downtime, during a meeting with the boss. This also means that sometimes they may demand flexibility in their regular nine-to-five schedule.

They Are Naturally Collaborative

Though makers might sound like the mad scientists of your department, it would be a mistake to think that they are solo adventurers or crazy loners. They are actually extremely good at working with others—whether encouraging people to join in their cause, or signing up for a cause they admire and helping it go much further than it would otherwise. Being a maker is not a singular activity, but an excuse to marshal resources, talents, interests, and passions in pursuit of a great idea. In fact, makers believe in unifying people—bringing them together—to discover the best outcomes, and they are more than willing to demolish silos and institutional barriers to do so.

This doesn't mean that makers are overtly confrontational or difficult. In fact, they are incredibly generative. I liken them to the talented people I have seen working in improv theater. One of the basic rules of improv is never to say "No," because that will kill the drill on the spot. Rather, in improv, it's encouraged to say "Yes, and" to keep the story going. In traditional organizations, families, and social settings, "No" is often the knee-jerk reaction to a new approach or a new path forward. We tend to say "No" because we feel we don't have the time, resources, or attention to spare, and we don't like change, new ideas, or variations on our preset agenda. Makers say "Yes," and when enough people in an organization respond positively like that, an atmosphere of opportunity and innovation results. "Yes" is the beating heart of collaborative, co-creative workplaces.

THE DIFFERENCE A DIFFERENCE MAKER MAKES

Every organization needs leadership to set the tone and management to make sure that imperative becomes the basis for action and execution by connecting people to resources, meaning, and purpose. Difference Makers leverage their own skills, passion, experience, resiliency, innovative spirit, and unstoppable drive to propel the organization forward. They are the energy source and the gears that make it possible for organizations to deliver on purpose, strategy, and business objectives.

In traditional organizations or organizations where Difference Makers are misaligned or not valued, being a Difference Maker is extraordinarily hard and stressful. It's a terrible thing to care more about your customers, brand, or work than your leadership or your organization does as a whole, and to then be impeded from making meaningful and productive change. This disconnect is especially confusing in organizations where the top leader is calling for dedication, passion, innovation, and drive, but where management stifles and punishes it—a condition that is far more common than I wish.

Effective Difference Makers are reflections or echoes of the cultures within which they thrive. They represent the company at its best to the customers they are close to, and leave the world with a lasting impression of what the organization stands for and strives to be. They are the brand of the business—the embodiment of its purpose and promise.

Unfortunately, too many organizations—even the best-intended ones—put barriers in the way of their people. In the next chapter, I want to show you how to avoid doing that, and not only get out of the way of your Difference Makers but actively support them and proliferate their ranks.

QUESTIONS FOR YOU TO CONSIDER:

* How successful are Difference Makers in your organization today?

* How well is your organization cultivating employees' abilities to make a difference?

10

THEY ENABLE A WORKFORCE THAT IS BOLD AND PLAYS BIG

IN THE 1980S, Roger Martin, a professor at the Rotman School of Management, and the author of *Playing to Win*, spent some time at a large retail bank shadowing customer service representatives (CSRs) as part of a consulting job. Martin was specifically studying how well the bank's strategy was flowing down to the branches and being executed at the tip of the spear by the primary customer-facing employees. CSRs were a particularly good measure of that "strategy flow" since they had no say in how they should act. As Martin wrote, "The CSRs are the choiceless doers. They follow a manual that tells them how to treat the customers, how to process transactions, which products to promote, and how to sell them. The hard work of making all those choices is left to the higher-ups. Those on the front lines don't have to choose at all—they just *do*."[1]

Expectations of obedience aside, Martin ran into one CSR who intrigued him because she was exceptionally effective. Her name was Mary, and she was the top teller in her branch, according to customer surveys. Over the course of a few weeks, Martin saw a pattern in the way Mary was dealing with customers, and it had nothing to do with the strategy flow of the bank. With some customers she was polite but very efficient. With others she would take longer, suggesting some new services or how to get a better yield on their savings. And with others she was extremely friendly and social. She would talk about their children, their vacations, their health—but say very little about banking and their finances.

It fascinated Martin that Mary was treating her customers in three distinct ways through a sophisticated segmentation strategy; yet, he knew that the teller manual did not provide anything like that kind of direction. When Martin questioned Mary about this discrepancy, she got upset at first, as if she were being called out for not doing a good job. But then she explained how she saw her customers and why she treated them one way versus another. Some customers, she said, didn't really like banking. They wanted Mary to be efficient and helpful but had no interest in advice or social conversations. Others weren't interested in being Mary's "friend" but thought of her as a personal financial-service manager and wanted specific answers to their questions and concerns. And finally, there was a group of people who viewed coming to the bank as a social event. They would wait for their favorite teller to be available even if there was a long line. If Mary didn't talk to them about their families, vacations, and hobbies, they would be disappointed with her service.

Martin was very impressed with this approach and suggested that other tellers and their customers could really benefit from learning about it. Mary thought this idea was pointless. "'Why would I ever do that?" she replied, suddenly impatient. "I'm just trying to do my job as best I can. They're not interested in what a teller has to say.'"

Although that was thirty years ago, I expect that many people working or consulting in organizations today can still relate to the contradictions and frustrations inherent in Mary's story. I ran into my own version recently, working with a large health-care company. The customer-care center people are blue-collar and minimum wage, and the company's implicit attitude toward them until recently was that they needed strict oversight—through intrusive managers and a 130-page training manual—to do their jobs.

In a pointless nod toward empowerment, CSRs at the company were allowed $250 per customer to solve complaints and problems, but that amount (determined years previously) was insufficient to cover any current procedures or events. On top of that, CSRs were written up and reported if they failed to follow procedures to the letter. Essentially, they had no flexibility or freedom in their jobs, were highly scrutinized by managers, and felt the burden of meeting the expectations of a rigid manual to accomplish work that was complex, unpredictable, and variable. Not surprisingly, CSRs felt frustrated, fearful, and disenfranchised.

Today at that company, there's some reprieve and hope. The instruction manual has been cut in half, managers are better trained to help rather than monitor, and CSRs now have up to $1,000 at their disposal to resolve claims on the spot. Interestingly, this last point has had an unexpectedly positive impact on the business. When claim disputes go unresolved, the claims process grinds to a halt. The paperwork is frozen for up to thirty days, during which time no action can take place, then a costly review is initiated. But around 27 percent of those claims can now be solved within five minutes when CSRs have $1,000 to use at their discretion. Now, more than a quarter of the company's problems get handled instantly at relatively little cost, eliminating extended delays and the protracted frustration of customers.

"Empowerment"—that word most of us can barely stand anymore—is not or should not be just for white-collar executives. It's widely accepted today that there's great value in harnessing and mobilizing the collective intelligence of the entire organization. But there is still a lot of uncertainty or confusion as to what organizations can, should, or must do to enable their people to have the greatest possible impact.

Best intentions aside, the roadblocks to mobilizing and enabling employees remain significant in most organizations. At one extreme, people like Mary end up doing what they do in spite of the system they work within. They care about the customer or the quality of their work, and they find ways to do what they do better, even though the organization does not really support them. I bet that even if Mary had a CEO extolling the very freedom and intelligence she was exercising in order to serve the customer better, she might still have managers or peers who would view her as a "pain" or worse for making their jobs more difficult. They might also, as Mary noted, be completely uninterested in her discoveries about the customer, and they could, as she probably feared, try to thwart, impede, or ostracize her as a result. In my experience, such things happen all the time and represent the sad reality of social systems that aren't positive or healthy. Too often, someone who actually cares about his or her work ends up fighting the organization to do a better job. If you've ever worked at such an organization, you probably remember how your positive feelings subsided over time, replaced by passivity, frustration, or dread. You may even remember thinking, when you see a new person come on board filled with energy, "He'll have the life sucked out of him soon enough." Those who last in such organizations learn not to care about their work, and get by "just doing their jobs."

CULTURE NEEDS CONSISTENT PEOPLE PRACTICES

I've also encountered many organizations with good intentions that fail to harness and mobilize their collective intelligence for different reasons. If I could sum it up, I would say they want the best people and the best outcomes, but they are not systematic or deliberate enough in their people practices to make that happen. They hire one type of person one week, and a different type the next, without understanding the power of fit or the confusion this inconsistency communicates to other employees. They make decisions one way in one situation, and a different way in another, allowing mixed messages to cascade throughout the organization. They are consequently misaligned around values, strategy, execution, and the customer.

Fixing one piece of that puzzle is never enough because the culture of the organization is being shaped and influenced from many different angles at once. That's difficult to explain to people because there's so much misunderstanding out there about what culture is and what it can and should do for an organization. Indeed, when a CEO comes to me with a request to "fix" her culture, what she really wants is for me to improve morale or shift widely held attitudes. When I hear that kind of request, I realize that the CEO doesn't see culture as core to the organization's success but as something that is off to the side and separate from the actual work of the organization. I explain to him or her that culture is everything the organization is and does. It's not intangible at all but surrounds the organization and permeates it because it is the sum total of how the people and leaders of the organization make decisions, set goals and priorities, collaborate and communicate, reward and punish, and hire and fire, and so on. The people practices in place are the means by which the organization reinforces that culture.

People practices—and HR practices in general—are sometimes viewed as the enemy, nemesis, or roadblock to a more agile, effective, innovative organization. A recent article in *Harvard Business Review* painted a picture showing why people practices can be so ineffective today. Commenting on hiring and promotion, the author notes: "Only a third or so of today's hires are internal. Companies engage executive search firms to fill most senior-level vacancies. One in four CEOs comes from the outside. And companies spend less time and effort than they used to mapping out the talent they'll need in the years to come: By the mid-2000s only a third were doing any planning in this area."[2] In other words, organizations have largely outsourced hiring and don't bother to make development or promotion plans for the people they do have on board.

Indeed, according to the author, few of the successful companies of yesteryear have held onto the people practices that made them great. GE was a notable exception. Microsoft, on the other hand, largely abandoned its investments in developing management skills, and many companies, such as the large banks and financial houses, permitted high-performers to put less of their attention on direct reports and more on their business results, while simultaneously gutting HR and shifting much of the nominal responsibility for hiring, firing, and performance management to the business and line managers. In other words, many organizations care less about whom they hire, how they manage, and whom they promote, but they still demand outstanding results.

That attitude makes it difficult, however, for an organization to position its people to achieve its strategic aims. As the author puts it, "One of traditional HR's biggest difficulties has been supporting business strategy, because it's such a moving target these days. Companies seldom have long-term plans with straightforward talent requirements. Instead they generate streams of projects and initiatives to address successive needs ... But HR is by nature a long-term play. Developing talent, heading off problems with regulations and turnover, building corporate culture, and addressing morale problems all take time. Often, leadership teams and priorities change before such initiatives have paid off. And when companies don't meet their performance goals for the quarter, those programs are among the first to go."

FEISTY COMPANIES DOUBLE DOWN
ON PEOPLE PRACTICES

In NFF companies, people practices are an organizational priority and stay that way. This is the case whether that company is Netflix, which is heralded for its progressive approach to people, or Amazon, which has been criticized for practices that are considered harsh. Such companies are deliberate, intentional, and strategic about their people practices. They start with a clear vision of the qualities, attitudes, and behaviors that help create and sustain their culture, and they build their hiring and career-development process in support of that. They bring this point of view into their firing and promotion decisions, conscientiously rewarding the leaders and employees who help the organization thrive and casting off the people who thwart collaboration or create misalignment, even when those people are otherwise highly effective at their jobs. They reinforce the vision constantly by celebrating small and big wins, and calling out employees for their commitment and contributions. And with this mix of big brush strokes and fine attention to detail, they turn their Difference Makers and their Courageous Connectors into a feisty workforce that is ready, willing, and able to be big and play bold.

What does it mean to be big and play bold? It means feeling inspired to think beyond immediate roles and job concerns and to pursue opportunities that can be game-changers for the company. It means being empowered to take action where action is needed and to have a highly developed sense of responsibility for fixing problems, finding solutions, executing with excellence, connecting with the customer, and driving innovation. NFF companies want people to be the opposite of "choiceless doers." They want people who feel free and flexible in accomplishing their work, and empowered to leverage their intelligence, insight, and good judgment rather than relying on managerial direction, corporate policies, or fixed rules.

This is why companies like Netflix and Google have rid themselves of as many rules as possible even as they've hired smart, committed, and creative people, and held them accountable to the values of the organization when making decisions or tackling problems. Netflix, Google, and the like are, in other words, values-based rather than rules-based companies. They won't tell you how to get somewhere, but they expect you to get to wherever that is on your own. Indeed, they even hope that you'll get somewhere better because you have the freedom and power to figure out the destination and the path. They know that people thrive in supportive, dynamic environments and that this flexibility helps lead the organization toward better paths, new approaches, and creative ideas.

This does not mean that there is a lack of accountability or discipline in such organizations. It's far from a free-for-all; but the discipline and accountability gets focused on outputs and behaviors, not processes. There are visible guardrails and transparent goals, and progress, impact, and results are quantified and measured to assess performance and success.

The Cheesecake Factory, for example, operates nearly 200 restaurants and serves more than 80 million customers per year. At the same time, it generates more than twice the return on capital of its competitors[3] and achieves 97.5 percent efficiency in food waste.[4] Given that level of performance, it would probably not be surprising if such a chain were literally a "factory," mass-producing meals under strict rules and supervision. In fact, the organization runs its kitchens very differently. Atul Gawande, the famed health-care writer, wrote a notable piece in the *New Yorker,* examining how the chain produces high-quality outcomes and why large hospitals should follow that approach. As Gawande observed, workflow was well organized, but there was plenty of play within those guidelines. "Two things struck me. First, the instructions were precise about the ingredients and the objectives...but not about how to get there...In producing complicated food, there might be recipes, but there was also a substantial amount of what's called 'tacit knowledge'—knowledge that has not been reduced to instructions."

This did not mean chefs were left alone to determine quality by their own standards. "At every Cheesecake Factory restaurant, a kitchen manager is stationed at the counter where the food comes off the line, and he rates the food on a scale of one to ten. A nine is near-perfect. An eight requires one or two corrections before going out to a guest. A seven needs three. A six is unacceptable and has to be redone." Clear instructions are given as to how the making of a meal should be improved, and those instructions are typically concerned with the quality and appeal of the product.

Perhaps not surprisingly, in an industry that burns through employees rapidly, Cheesecake Factory is regularly rated as one of the top 100 places to work in the country.

So how do NFF companies harness intelligence, energy, passion, commitment, innovation, and diligence in pursuit of big and bold goals? Let's take a look.

THEY MAKE HIRING A TEAM A SPORT

NFF companies have a clear vision of the skills, attitudes, and behaviors their culture needs, and they intentionally hire, fire, and promote in alignment with those qualities. In other words, they work hard to try to figure out whether an employee is a good culture fit before hiring, and they are willing to fire that employee if he or she does not actually prove to be a good fit over time. Along the way, they're also promoting people who demonstrate that culture fit through the work they do to help the company live its culture and achieve its goals. This promotion policy sends a powerful message to employees by reinforcing what success looks like and how it is achieved.

Companies that hire for culture fit know they can't determine a good match just by sitting a single interviewer and a candidate in a room together in a one-off event. To get a feel for the candidate, and to give the candidate a good feel for the organization's culture, they typically involve a team of people, often from different levels and parts of the organization. Anurag Gupta, general manager of Amazon Redshift and Amazon Aura, says Amazon assigns each interviewer on the hiring team a different cultural competency to focus on when interviewing candidates. "Half your onsite interview time should focus on culture," he adds.[5]

Tesla uses a collaborative hiring process in which the candidate is introduced to the entire company when he or she comes in to interview. Prospective employees spend an entire day with staff getting to know the organization while going through multiple interviewers.[6] Not surprisingly, Apple treats hiring as a team sport, too. Steve Jobs once said, "You need to have a collaborative hiring process." As he explained, "When we hire someone, even if they are going to be in marketing, I will have them talk to the design folks and the engineers."[7]

Salesforce.com, the extremely successful cloud-computing company based in San Francisco, takes this team-sport aspect to another level. It has a "Build Your Own Dream Team" event where candidates are encouraged to bring a group of people they would like to work with. They participate in happy hours and collaborative activities and assignments to identify skills and potential strengths. Grand-prize winners are offered jobs. The approach is a reflection of the very social culture at Salesforce.

THEY PROMOTE EQ AS MUCH AS BQ

As I've said from the beginning of this book, at NFF companies the "how" is more important than the "what." We're used to thinking of people at successful companies as being hyper-bright—and, frankly, they often do demonstrate high BQ or business intelligence, strategic savvy, technical excellence, and innovative agility. But just as importantly, those people also tend to have high EQ or emotional intelligence. They're emotionally grounded or at least solid, good at relationships, self-aware, and sensitive to the needs and feelings of others. Why is that important? Because fast-paced, highly collaborative, and innovative companies need people who work and play well with others, without crushing spirits and bruising feelings in the process.

In traditional companies, the latter is a nice-to-have and not considered a predictor of success. Usually, organizations focus on promoting individual contributors and managers who are the strongest executors. They are the performance stars who meet and exceed targets, and can be counted on to drive themselves and others to deliver on goals. An industry of behavior coaching and counseling has cropped up as a result to help change the behaviors and personalities of exceptional contributors and results-oriented managers when they step into positions that require a lot more leadership and a need to focus on the how as much as the what. The ability to motivate, inspire, and develop trusting relationships is fundamental to the best leadership but, according to Gallup, only one in ten people has such characteristics.[8]

NFF companies ensure that 10 percent thrives in their organization. They know that a nimble and feisty environment is based on a culture of advancement in which employees learn and grow, not only in their areas of technical expertise but, more important, as human beings capable of leading others, as they rise through the ranks. Google runs an incredibly popular program on developing EQ called The "Search Inside Yourself"

Institute. As one participant in the course puts it, "Emotional-intelligence skills support collaboration, more open communication, more transparency and less posturing, less ego, and more people working for the greater good and for the purpose of the organization succeeding."[9]

On the flip side of that, NFF companies are not afraid or are at least willing to "fire brilliant jerks." In other words, they deliberately rid themselves of people who are toxic to others and the culture even if they are stellar performers.

I sometimes encounter resistance to this idea. Don't we want brilliant people? Shouldn't we be willing to suffer for results? In some cultures—yes. If that's what you value and success requires it. But in most cases, such resistance tells me that the manager or leader is buying in to the brilliant jerk's aura of importance and entitlement. In fact, few things are more detrimental to a team or an organization than a star who seems indispensable because of the results he or she delivers, and yet that star violates the organization's values and beliefs and hurts others in the process. Too often, such people are bullies who destroy collaboration, diminish or stifle the contributions of those around them, and lower the overall performance of the group. Once they're gone, it is almost always the case that performance levels will rise, individually and collectively, even as morale and engagement shoot higher, and the culture becomes a strength again and not a problem.

Netflix has been the flag-bearer for a "no brilliant jerk" policy. It says, "Some companies tolerate them. For us, the cost of teamwork is too high." Jack Welch, no one's idea of a softy in the executive suite, has written similarly about the negative effect of "jerks" or "bullies" from his personal experience. At GE, such people were referred to as Type 4 managers. The Type 4 is "the person who delivers on all the commitments, makes the numbers, but doesn't share the values." In 1992, Welch made a dramatic announcement at a company-wide meeting: Four out of the five managers being asked to leave the company had delivered good financial performance but were shown the door because they "didn't practice our values."[10]

Since these firings took place twelve years after Welch assumed his role as CEO, I can imagine that making the decision to get rid of four brilliant jerks was not an easy one, even for Welch. The message to employees, however, and the reinforcement of GE culture was much more important in the long term. As we can see, GE has done just fine since.

THEY VALUE DIVERSITY OF THOUGHT, EXPERIENCE, AND PERSPECTIVE

NFF companies believe in diversity but it's a different sort than the quota-based diversity of traditional twentieth-century organizations. In addition to simply endeavoring to reach targets for a certain number of women or minorities among their employee population and leadership ranks, NFF organizations value diversity of thought and take innovative approaches to ensure a mix is in place and can be leveraged effectively.

One effective way to ensure diversity of thought is to include people of diverse backgrounds, experiences, and perspectives in the organization. While that diversity can be achieved through traditional quotas, the crucial piece is to look beyond surface comparisons and identify people who add to the mix in a way that makes a difference. To that end, some organizations make sure that people who have different skill bases or outlooks on the customer or product are rotated into unusual roles and given a voice. Other organizations do a form of reverse mentoring in which minorities or Millennials are given the responsibility of mentoring top executives about the concerns or perspectives that might be lacking in decision-makers. Dartmouth Tuck School of Business professor Vijay Govindarajan recommends what he calls the "30-30 Rule." It requires that at least 30 percent of the people who make strategic decisions in an organization be thirty years old or younger.

Recently, I came across an organization that had, as one of its values, that people should be able to achieve personal prosperity through their work. Yet, that organization was mystified that it had an astounding 99 percent one-year turnover in its retail staff. When we looked into the circumstances contributing to this appalling number, one thing we learned was that the organization was paying its retail employees minimum wage. No one on the leadership team had any real understanding of the hardships this level of compensation caused or the message it actually sent. A voice in the room coming from a different background or experience might have at least identified this problem for the others.

THEY MOTIVATE WITH MEANING, NOT JUST MONEY

Meaning is the new money...well, let's not go crazy. Money remains very important for most of us. It's a measure of recognition and achievement, as well as a necessity to live comfortably while mitigating some of the stress of life. But more money does not necessarily buy more motivation. It reminds me of the happiness study that declared that as long as a certain threshold of income is reached, gradations of happiness become less substantial. The point about motivation is: you may leave one organization for another because the money is better, but you won't necessarily be more motivated than before.

In 2010, Tim Judge and a few of his colleagues reviewed 120 years of research to synthesize the findings from ninety-two quantitative studies—a dataset that included more than 15,000 individuals. The results indicated that the association between salary and job satisfaction is very weak. The correlation shows that there is less than 2 percent overlap between pay and job-satisfaction levels. Companies that are encouraging, rewarding, and recognizing employees primarily through financial incentives miss important motivational levers like purpose, passion, transparency, and meaningful work.

In traditional companies, the premise has always been, "We're paying you so that you will produce for us." As Don in *Mad Men* famously said, "That's what the money is for!" In new-era companies, fulfillment and the pursuit of purpose is something that people seek not only in their lives but also—and perhaps mostly—in their careers. Talented employees today can go anywhere for a job. What they want is work that allows them to make a contribution for an organization that makes a difference.

Talented employees today can go anywhere for a job. What they want is work that allows them to make a contribution for an organization that makes a difference.

Millennials are particularly driven by purpose. For six in ten Millennials, a "sense of purpose" is part of the reason they chose to work for their current employers.[11] The emerging workforce is more interested in how companies affect society than they are about profitability. Companies that meet this need have a committed, engaged, and motivated workforce as a result.

Interestingly, studies on what motivates people to play games seem to show interesting insights into what makes us tick as employees and individuals when it comes to workplace motivations. These studies have shown that four primary drivers motivate different individuals. By targeting what makes our employees tick, we have the ability to harness their passions in pursuit of a shared purpose.

The four drivers are:

- **Exploration**—These individuals need autonomy and freedom in their work and lives.
- **Achievement**—These individuals are driven by goals, and relish completing tasks, mastering situations, advancing in work, and getting individual incentives.
- **Socialization**—These people find connection through groups and teamwork; they like to build strong, personal relationships in the workplace.
- **Impact**—These are the individuals who are most driven by meaning and purpose, and feel a need to influence and encourage others.

LinkedIn does a great job of creating varying motivators to spark different kinds of people. Their InDays events, which take place one Friday a month, give employees the time to think creatively, work on projects, and invest in their careers and personal interests outside of the responsibilities of their jobs. They can work on something they care about, participate in a hack, or spend time volunteering. Those activities aren't explicitly tied to LinkedIn's organizational purpose of "creating economic opportunity for every member of the global workforce," but they demonstrate that LinkedIn believes in "walking the talk." More-engaged and passionate employees help the organization align with its purpose in many different ways, and those moments when someone is able to escape the daily grind are incredibly valuable when it comes to surfacing new ideas, innovations, or replenishing energy sources.

The point is that people are motivated differently, and a good manager and a nuanced organization will make efforts to determine what works best. NFF companies also tend to focus on motivators that create unifying goals rather than pit people against one another. In the stereotypical Glengarry Glen Ross culture, competition is used to motivate performance. Everyone on the sales team looks to the leader board to see not only who is going to win but also who is going to be fired. Competition may work well in certain environments, but it's not often going to be helpful in developing a supportive, collaborative, or creative culture.

THEY CELEBRATE WHAT THEY VALUE

What does your company say it values? Now compare that to what it celebrates. Traditional companies talk about integrity or innovation or making the tough decision, but they reward results, numbers, profitability measures, etc. On the other side of the coin, research suggests that 87 percent of recognition systems focus on tenure, rewarding those who stick around.[12] There is nothing wrong with scoreboard-watching or appreciating commitment, but your organization must celebrate people who do what you say you value or that message will become lost and meaningless.

At Novartis, for example, career tracks are broad and big so it is difficult to reward the scientists who work there with advancement or promotion. Novartis has figured out how to recognize and celebrate people in meaningful ways, however. It instituted a new recognition program a few years ago that works from a basic online portal. Anyone can go and recognize anyone else, whether within his division or anywhere else in the global organization, with points that can be exchanged for money. The approval process is admirably lacking in bureaucratic restrictions. Up to a certain level of recognition no approvals are required, and above that, approval is still easy to obtain. It seems to mean more to employees to be recognized so directly by others, and that celebration has more impact than a bonus program. Zappos has a similar program that enables peer recognition for outstanding efforts that translates into Zappos dollars. It also has a Hero award for the employee who embraces Zappos' core values to the fullest.

Intuit values innovation and risk-taking so much that it hosts a company-wide ceremony to bestow a "Failure Award" to a team whose unsuccessful idea resulted in valuable learning. Similarly, W.L. Gore hosts a celebration with beer or champagne when they kill a failing project, giving it as much praise as if the project had succeeded.[13] A similar celebration is GE's Power to Pivot Award. It's important to identify and elevate the real heroes of an organization.

Celebration is one of the most overlooked areas of building a unified culture. Organizations drive hard toward their quarterly results and rarely take the time to celebrate personal, team, and organizational achievements. But celebration is part of our social nature, and it helps us bring our entire selves to work.

I've encountered a few wonderful instances of celebration over the years. For example, I heard a story at Lowe's of an employee who finished college but was unable to take the time or spend the money to travel to his graduation because he had a family and was on a tight budget. So, his team organized a surprise graduation ceremony for him. They had an employee who played trumpet play a graduation song, and they celebrated with cake and made a diploma to give the graduate. It created a special memory for everyone involved and was an important team bonding experience.

We need to reward and recognize people more for the things they do right and not focus solely on providing feedback or correction for the things they do wrong. Parents, teachers, and animal trainers understand that positive reinforcement works better at improving performance than negative feedback. Another example comes from the world of policing. In British Columbia, the Royal Canadian Mounted Police decided to distribute positive tickets to at-risk teens who stayed out of trouble or did something right rather than always targeting those doing something wrong. The result was that youth-related service calls dropped by 50 percent.[14]

THEY DEVELOP PEOPLE, NOT JOB COMPETENCIES

In traditional companies, development has been focused on the job and rooted in the past. Performance management has been an example of this approach. The annual talk between supervisor and supervisee is a standard means to assess whether objectives over the year have been met and, more likely than not, to assign blame and deficiency to the supervisee over whatever failures have occurred. This approach does remarkably little to improve future performance, however. There's also no onus put on the manager to be accountable for the results of the employee. The employee is right to wonder, "Where were you when I needed you most?"

A particularly unhelpful version of performance management is "stack ranking," which assigns employees in a group a score or ranking relative to their colleagues. The idea is to apply comparisons as a motivational tool to encourage improvements in low performers and get the top performers to keep their edge. In the most austere of work environments, the lower performers are automatically let go annually as a means of "culling the herd." Known as "rank and yank," this approach to worker development and engagement was made famous by Jack Welch at GE.

In very practical terms, rank and yank and stack-ranking don't work. They cause mediocrity to prosper rather than excellence, don't recognize the potential that all people, even poor performers, have to develop, nor the responsibility of leaders to develop them, discourage collaboration and risk-taking, invite backstabbing and self-protection, and generally confuse the strategy and aims of the organization with the imperatives of survival of the fittest.[15]

GE got rid of that approach when it proved inadequate in the new economy, replacing it with a mobile system that encourages continuous feedback as a way of coaching sustainable performance improvement in line with business objectives and values.[16] Dolby, Accenture, and Adobe similarly got rid of their performance-management and review systems because they failed to achieve the goals of performance improvement. Deloitte instituted a simple four-question test for managing performance that essentially asks the same question that Netflix asks to identify Keepers: "Which of my people, if they told me they were leaving for a similar job at another company, would I fight hard to keep?"

New-era organizations understand that they must shift their emphasis and tactics on how they develop their people. They know that Difference Makers care about lattice just as much as they do ladder, and expect to be pushed and given opportunities to develop themselves in a rich variety of ways. This has led organizations to move on from prototypical "employee and leadership development" just for the sake of bettering the business, to truly focusing on how to develop people in their personal, professional, and communal lives. While old-era workers sincerely believed that if they put in the time, they would deserve promotion and recognition, new-era workers want to learn as much as possible. As Difference Makers, they believe in self-growth and expect to be challenged so that they can develop rapidly and meaningfully.

With so many options and opportunities available to them, and the Internet in the palm of their hand, Difference Makers are broadly curious and energized by change, opportunity, and growth. Companies bore or confine them at their peril, and promotions or carrot offerings that feel inauthentic will not appease their quest for meaning.

The most astute new-era companies don't believe in generic development paths. They know that cultivated growth programs tailored to individuals, both within their current roles and beyond, are necessary to satisfy curiosity, growth, and the need for introspection. Zappos is an organization that gets this need. It runs an innovative rotation program that combines leading-edge training with work environments that stimulate opportunities and growth. In fact, in support of its fifth Core Value— Pursue Growth and Learning—Zappos launched ZapposU in 2008 as a department that focuses on employee development. It started with two classes, Project Culture and Communication, but now it has expanded to such offerings as The Art of Storytelling, Excel, Pimp My PowerPoint, and the Science of Happiness.

P&G has been recognized as one of the best companies for leadership development. Its program is closely related to how it coaches people to uphold the company's Purpose, Values, and Principles. As the company puts it, "P&G's formal training, known as our proven leadership development model, can be summed up like this: We hire the best, brightest, and most diverse talent from throughout the world, teach them through hands-on responsibility, and coach them to drive the model to new levels of success, while always operating by our deeply held Purpose, Values, and Principles." It also enlists a development framework called "Li-La-La" for learning intent, learning action, and learning application.[17]

Difference Makers are focused on personal development beyond the job because that is how they are wired. New-era companies that want to attract and engage such people know they must respond in kind. I know one person at LinkedIn who was able to hit pause on her career in order to go to culinary school. While that had little or no connection to her work, it's doubtful that staying in a job and stifling her dream would have made her a better employee. Instead, getting the opportunity to explore a passion gave her a richer understanding of the passion of LinkedIn users and prompted more loyalty and gratitude toward her employer, boss, and coworkers. LinkedIn also regularly hosts speaker series and workshops to help stimulate and enrich its people, culture, and workplace.

Google is another company that recognizes the importance of bringing the whole self to work. At a hard-core engineering firm, such notions may seem unlikely to go over well. But the program "Search Inside Yourself" was designed by an engineer for engineers as a way of stimulating reflection and mindfulness in the workplace. It's been a tremendous hit with Google's workforce.[18]

THEY TREAT EMPLOYEES LIKE THE ADULTS THEY ARE

In traditional companies, it sometimes feels as though the punch clock still exists. There's an expectation that your time is owned by the company, and while you are on company time you are to think of nothing but company business. Outside concerns are to be compartmentalized. How early you come in and how late you leave are indicators of how committed you are to the organization. And today, with the ubiquity of connectivity, some organizations expect their people to respond to emails within minutes no matter the time of day or night, or whether it's the weekend or the Fourth of July.

NFF companies have a deep belief in freedom and flexibility. They encourage flexible work arrangements because they care a lot less about owning your time than about needing your results. They trust that people work in different ways, can be productive over different time spans or at different hours, and will feel accountability to strive for outcomes and results. They allow for telecommuting because they know it drives higher productivity and less attrition.[19] They give employees freedom to take as much vacation or child-care leave as necessary; and indeed, they often find that they have to enforce such leave rather than worry about its abuse, because most people today are so committed to their work they tend to cut time off short.

The famous perks that new-era companies offer employees, such as gym memberships, quality food, child care, and laundry services, are not luxuries designed to "outbid" competitors but gestures of recognition that employees are people who have lives. Instead of separating or compartmentalizing your work life from your life outside of work, NFF companies want you to bring your whole life to work. They know you can't be a whole person on the job if your life is divided in two because the disconnect creates stress and burden. They want you fully present and secure so that you can engage on the work and the problems that matter, not the distractions.

PRACTICES THAT MAKE THE RIGHT DIFFERENCE

All organizations—traditional and new era—go to tremendous lengths to organize, manage, and motivate their people. But NFF companies are more conscious and aware that people practices not only serve to direct employees' attention and drive their performance; they also shape and build the culture of the organization. When people practices are designed and executed to connect the organizational culture with its values and strategic objectives, great things become possible. In that kind of coherent and aligned workplace, where people are selected, developed, motivated, and celebrated according to a cultural vision, they are given the freedom and the support needed to be bold and play big.

QUESTIONS FOR YOU TO CONSIDER:

* How well do you recruit, hire, retain, and promote Difference Makers in your company?

* Which of your current practices encourage freedom and flexibility? And which practices stifle them?

* How well does your company celebrate what it says it values?

PART 2

ORGANIZATIONS THAT WIN: HOW TO CREATE THEM

11

ARCHITECTING CULTURE: A FRAMEWORK FOR BUILDING YOUR CULTURE

HOW DO YOU BUILD a culture that is "nimble, focused, and feisty"? Throughout this book, I've described the approaches, outlooks, mindsets, and attributes of NFF organizations, and loaded you with examples of thriving organizations that have come to dominate their markets and meet the needs of employees and customers in a new way as a result. Now, it's time to learn how to bring this work into your organization and make it your own.

Today, the most successful and dynamic organizations know that culture must be architected and adapted intentionally for an organization to grow in the right way, meet its strategic objectives, and ultimately produce those bottom-line results.

Sure, cultures can and will develop naturally from the unintentional emergence of beliefs and behaviors surrounding the way the company operates from day to day. However, going the route of "let's just let it evolve" leaves things to chance, and in my opinion, not in a good way. Most times these beliefs and behaviors are not very aligned with what the company needs to be successful. Architected cultures, in contrast, are proactive about unearthing their *why* and shaping the attitudes, actions, and practices that collectively form their *how* in support of their why.

In addition to consciously architecting their cultures, new-era companies know that culture isn't immutable. They know "culture once and done" isn't an eternal advantage and that it must be cultivated, shaped, and adapted over time. They make shaping culture a constant and continual practice. Their CEOs not only see the need to disruptively innovate their product line, go global, or adopt Six Sigma principles, but they are also constantly thinking about their culture as the operating muscle to guide those strategies, innovations, and plans. They lead, direct, challenge, and push on culture, never letting up. It's an imperative just like any other part of their business.

> "Your beliefs become your thoughts, your thoughts become your words, your words become your actions, your actions become your habits, your habits become your values, your values become your destiny."
> —Mahatma Gandhi

The way these companies embed this practice into their organizational DNA includes a process of unpacking, challenging, articulating, and continually driving toward specific beliefs and behaviors that help to reach their intended business outcomes. Many of the companies discussed throughout this book have done this in one form or another, intentionally shaping their cultures to drive their future visions. This intentionality provides them with a clear path to make decisions and have an intentional impact. Whether or not organizations are deliberate or organic in their approach to culture, the implicit and explicit beliefs threaded throughout the organization will inevitably influence its direction, or as Gandhi points out, its shared destiny. This is why whether you are just breaking ground with a new startup, or working to influence an organizational culture of tens of thousands of people, addressing core beliefs is one of the most critical things you can do as a cultural influencer.

After years of studying and shaping the critical elements that compose culture, I created the Architecture of Culture™ model to serve as an actionable framework to help organizations architect and build their cultures. The model is built on many of the credos and constructs I've learned through my experience as a cultural designer:

Whether you are just breaking ground with a new startup, or working to influence an organizational culture of tens of thousands of people, addressing core beliefs is one of the most critical things you can do as a cultural influencer.

- Your purpose: The first step to creating a culture is getting clear on "why" and then building the culture through the lens of your organization's purpose.
- Your organization philosophy and values: The most effective cultures are guided by clear philosophies and values to help guide behavior.
- Your narrative: A company's purpose, philosophy, and values— what I call its "narrative"—should guide the beliefs and behaviors of leaders and employees.
- Your metrics + indicators: Companies must create clear metrics that align with the company's intentions and help drive accountability to these cultural expectations.

In essence, organizations first must get clear on what they stand for. After this has been established, communicated, and internalized to provide focus, it's important to shift the necessary mechanisms to drive toward these beliefs. This means getting clear on the kind of leadership, employee behaviors, and organizational practices that will bring the culture to life. Such a capacity will help you stay true to a core direction while being responsive to unexpected opportunities and challenges.

So how do you establish that kind of consistency, clarity, and dynamic energy for your organization? Step into your first class on architecting culture. I'll start by describing the key elements of clarifying the future culture you want to create, and then in the following chapters provide insight into how to drive your organizations toward this future.

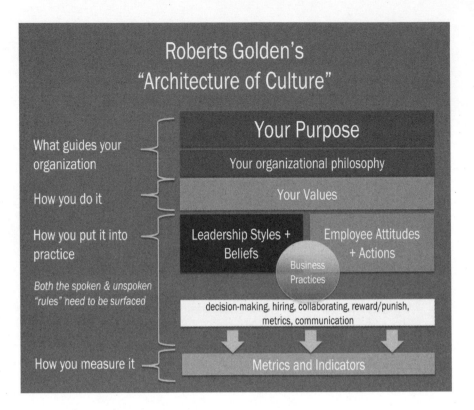

YOUR PURPOSE

If you look up the word "intentional" in the dictionary, you'll see its definition is something that is "done on purpose." I find that notion very satisfying, as "purpose" is the foremost thing my consultants and I encourage companies to consciously define and set for themselves as they go about intentionally designing the culture they want.

Culture should take root from the organization's clear purpose, its reason for existing. The first step in architecting culture is clarifying that purpose. We've discussed purpose at length in the book, so I can spare you an elaborate deep-dive into its power. But I want to provide you with a few reminders. *Purpose expresses the core of why you exist, what you are organized to accomplish, and who or what you aim to serve.* For this reason, although purpose is deep at the core of your organizational foundation, it is also directed outward to bring your customers and market into a laser-like focus. Purpose is also timeless. It aims to transcend your company's mission.

Greg Ellis, former CEO and managing director of REA Group, described purpose this way: "Your purpose is . . . what you're doing for someone else."[1] Ellis adds that it is not just about the importance of understanding and serving customer needs but should also be about putting leaders, managers, and employees in the customers' shoes.

In other words, defining and living your purpose helps your organization be outrospective, forward-directed, strategic, and competitive.

YOUR ORGANIZATIONAL PHILOSOPHY AND VALUES

Your Organizational Philosophy

Without a clear business philosophy to support your purpose, your company will lack direction and identity in how it will actually deliver on that purpose. Your purpose doesn't make your company automatically unique and authentic. Two health-care organizations could share a similar purpose of delivering world-class care for patients. But their philosophies on "how" they will deliver on that purpose will distinguish them. Purpose doesn't necessarily differentiate a Walmart from a Target or a Whole Foods from a Safeway, but the way these companies uniquely interpret and go about fulfilling their purpose creates the distinctions we can all see and feel.

I think about the relationship between purpose and philosophy from my experience as a mom. As parents, we all share a similar purpose: to provide our children with the best lives possible. But parents differ greatly from each other in "how" they fulfill this purpose. What is (or would be) your parenting style? How would you raise your children? How strict or lenient would you be? Where would you focus your attention? How supportive, nurturing, giving, authoritative, permissive, and involved would you be?

We face similar decisions when crafting organizational philosophy. Purpose takes a very outward focus, declaring what an organization aspires to do for its customers and the world; but the philosophy blends an outside-in perspective, declaring "how" the organization will show up for customers and employees. To make this distinction explicit, you must get very clear on two key questions:

1. Who are you going to be for your customers?
2. Who are you going to be for your employees?

I stress to our clients that this outside-in approach is important to contemplate and continually hone as they build, grow, and shift.

We talked about mindsets earlier in the book. Specifically, we talked about how "nimble, focused, and feisty" organizations share certain mindsets in that they believe inherently that "fast is better than big" while focusing on "possibility over profitability," and being "hungry and outrospective" by nature. These are general characteristics of new-era organizations, and intrinsic to how they think about and see the world, and the best way to be successful in it. But, while they are closely related to organizational philosophy, they are different in a nuanced way. While mindsets are general, and can be shared in common by any number of organizations, organizational philosophy is particular to each unique organization. An analogy might be that Western capitalist democracies generally believe in individual rights, separation of church and state, and the sanctity of private property and capital; yet the specific interpretation of those beliefs is manifested differently in the US than it is in France or Switzerland.

I've seen organizational philosophies take many forms. Some firms define their organizational philosophies through their credos; others, like GE, state them as The GE Beliefs. Some firms, like Google, outline a manifesto of sorts that shares the firm's beliefs and how they intend to operate, as in the IPO prospectus I shared in the Mindsets chapter. In my experience, there is no one right way to declare your organizational philosophy. Every organization is different and may articulate that philosophy in different ways. The essential thing is to actually determine one. It's not sufficient to have a mission, vision, purpose, and values. Defining your organizational philosophy—your core guiding principles—is the single most important thing you can do to create a unique and differentiated company and culture.

A major retailer and consumer packaged-goods company we've worked with was changing an aspect of its organizational philosophy from "Not disappointing one customer" to "Delighting as many customers as possible." That shift had major implications for its culture and, ultimately, its strategy. Its new strategy was "Serve the best coffee in the most places to as many people as possible." As a result, it is shifting from an old, slow-growth company to a more aggressive, fast-growth company.

As I mentioned, Google has a clear philosophy born from the hard work of narrowing in on its beliefs and taking the time to articulate its mindset. You'll notice Google's philosophy takes an outside-in approach, clearly affecting both customers and employees. Its philosophy is articulated through "10 things" they know to be true:

1. Focus on the user and all else will follow.
2. It's best to do one thing really, really well.
3. Fast is better than slow.
4. Democracy on the web works.
5. You don't need to be at your desk to need an answer.
6. You can make money without doing evil.
7. There's always more information out there.
8. The need for information crosses all borders.
9. You can be serious without a suit.
10. Great just isn't good enough.[2]

Google clearly articulates its core beliefs in a way that guides its strategy, culture, and way of working. The organization firmly believes in possibility over profitability, fast beating big, and taking an outrospective focus, and it translates these into core beliefs. This laser-like focus and clarity helps to create a philosophy that can be used to shape its culture in order to guide the organization.

Your Values

We have also discussed the power of values throughout this book. Values help employees live the purpose of the organization by serving as clear decision-making guides. Values help employees at LinkedIn, for example, understand that members come first and they remind Zappos employees to deliver their definition of WOW service. Values have the power to eliminate, replace, and upstage the stringent rules and processes that many organizations cling to, balancing the power of providing direction while also encouraging autonomy and flexibility.

Today, the vast majority of organizations already have values in place, so it is likely that your organization does, too. What is important, however, is to determine whether those values are indeed true to your organization, core to the ideals you need to uphold to achieve your objectives, and expressed in words that resonate with your employees and stakeholders.

In *How Google Works*, Eric Schmidt and Jonathan Rosenberg complain that most organizations don't do a good job of really defining their core values, so the task falls on human resources to come up with a bunch of pithy statements that aren't distinctive to the organization and, frankly, they reflect the same values as most other organizations. "The difference between successful companies and unsuccessful ones," they say, "is whether employees believe the words."[3]

Your values must be the strongest representation of your organization's purpose and culture. In the process, you are not echoing or repurposing your mission statement but actually internalizing and exemplifying what your company stands for. A study on corporate culture, conducted by a group of university professors, showed that 85 percent of S&P 500 companies have a section on their website dedicated to corporate culture, and the principles and values that should inform the behavior of the employees at these companies.[4] Eighty percent of companies mentioned innovation as a value; 70 percent went with integrity and respect. These "advertised values" not only do a poor job of guiding behaviors and actions (do we all know what it would mean to be "innovative" in our jobs?), but they also don't have a direct correlation to the short- and long-term performance of these firms. It is time to rethink the way we identify, communicate, and act upon our core values as organizations.

In our work, we encourage organizations to be very explicit and clear with their values by expressing them in terms that provide direction and act as a behavioral guide for the organization versus simply broad words that are left open to interpretation.

Let's think about the values of Zappos, a very distinctive organization with a unique way of treating customers. It clearly defines its values in a way that leaves little room for interpretation, little chance of misunderstanding. Consider #6 of its ten core values: "Build Open and Honest Relationships with Communication." It goes on to describe the importance of building emotional connections, to be an open and honest communicator, to listen intently. This value serves both as the behavioral guide for the organization and the glue that reinforces how to work with and treat one another and its customers.

I've always wholeheartedly believed that when an organization really cares about culture and that culture is demonstrated outside-in, it translates into substantial brand value. As consumers, we give Zappos a lot of credit because it does an incredible job at creating a consistent and authentic experience. Check out this email I received from Zappos when it messed up on my order:

Dear Sara—

So, this is embarrassing... behind the scenes, we had a perfect storm of things that went wrong at our warehouses and your order will arrive one day later than we originally promised. We tracked down part of the issue which was the result of human error which partly caused us to do the wrong thing. We just did the math and about 13,000 customers were affected by this, which frankly makes this completely unacceptable since we normally try to underpromise and overdeliver, but that clearly wasn't the case today.

So, instead of your order being delivered by Tuesday, July 8th, as promised, it's now expected to be delivered by Wednesday, July 9th instead. If this is causing you undue hardship, please call us at 800-927-7671 or email us at cs@zappos.com and we will bend over backwards to make it right. We promise.

If this isn't causing you undue hardship but is just extremely annoying, please call us and ask whoever answers the phone to do something weird or embarrassing, like sing "I'm A Little Teacup" or do their best audio impression of a cute little kitten.

You trusted us, and we failed this time...

https://www.youtube.com/watch?v=wPOgvzVOQig

Our goal is to always WOW our customers... while we can't change the past and the human error, what we can do is change the present and the future.

If there's anything we can do to get a little smile out of you, just let us know what it is and we'll do our best to accommodate.

—Tony (Zappos.com CEO)

It's so true to who they are. As a customer outside the company, this is what you would expect their internal culture to feel like. From what I understand, it's precisely this same culture that gets manifested externally.

Tony or Tony's people at the very top, no doubt, generated that email. But I suspect that, like airline attendants on Southwest Airlines who sound an awful lot like former CEO Herb Kelleher when they make corny jokes, anyone writing me an email from Zappos would take a similar tone and approach. And the writer wouldn't need the communication cleared, and wouldn't need it cut and pasted. When a company is rooted in values as opposed to rules, there is much less emphasis on attempting to control or direct peoples' thoughts or behaviors through defining every little step and process, and there is much more of a focus on aligning and enabling team members around those values, trusting that if the values are clearly stated and well-internalized, they guide employees' strategies, decisions, and actions. This embedding of values encourages empowerment and engagement versus conformity and bureaucracy. Zappos' core values provide enough specificity and authenticity to act upon—and also ensure there isn't a wide deviation in how people in the organization show up.

YOUR NARRATIVE

Why is the personality of a company like Zappos so clear? Obviously, it's forthright and wears its personality in its communications and in the way service representatives talk to customers. But there are companies that are far less communicative and extroverted that still manage to project their personality clearly. Apple, for example, is far less loose than Zappos, but everyone gets the Apple message and story. Amazon provides next to no direct contact with customers, yet it has the same clarity of purpose and values. GE is far more traditional in a corporate sense and somehow also manages to project what it's about, what it stands for, and how it thinks about the world.

What these and other culturally strong organizations have in common is that their purpose, organizational philosophy, and values are tightly aligned. These three strands are woven into a tapestry that tells a distinct and differentiated organizational story. I call this story the narrative of the organization.

I said earlier that culture serves as the guide and glue of an organization. Your narrative is an ongoing story that not only gives you direction, but it also describes in tangible and concrete ways how your culture gets put into effect. This narrative in turn reinforces the glue for your organization.

The narrative, in other words, brings everything together. It is simply your organizational point of view for your culture. It describes in a visceral, emotionally connecting way what your company stands for, why it exists, how it will deliver on its purpose, and which core values it holds near and dear. It should resonate throughout the organization and be reflected through the day-to-day interactions, decisions, and atmosphere that your company builds. In addition, your narrative should provide a sense of focus and clarity to your company, a core understanding that should be constantly discussed and ultimately integrated into your cultural fabric. Your narrative helps your company find its uniqueness and communicate the culture that supports your objectives.

Think about the dangers of not having a point of view as a company. People would be left floating in the unknown, forced to deal with an ambiguous environment and future without clear direction from the organization. Decision-making would become murky, and employees would question leaders' guidance and vision. The results could be devastating. Sadly, this is the reality more times than not. Strategy is the belle of the ball, and culture is left sitting on the sidelines to fend for itself.

Crafting a narrative goes beyond the power of just telling a nice story. John Hagel, one of the co-founders of the Deloitte Center for the Edge of Innovation, points out these differences. "Stories are self-contained," he says. "They have a beginning, a middle and an end. Narratives on the other hand are open-ended—the outcome is unresolved, yet to be determined. Second, stories are about me, the story-teller, or other people; they are not about you. In contrast, the resolution of narratives depends on the choice you make and the actions you take—you will determine the outcome."[5] The narrative serves as both a guide and a call to action, encouraging and engaging employees to help take your organization to unforeseen heights. In the end, companies with a clear narrative have a distinct advantage over those that don't. It is one of the most crucial tools you can have in your tool belt when constructing a culture that will win in the new era.

If you think the process of developing a coherent, positive narrative is easy, consider how infrequently it happens in our own personal lives.

Many of us go through each day without taking the time to consider what we truly believe in, why we think or act the way we do, whether we hold assumptions or beliefs that are holding us back and keeping us from achieving some deeper purpose or desire. Few of us ask, "Are my actions and decisions reflective of my core belief system? Am I passionately pursuing my purpose every day?" Few of us are even able to create consistency in our personality through all settings and circumstances.

New-era companies take the time to ask these questions and provide the time, space, and clarity for employees to answer them as well. They understand that if they don't, they will leave their culture up to chance, without a map for their organization to follow. They understand that without the bigger picture, a narrative that employees can hear, see, and feel, they are at risk of creating a culture defined by day-to-day minutiae and a workforce inherently unsatisfied and unconsciously searching for a higher purpose.

YOUR BUSINESS PRACTICES

Once you create a narrative composed of the first three elements of the Architecture of Culture (purpose, philosophy, and values), it is time to operationalize the narrative, so to speak, making it so clear and coherent that it informs the other critical elements that form your culture.

How do you get started on invoking this narrative? You need to outline your desired leadership styles and beliefs, your employees' attitudes and actions, and the major programs and practices to align and support what you want to occur. Practically speaking, when your leaders and team members are doing their everyday activities to run and execute on your business, your culture is being formed and cemented through activities such as setting and acting on priorities, sharing or potentially hoarding information or ideas, making decisions or waiting for decisions, delegating or relegating, rewarding or punishing behavior, encouraging or discouraging risk, handling mistakes, celebrating successes, and so on.

To put yourself on the right track, you need to understand how your current styles and practices are promoting or detracting from the organization and culture you need in order to be successful. All of these attitudes and actions (at every level) need to be pointed toward your purpose as a company.

With this in mind, working to implement your narrative and create a more "nimble, focused, and feisty" organization takes three primary areas of focus that can be boiled down to a simple credo: "Lead, Align, Engage." These three link directly to the next three elements of the Architecture of Culture™:

- **LEAD**—How leaders and managers model, catalyze, and engage to deliver the intended culture (Leadership Styles + Beliefs)
- **ALIGN**—How the business practices are aligned with and support the intended culture (The formal + informal Business Practices)
- **ENGAGE**—How to appeal to employees in a heartfelt manner to inspire action, and clarify the necessary attitudes and actions to deliver the intended culture (Employees' Attitudes + Actions)

Crafting a narrative is focused on clarifying and articulating the culture you want to create. The three elements above, however, focus on activating the desired culture. During major change efforts, many organizations typically concentrate on one of the areas of focus while giving short shrift to the others. For instance, it's fairly common for organizations to focus on the communications and employee-engagement activities during a time of change, reverting to a typical "change management" and communication approach. But this doesn't shift a culture. Work must go beyond a communication plan or a fun, catchy campaign with new posters, pamphlets, swag, and toolkits. This means that the work must be comprehensive and balanced, not strictly limited to the "Engage" areas of focus.

In fact, when constructing a culture, it is best to focus on the "Lead" and "Align" areas first. By ensuring leaders are leading in an authentic, believable way that builds credibility with employees, while also ensuring programs and practices are aligned and contributing to the purpose and the organization's ability to move quickly, the "Engage" efforts will be more genuine and have greater impact. Organizations with low levels of trust and positive morale should focus on key shifts within the leadership team and major programs to refocus the organization and provide some proof points that the organization is committed to changing. Doing this will help inspire a movement and create momentum for meaningful and lasting change.

Lead (Leadership Styles + Beliefs)

A critical element of building a strong foundation is developing Courageous Connectors who set the pace, tone, and ultimately the culture for an organization. Leaders should exhibit and reflect the mindsets inherent within an organization, and embody the purpose and values that serve as cultural guides. Leaders play a fundamental role in shaping the way people think and act, and the way they provide direction, implement plans, and motivate people should be in harmony with the company's direction and objectives.

People experience and learn about their culture and the purpose through the behaviors they observe in their leaders—what they say, what they do, whom they acknowledge, and how they personally contribute to the purpose. Leaders are critically important to bringing the purpose to life and providing opportunities for employees to contribute and follow their personal purpose.

It takes a collective, aligned leadership team to make the purpose believable and inspirational, to share stories of how the company is delivering on the purpose, to infuse the customer into every discussion, even if a leader heads a non-customer-facing function, to make its decisions based upon values rather than rules, and to challenge its teams to constantly think of new ways to better serve customers.

Josh Bersin, the founder and principal of Bersin by Deloitte, conducted research on hundreds of companies and correlated their business performance with a variety of different people and talent practices. One of his major findings was that high-performing organizations take the time to develop their leadership philosophies. This means they develop unique, research-based leadership models that are aligned and unique to their cultures. Getting clear on the critical and consistent leadership beliefs, behaviors, decisions, and actions helps create high-performing cultures that guide organizational strategy. "Regardless of who the CEO may be, operational execution takes place at the mid-level and supervisory level," Bersin writes. "When these individuals are well aligned, coached, and trained, the business thrives. High performing companies understand this, and they build a leadership development program that uniquely trains, supports, and selects people who drive their business's strategy. By doing this, they build execution into the culture."[6]

The Lead area of focus focuses on aligning leaders with one another on the desired future of the company and the role leaders will play. It takes time to create the leadership understanding, capability, and commitment to craft a more "nimble, focused, and feisty" organization. It serves as the first sign that shifts are taking place within an organization and marks the first step in building credibility. These changes often come in the shape of leaders forming one new positive habit at a time. When thinking about shaping this area of focus, there are a few critical questions to ask:

- How would we describe the collective leadership style at our company?
- How do our leaders' behaviors currently support or not support our purpose and values?
- What are the leadership beliefs and behaviors we currently reward, measure, and hire for? How do these affect our organization?
- How might our leaders' behaviors and actions need to shift to support the culture we want to create?
- What are some key actions leaders might take to better support the culture?

Align (Informal + Formal Practices)

This is probably not news to you, but the internal programs, processes, practices, methods, and rules that are used within an organization have a dramatic effect on the culture. These include formal and explicit programs and processes that have been intentionally set to influence an organization, as well as informal practices that are less explicit and mechanized but still guide daily rules and routines within an organization. These programs and practices guide the type of people an organization attracts, hires and fires, promotes, how it rewards, punishes and incentivizes, how decisions and strategy get made, how it communicates and collaborates, and how feedback and conflict are handled. The "Align" area of focus focuses on aligning these programs, process, and practices with an organization's purpose and intended culture. It's important that these support mechanisms work as enablers to support how you want your organization to look in the future, rather than getting in the way or contradicting the desired results.

The way programs and practices are structured, and the behaviors and actions they drive throughout an organization, dictate how empowered and engaged employees feel to deliver on an organization's purpose and most critical objectives. These elements have the power to free an organization to innovate or cripple it with bureaucracy and confusion. They must also evolve along with a company's maturity and the environment's demands, working to push the organization forward rather than strangle its evolution. Some important questions to ask and answer in this area of focus include:

- How do our formal business practices (rewards, punishments, hiring and promotion, decision-making, and so on) have an impact on our culture? What are the positive and negative impacts?
- What are some of the informal ways we reward, punish, hire and promote, and make decisions within our organization? How do these conflict with our formal practices?
- How might our formal and informal business practices need to shift in order to lead our organization toward our desired future?
- What are a few key programs or practices we could change quickly to better deliver on our purpose? What could we shift to strengthen the internal climate and culture of our organization?

Engage (Employees Attitudes + Actions)

The "Engage" area of focus largely focuses on emotionally engaging with employees on the heels of new leadership behaviors and changes to key programs, processes, and practices and working to activate and mobilize action. The work requires creating experiences, forums, and messaging that reinforces desired behaviors and actions by helping employees to become aware and engaged while internalizing the desired changes for the future. This includes aligning senior leaders' core messages, communicating bright spots, and creating a variety of experiences that may feel new or different for employees.

It's about creating rich experiences and dialogue that signify change and inspire employees, shifting from top-down communication to an organizational conversation of what it will take to create movement within the organization.

The work is also about enabling employees to drive the culture forward. To enact meaningful and lasting change, it is important that the focus go beyond leaders and programs. It is equally important to provide employees with the freedom and flexibility to shape the culture as they see fit and work with them to expand or refocus their roles to create greater impact. This takes commitment from leaders and managers to provide opportunities for employees to envision how their roles may shift, enrolling a group of influential employee frontrunners to lead the charge. This work helps lead to a great understanding and commitment to:

- the organization's purpose, philosophy, and values;
- the role and importance of culture;
- the major changes taking place within an organization and the "why" behind these changes; and
- the expected behaviors and actions of employees and their key roles in driving the organization moving forward.

Some important questions to consider within this area of focus:

- How do our employees describe our current culture?
- How would we characterize the overall attitudes of employees at our company?
- How do our employees' behaviors support or not support our purpose and values?
- How might our employees' behaviors and actions need to shift to support the culture we want to create?
- How will we enable our employees to positively influence the culture moving forward? How will we empower them to better deliver on the purpose?

YOUR METRICS + INDICATORS

The final piece of the puzzle is to put metrics in place that serve as a true indication of your organization's adherence to its own narrative. As the saying goes, you manage what you measure. Many organizations fall into the trap of setting out to build their culture, but impede their own progress by driving toward measures that don't actually contribute to what they are trying to build. The metrics you select must serve as a reflection of what your company values. If your narrative and your metrics are misaligned, you create an organization that preaches one thing and practices another in the most fundamental sense.

Metrics and measurements, and how they are respectively communicated and talked about, often indicate what a company truly values and many times are misaligned with a company's purpose, values, and intended culture. Metrics are a reflection of organizational beliefs and drive the behaviors, decisions, and actions throughout an organization. If financials are all that are talked about and emphasized, for example, this emphasis will inevitably affect how a manager talks with her employees, how communications teams talk about change, or how a customer-facing associate views his relationship with the customer.

Shifting an organization's metrics has a dramatic effect on culture, but it's the area that is most often neglected during times of change. Even during the most heart-centered of initiatives, such as creating and communicating a new purpose and values within an organization, metrics can fall flat. They are brought up last or not at all, given a shrug or lack of attention throughout the process, and framed as "nice to have" rather than "need to do." But changing metrics are the proof of an organization walking the talk. It's critical for organizations to point their employees and leaders toward business metrics that will ultimately benefit the customer and deliver on the purpose, not just the company's bottom line. This is a major undertaking that can and should not be overlooked to build or change a culture.

Shifting metrics is a major action to take to help shift a culture. But there are also ways to measure how a culture is shifting over time. Stories serve as key indicators of a company culture and can be used to get an overall pulse check of the organization. When you sit down and ask someone, "Can you share a story that best describes your company culture?" it's usually a very good way to gauge his or her perceptions of the culture. Does it cast the company in a positive or a negative light? How old or new is the story? What are the values being portrayed in the story? For larger and older organizations, the stories being told are often old and outdated, an ode to the heritage and "golden days" of an organization. This is perfectly fine; stories at their core are ways to preserve and protect the past, and as humans we also have a natural tendency to glorify the past. But it's important to move the organization to create and generate new stories that reflect the current culture and guide the future culture rather than the past.

Change only sticks when it becomes "the way we do things," and unless it is clearly measured, it's hard to know how the change is progressing.

Here are some questions to consider when thinking how your company metrics may need to shift:

- What metrics are most important to our organization? How does this reflect what we value?
- How might our metrics shift to better reflect what we truly value as an organization?
- How do our metrics affect our leaders' and employees' behaviors and actions?
- What are our customer metrics? How can our metrics shift to help drive a deeper sense of customer-centricity throughout the organization?
- What stories do employees tell to describe our current culture? What kinds of stories would we be hearing if our culture were as we desire?

Now that the critical elements for envisioning, architecting, and shifting a culture are clear, the real work begins. It's time to step into the process of creating your narrative to guide your organization's collective future.

12

ENVISIONING YOUR CULTURE: YOUR FIRST STEP

ENVISIONING AND ARCHITECTING a culture starts with clarifying the mindsets and values your organization holds near and dear. You've probably heard Lewis Carroll's quote, "If you don't know where you're going, any road will take you there." This isn't just the case for Alice in Wonderland; it applies to culture-building as well.

Expressing the future is a critical first step. Your organizational narrative, guided by a shared purpose, is what serves as a compass for your cultural journey, regardless of where you may be currently. But to create this narrative, it's necessary to do some real "roll up your sleeves" work on the front end to get an understanding of the current state of your company culture and to create alignment around what the future should look like.

Regarding process, you can certainly think about it as more art than science. Unfortunately you can't rigidly follow a process map or take calculated steps to find a perfect, one-size-fits-all narrative. However, in this chapter I hope to offer some tools and frameworks for you to think about, to structure a way to get to the best outcome for you. From my experience, the best approach is to involve a lot of voices in the organization to ideate, create, and refine the narrative that resonates throughout the organization. This means sticking to a multi-directional ideal that brings leaders, managers, and employees together to share their differentiated points of view in order to create something that is relevant and rousing at the same time.

Generally, I like to kick off the process with leaders to help pave the path.

Envisioning Culture with Leaders and Managers

Facilitated sessions and discussions with leaders to envision the future of the organization and culture provides critical input to this effort. It's important to understand where the organization is, what it will take to guide it toward a successful future, and what it means to operate the organization with a clear understanding of its purpose, philosophy, and values. Whether or not you have already undertaken the hard work to create a purpose statement or define your organizational values, these discussions will help clarify points of alignment and misalignment.

The main purpose of these discussions is to create a unified voice and direction for leadership by uncovering and discovering different leaders' points of view. Discussions can take place one-on-one or with small groups. If your company's leaders are not naturally collaborative and transparent with one another, I encourage starting with one-on-one interviews and waiting to have small sessions to focus on aligning leaders later on down the road.

Generally, you should target the most senior leaders and a small subset of managers for these discussions. Please note that before having these discussions it's helpful to give them a definition and some context about how the organization thinks about and defines culture so that everyone has the same view during the discussions. Some key questions to ask in these sessions include:

Culture
- How would you describe our current culture?
- What are the bright spots of our culture? What are the barriers?
- What is the type of culture we want to create?
- What are the cultural attributes that have been most important to our past and current success? What are the cultural attributes that will be most important to our future success?
- How far removed is our culture from the one we need for the future?
- Who are we when we are at our best?

Purpose
- Why does our company exist?
- Whom do we serve? Who is our customer? What does the customer care about?
- What does it mean to be a purpose-driven company?

Philosophy
- What is our philosophy as leaders?
- How must we show up for our customers to be successful? How must we show up for our employees to be successful?

Values
- What do you value? What does our company value? What do our people value?
- How do you feel about our existing values? Which resonate, which do not?
- How are our current values being lived?
- Which are more important—values or rules? Which are more apparent in our culture today?

POLLING THE PEOPLE

It takes a multi-directional approach to create a movement that will in turn shape the future of an organization. It takes senior leaders setting clear expectations and a common vision for the organization, managers helping to deepen this vision, and employees taking action to bring that vision to life. It's not just top-down, but middle-out and bottom-up, as well. Bringing a variety of stakeholders to the table to collaborate and debate, shape, and drive these efforts is a huge component of the process. It's what makes it holistic. But most important, I think this act of polling is what helps to create a climate of trust. Something that is much needed, especially if you're trying to drive substantially different ways of doing things in your organization. It's critically important that "how" you actually plan for and implement culture efforts embodies the very behaviors and practices you want to create in your organization.

We often use a multi-directional approach to gather input from a cross-section of different people throughout the organization. This can be done via discussions, surveys, and polls, and internal collaboration tools that surface meaningful feedback across an enterprise. If you have the time and resources available, I recommend utilizing as many channels as possible to surface this feedback. The more channels you use, the more it ensures comprehensive representation from all different roles, levels, and functions across your organization since not any one communication channel reaches everyone.

Culture Roundtables

Inviting various leaders, managers, and employees to join in a "Culture Roundtable" discussion is a great way to surface perceptions through deeper dialogue. Make sure attendees are good representatives of the type of culture you want to create and can serve as "frontrunners" for pushing the organization forward by positively influencing others. It's best to structure these sessions as informal, sit-down conversations where individuals can share their perceptions of the cultural bright spots and barriers without judgment.

After discussing the purpose of the conversation, focus on some key questions for the discussion and see what happens:

- What do you believe is our core reason for existing?
- What do you believe makes our company different from our competitors?
- What does our company value? How do our company values align with the personal values of our people?
- What do our leaders believe is important? What do our employees believe is important? How are these beliefs similar or different?
- Can you share a personal story that reflects why what we do as a company is important? Can you share a personal story that reflects our culture, good or bad?

Getting Feedback from the Crowd

Creating open and direct conversation is a key component in getting to the heart of the purpose, philosophy, and values and making the narrative real for an organization. Also involving employees early on in the process signifies and deepens transparency and trust and creates an urgency that positions an organization toward action. Once you open up the discussion, employees will naturally expect to see and hopefully will take part in driving changes. If done well, this participation can reinvigorate a culture and create a movement that compels employees to join. Let me give you an example.

When Sam Palmisano became IBM CEO in 2002, he recognized that major shifts were about to take place in technology and the global economy in a world still spinning from the recent dot-com bubble-burst. Palmisano and his team believed that if IBM was to stay relevant, it would need to transform to keep up with the times. "This is why we decided, nearly a decade ago, that returning IBM to greatness required getting back in touch with our DNA. So, one of the first things I did as CEO was to initiate an effort to reexamine our core values." The leaders didn't sit in their ivory towers, though; they used the power of the crowd. They turned a digital crowdsourcing event that the company had started in 2001 with its 300,000 employees around the globe into a "jam" that allowed people to ideate, explore, and problem solve. This effort evolved into "ValuesJam," a three-day online event that encouraged any IBM employee anywhere in the world to provide ideas on what IBM should stand for and suggest guides for how they should operate. The core of the discussion focused on what aspects were worth preserving and what needed to be changed.

Some of the feedback was incredibly tough, even prompting some executives to suggest shutting the event down, but Palmisano let it play out. Indeed, if he had smothered, censored, or diverted attention from honest criticism, he would have destroyed the very trust he was trying to foster. Instead, he stayed the course and the new values were surfaced and announced to employees later that year. Since then, they have been integrated into the company's policies, processes, daily operations, and ultimately culture. In fact, IBM held "WorldJam 2004" to identify new policies and practices that would be changed or adopted to help operationalize and make the values a reality.[1]

Palmisano's action quickly demonstrated to employees that he was dedicated to righting the company's ship, and empowering the collective voice of its people. I think IBM serves as a strong example of using employee insights to create shared values. I'm a firm believer in crafting a narrative outside of that leadership ivory tower. It's the people who make the day-to-day decisions and take the day-to-day actions who will ultimately shape a company's culture best.

IBM represents one side of the spectrum in empowering the crowd to create the cultural pillars that will drive your organization. You can move toward the middle, of course, to strike a balance between comfort and pressure levels. This could involve reaching out to specific employee and manager segments through targeted surveys and focus groups, or holding online "group chats." These practices can help get input and insight from a variety of people that major change is coming.

I encourage you to work with a diverse set of stakeholders and channels—such as internal collaboration tools and social networks, focus groups and "Culture Roundtables," and one-on-one interviews to narrow down on the values. Once this has occurred, and you have zeroed in on the values, you can test the values with senior leaders to secure approval and ensure they fit within their vision of the company culture, and whether or not they are willing to drive these values throughout the organization to guide decisions and key practices, such as hiring and firing decisions.

Consider Other Sources

I believe getting feedback from leaders, managers, and employees is critically important; however, there are some additional ways I would recommend that you surface information from other stakeholders:

Customer conversations

Since the purpose and the customer are so deeply linked, conversations with customers often yield fruitful results. If you can, have a few conversations or sessions with customers to deepen your understanding of why they work with you or buy from you, what makes your company different, and how you make them feel. Customers also generally have high-quality insights into the values of your people; prod them on the clear actions or behaviors that stick out to them through their interactions with your company.

Conversations with companies with purpose

Talk with other companies that demonstrate a clear purpose, philosophy, or values. Are there any outside enterprises that your organization holds in high esteem? Organizations with strong cultures are often happy to discuss their process and journeys with other organizations. Some of the most valuable experiences I've had through the years involved bringing clients together from different organizations to participate in "Benchmarking, Brainstorming, and Best-Practice Sharing" sessions to share insights into their worlds and think through the problems that trip up so many organizations. Leaders and practitioners are often left feeling isolated on their own islands within their organizations; connecting with others on the "outside" is one of the best ways to overcome this feeling. Don't be afraid to reach out!

Get back to your roots

Your "why" is often more clear the closer to the date of company inception. Take a look back at your company history and early artifacts to get a clearer sense of why you came to be in the first place. While an organization's philosophy and values may shift over time, the founding beliefs may provide inspiration and direction moving forward.

Scan the social channels

Stories often serve as a great reflection of your organizational culture and your organization's purpose, philosophy, and values. Look through external social media channels (and internal as well if you have them) for personal stories that may provide some insight.

Distill the data and look for key insights

After gathering as much information as possible, it's time to sit down with your project team to sort through the findings and funnel them into common themes. Some key questions to consider:

- During the process, what were the statements, stories, or moments that seemed to resonate with everyone?
- What were the words or themes that seemed to be reiterated over and over?
- What do employees and customers think makes us different?
- Why do our employees show up for work every day?
- What were the values, characteristics, or beliefs that were reflected or articulated throughout the process?

- What did we learn from leaders? What did we learn from employees? Are there big disconnects in how these different groups view the culture, and what are they?

You can think of this part of the process as similar to the work of an archaeologist or anthropologist. You'll want to excavate and "dig" for important themes, words, and facts. The key is to look at all of the data that has been recorded, and draw clear linkages and themes while remaining as unbiased as possible. This is essentially the process of ethnography, in which researchers immerse themselves in other cultures to conduct qualitative research to provide a detailed and in-depth look at everyday life and practices. The ultimate purpose of ethnography is to define and represent the culture of a group, which is fitting and very similar to the process of uncovering and crafting a narrative.

After Sam Palmisano guided the three-day "ValuesJam" at IBM, company analysts mined more than a million words of text for key themes. After this, a small team that included Palmisano developed the revised set of corporate values.[2] It was the perfect anthropological "dig," composed of empowering the crowd to provide the input and insights into the culture, collecting the information intelligently, working to sort through the data, and distilling it into clear, guiding tenets.

CRAFTING YOUR NARRATIVE

Once you've undergone the work of uncovering the beliefs and values that will guide your organization into the future, it's time to craft your narrative. As we've discussed, the narrative is composed of the first three components of the Architecture of Culture (purpose, philosophy, and values) and will help guide the remaining components of the culture you hope to bring to life—the leadership styles and beliefs your company values and promotes, the employee attitudes and actions you consciously hire and reward for, and the way you structure your business practices and programs to reach your desired future. The narrative sets the stage.

	Purpose	Philosophy	Values
What is it:	The fundamental reason for an organization existing	The holistic view of "how" an organization works, acts, and operates to support its purpose	The moral compass and decision-making guides that provide direction for individuals on how to act and behave within an organization
What does it answer:	Why do we exist? Whom do we aim to serve?	What do we believe? Who are we going to be for our customers? Who are we going to be for our employees?	What do we value? What guides our decisions? What are the behaviors we most value from leaders and employees?
Suggested Length:	One sentence	A few sentences to a paragraph, or a few bullets	Five to ten core values
Helpful Tips:	Ensure the customer and purpose are linked	Ensure the philosophy and organizational mindsets are linked	Ensure they're actionable

Purpose

If you already have a clear and stated purpose, then you have completed the first step toward building your future culture. If it doesn't center completely and totally on your customer and walking in his or her shoes, though, I would ask you to reconsider it. All organizations, large and small, are at different stages of their cultural journey, and whether or not your organization has been in operation for fifty years or fifty days, a purpose centered on your customer may be a bridge you have not come across yet. Whether you are looking to unearth, rediscover, strengthen, or stick with your purpose statement, there are some general rules of the road to consider in order to make it as clear, concise, and inspirational as possible.

Tips for your purpose statement:
1. **Link it with the Customer**. Your purpose should address "why" you exist and "whom" you exist for.
2. **Say it Succinctly**. The best purpose statements make the point in one sentence or less.

3. **Get Deep**. Get into the heart of why (the deeper why) your company exists.
4. **Make it Timeless**. Make sure your purpose can stand the test of time regardless of strategy, product, or service offering.
5. **Button up the Basics**. We all interpret certain language differently. But some words are more ambiguous than others. For instance, I may interpret "natural" a bit differently than you may. Make sure all of the words you are using are leading toward the intended outcome.
6. **Make it Altruistic**. Focus on improving something other than the company's bottom line.
7. **Make it Believable**. Make sure the purpose is believable and authentic to those that matter most—your employees and customers.

Key questions to ask when thinking about shaping your purpose:
- Why do we exist?
- Whom do we aim to serve?
- Why do our employees come to work each day? Not just why do they come to work, but why do they come to work for our company?
- What do we hope to accomplish as an organization?
- What do we want to be known for?

EXERCISE: RANDOM CORPORATE SERIAL KILLER

A great way to get to the heart of the purpose is to play the "Random Corporate Serial Killer" game. I mentioned this before in the They Lead with Purpose chapter (chapter six). This is how it works:

Pose the following scenario to the group: Imagine that a potential buyer approached us and offered to buy the company for a generous price. The buyer would guarantee that all employees would keep their jobs at the same pay scale, but with no guarantee that those jobs would be in the same industry. Then imagine the buyer plans to kill the company after the purchase—our products and services would be discontinued, our operations would be shut down, and on and on. We would completely cease to exist.

Ask the group: Would you accept this offer? Why or why not? What would be lost if the company no longer existed? Why is it important that we continue to exist?[3]

Exercises like this help people get outside the box to imagine and reflect on the company's deeper reason for being. During these sessions, make sure to record key insights and themes to distill later on.

Purpose Statements

- **CVS:** "Helping people on their path to better health"
- **Roche Genentech:** "Doing now what patients need next"
- **John Deere:** "Serve those linked to the land, thereby helping to improve living standards for people everywhere"
- **Lowe's:** "To help people love where they live"
- **Unilever:** "To make sustainable living commonplace"

Craft your purpose statement
- (A)   What does your company do for its customers?
- (B)   Who are your customers?
- (C)   What is the positive impact you have on them and the world?

Put it together and Refine: <u>A + B + C =</u>

Philosophy

Creating an organizational philosophy that supports your purpose and drives your organization forward hinges on your ability to clearly articulate leadership's differentiated point of view and mindset. Providing leadership with the time and space to develop this point of view is a critical part of the process.

Key questions to help frame how you think and develop your philosophy:
- What must we believe in order to live our purpose? What are the cultural attributes that are most important to delivering on our purpose?

- What are the five most important and fundamental beliefs that drive who we are as a company? Two examples from one of our clients: "We as leaders must ensure the why is clear, and that the what and the how are owned by many," and "We recognize that in order to succeed, we must be willing to fail."
- What are the key mindsets that we must embrace for the future? (*Remember fast is better than big, possibility over profitability, and hungry and outrospective.)
- What will we not tolerate as an organization?

Tips for your philosophy:
1. **Make it digestible.** It should be said within a few sentences to a paragraph, or a few bullet points. If it goes longer, you're most likely saying too much and yet being too vague in the process.
2. **Ensure it supports the purpose.** It should further clarify rather than confuse the purpose. Remember it should help contextualize the purpose.
3. **Make it matter outside and in.** The philosophy should focus outside-in—clarifying who you will be for your customers and employees.
4. **Make it the organizational guide.** The philosophy takes a higher altitude than the values. While values help clarify the expected leader and employee behaviors and decisions, the philosophy clarifies the core identity of the organization.

EXERCISE: COMPARE AND CONTRAST TO CLARIFY PHILOSOPHY

It can be difficult to get really clear on the beliefs and actions that will shape your organizational philosophy. If this happens, it's helpful to take a step back to think about how your philosophy differs from a competitor's. This process helps to clarify the way your organization uniquely delivers on its purpose.

The process:
- **Identify:** Your most direct and largest competitor
- **Imagine:** Your company and your competitor have the same purpose (your organization's purpose)

- **Ask:** How would we each uniquely go about fulfilling our purpose? What would be the differences in our beliefs about delivering on our purpose? How would we vary in our approach to customers? How would we vary in our approach to employees?
  - **Scribble:** As many thoughts as you can in 3 to 5 minutes
  - **Discuss:** With team members to align on the similarities and differences to help solidify the overarching beliefs that serve as the foundation for the philosophy

*This process can be repeated a number of times to help clarify the philosophy even further. Sometimes it's helpful to choose an organization with a fairly distinctive philosophy, radically different from your own, to compare with (Amazon? Google? Disney? Walmart? Zappos? ExxonMobil? Southwest Airlines? Facebook? The Army? Goodwill? Starbucks? Apple? Uber? McDonald's?)

Craft Your Organizational Philosophy

We believe _____ because _____

We believe _____ because _____

We believe _____ because _____

Values

Values are the ideals your organization holds close, and they represent the key attributes that your organization wants to create in its culture. As statements, your values are your way of expressing the qualities that will be most important in the way you get things done to achieve your results.

After years of working with dozens upon dozens of companies, I can tell you that values such as "innovation" and "integrity" are still commonly used throughout the business landscape. I firmly believe that in order to create value-based cultures we must shift the values of organizations to make them more actionable and specific so they can be leveraged as guides for all employees to embrace and deliver on the purpose. This is the first tenet in crafting values, but certainly not the only one.

Tips for Your Values:
You will want to create values that are:

1. **Actionable Guides** – Ask yourself, "As an employee of my company, if I was seeing this value for the first time, would I understand how to act in accordance with the value?" If not, work to sharpen and clarify the value.
2. **Tie to the Purpose** – Values must help clarify and describe how your organization will act to support the purpose. Make sure there is a clear link between the purpose and values.
3. **Simple and Enduring** – Unlike the purpose, values can shift over time in order to reinforce the desired behaviors and actions needed for that particular point in the organization's trajectory. However, by and large, I believe values can endure for the long haul but the definitions of how those come to life change to emphasize important traits for the times.
4. **Authentic and Believable** – Do the values speak to your unique company culture? Does everyone believe in them because they symbolize what's important to the organization? Are the values authentically lived by leaders and employees alike?

Quick Fix for "Non-Actionable, Single-Word Values" and the Power of Value Statements

What if your organization has non-actionable, single-word values such as "innovation" and "integrity," but you don't have the organizational appetite to change those values? Maybe because your values are already strewn across all your office walls, company swag, and website, you see there is just no way they are going to change. While I think sticking with such values is shortsighted, and I firmly believe that retooling your values will help them serve as guides to creating your desired culture, I understand the fear of backlash. And there is a way to reconcile that problem.

The trick is to deepen those values by creating "Value Statements"; these are statements that provide further direction for how to fulfill the values within your desired culture. In this way, you turn a value such as "innovation" into something that can actually guide day-to-day behaviors and decisions. Netflix provides a good example of this. The movie provider actually has nine values, including "passion," "courage," "honesty," "communication," and yes, "innovation." However, Netflix doesn't leave it to its employees to figure out what it means by each of those values. Instead, the company deepens each of the values with a set of value statements. For instance, the concept of innovation becomes actionable with four value statements to support it. At Netflix, "innovation" means:

- you reconceptualize issues to discover practical solutions to hard problems,
- you challenge prevailing assumptions when warranted and suggest better approaches,
- you create new ideas that prove useful, and
- you keep us nimble by minimizing complexity and finding time to simplify.

Developing value statements that provide this behavioral lens is critical to deepening values that aren't direct or clear enough to guide our decisions and actions. Netflix's values get to a level of specificity that is key to guiding a culture; it provides key tenets that can be driven from a behavioral and programmatic standpoint. Using a value statement such as, "You keep us nimble by minimizing complexity and finding time to simplify" is something that can be internalized and acted out by employees and managers, as well as something that can be driven programmatically to measure these behaviors and ensure the programs, processes, and practices of the company are leading toward this value. All in all, this specificity is hugely helpful.

Some Key Questions for Assessing Current Values + Sprouting New Values

Whether you are assessing your organization's current values or creating new values for the future, equipping yourself with questions that get to the heart of your company's values will help you during the process. Below are a number of questions that I've found to be very helpful when working with stakeholders throughout the organization.

Assessing Current Values:

1. Are our current values aligned with the company and culture we want to create?
2. How do our values show up or not show up in our day-to-day actions and decisions?

Continued on next page

Continued from previous page

3. How do our values currently support our purpose?
4. How do our values align with the personal values of our people?

Sprouting New Values:
1. Think about a time that made you proud to work for our company. What were the values present that made you so satisfied or proud?
2. What is important at our company? What do we value?
3. If there is one thing that makes our company different from others, what would you say that thing is?
4. What are the positive aspects of our culture? What are the negative aspects?
5. How must we act and behave in order to better support our purpose and customers?

EXERCISE: CURRENT AND FUTURE VALUES

One group exercise that I've found to be helpful is to ask all participants to individually draw a line down the middle of a piece of paper. On one side have them list the current company values. On the other side ask them to jot down the values or characteristics needed to make your company successful moving forward. Have a discussion on which values are aligned with the company and culture you want to create, which values may need to shift, and which values are missing completely.

Craft Your Values

1. What is the Core Value (1 to 2 words): _____

   • Make it actionable: _____

   • Make it culturally relevant: _____

   • Final value: _____

2. What is the Core Value (1 to 2 words): _____

   • Make it actionable: _____

   • Make it culturally relevant: _____

   • Final value: _____

Putting the Pieces Together:
Our Organizational Narrative

Purpose: _____

Philosophy: _____

Values: _____

VALIDATING YOUR NARRATIVE

To ensure you are sticking to a co-creative approach, it's important to validate the narrative with stakeholders throughout the organization before communicating and integrating it into your organization. This does not need to be an overly complicated or over-engineered process. It can be as simple as socializing the narrative with the leaders, managers, and employees you have worked with throughout the process to get their feedback and suggestions. This can take place through quick surveys, pulse checks, or in-person meetings. Once this feedback is surfaced, final refinements to the narrative should be made, paving the way for work to begin in aligning leadership to drive the narrative forward.

13

LEAD: BUILDING LEADERS FOR YOUR NEW CULTURE

MANY "FUTURE OF WORK" PUNDITS dismiss the importance of leadership for the new-era company. They say that today's dynamic work environments can be leaderless and managerless; i.e., self-organizing, self-managed, peer-to-peer, or emergent. I believe the role of leadership in the new era has become even more important—but it is fundamentally different than in the past. Leaders of the new era are no longer commanders but culture code-setters for their organizations.

Today's leaders must still focus on the interdependence of strategy, execution, and culture—and also consciously examine and expand their own role in leading and modeling culture. They know that culture is critical to becoming agile, innovative, and bold so they deliberately model and amplify those cultural strengths through their actions and behaviors.

Becoming the kind of leader who can do that is not easy, however. It requires "unlearning" many of the traditional strengths and capabilities the leader has come to rely on over the years, while also becoming better at more personal skills such as self-examination and developing an awareness of how others are affected by behaviors and attitudes. Leaders must deeply and truly know "who they are" and "what they believe" in order to deliberately and actively model and manage the organization's desired culture. But if the leaders do not shift and grow internally to match the desired cultures, then they will not act consistently or authentically in modeling those behaviors. When this happens, people who take their cues from the leaders will be confused about how they, too, should act. As a result, the changes to the organization's culture will not stick.

In this chapter, I will define a path leaders can take to unlearn old processes and learn to become introspective, self-aware, and deliberate about their own change and growth while also gaining the courage needed to lead a new-era organization.

THE CHANGE CURVE

Over decades of advising clients, I have developed a "change curve" for leaders that helps them move along a specific path as they make shifts and build new habits and capabilities. Along the way, they must also often unlearn other habits and capabilities. This may be because the source of a leader's success—relentless drive or an ability to execute—can also become a great impediment, limitation, or barrier preventing future effectiveness. As one software CEO once told me, "Our core capability is thirty years of engineering know-how and building software." Building on highly successful but entrenched skills to develop new capabilities is no easy task but may be essential nevertheless. How can an organization learn to become more innovative and customer-focused, for example, if its leadership still inherently believes that rapid execution is critical for success? Learning to recognize and be aware of such "liabilities" is necessary when companies take on new ways of thinking and behaving.

Before I dive into the key steps, let me share an overview of the process. Recognize, however, that the process is not exactly a linear path. In certain phases, in fact, many of the pieces of this process will be happening simultaneously.

	Phase	Description	Why do you do it	How you do it and estimated timing
1	**Expanding** (Through learning and unlearning)	This is where leaders reflect on the organizational narrative, outline what it means for their desired culture, and begin to confront and break down the current culture to surface collective and individual beliefs and assumptions about the organization and its people and capabilities. It's also where new core assumptions can be built that will act as guardrails moving forward.	If existing beliefs and assumptions aren't surfaced and challenged, it's impossible to build a new foundation.	Sessions with and across leadership It can take from 1–2 months to get senior leaders together to develop guardrails.
2	**Examining** (Learning about themselves)	This is where leadership assessments and feedback come into play. This process starts to become more personal to the individual leader.	Getting leaders to examine who they are and how they're showing up helps them to understand their own personal roadmap. It also helps them begin to build a foundation of trust necessary for a new culture.	This is typically a more individualized activity for leaders and managers to assess themselves and facilitate discussion with their teams and peers. It can take 2–3 months for leaders to have the opportunity to hold discussions and properly reflect.
3	**Experiencing** (Developing new capabilities + awareness, relearning what will work and what won't)	This is about learning new behaviors, building upon existing ones, and developing new capabilities through a variety of ways including educating, immersing, supporting, and modeling.	Leaders immerse themselves in developmental experiences that stretch, challenge thinking, and build new capabilities through doing that help make it more tangible and connected to day-to-day practices.	Often done through immersive experiences. Best to hold a series of sessions over 6–8 months to work on culture and capability efforts. We subsequently encourage these experiences to be part of ongoing leadership development moving forward.

	Phase	Description	Why do you do it	How you do it and estimated timing
4	**Ingraining** (Embedding + reinforcing)	This is where leaders start to internalize and cement new habits. They typically do this through setting intentions, creating accountability, and incorporating ways in their lives to reflect and make adjustments.	Intellectual understanding of the need to personally change and build new skills is not enough to make culture change stick. Leaders must adopt mechanisms to stay accountable and reflective. Otherwise, new habits don't form and emphasis fades, turning the culture change into another "flavor of the month" initiative.	We do this by creating various ways to keep the culture change visible and important, while holding leaders accountable to what they said they would do. We often ask leaders to take this on for a minimum of 90 days to keep new practices visible and top of mind.
5	**Enrolling others**	This is where leaders come to not only personify new attitudes and behaviors but become ardent advocates and actively enroll others. To "scale culture," leaders must consistently serve as visible culture code-setters and pass those expectations to their teams.	The impact starts to spread when ownership is disseminated through the ranks. Culture change can't be perceived as a "from the top" initiative. Management is often the biggest influencer in an employee's daily reality. People take most of their cues and direction on what's important from their managers.	We do this by having leaders teach other leaders, and enabling them to make the message and action their own. Timing varies depending on how many levels of management are in the organization. Most organizations do this in a very concerted way for at least a year.

How do people change in such a way that it sticks over time? Imagine you want to get healthier, lose weight, and get fit. Logically, the first step is to envision what that future would look like, expanding your idea of "what could be." You're feeling it, imagining it, trying it on, so to speak. Perhaps you clip out an image of an ultra-fit person from a magazine and use that for inspiration.

Envisioning yourself in the future requires just such a picture—a clear image of what that future would look and feel like if you were behaving in a specific way. Equally important is building a working plan, or map of how to get there. Often we need a personal trainer or a coach to help keep us accountable. After all, we're trying to break some deeply ingrained habits and build new routines and behaviors. Critically, though, it's not enough to envision that new body or to have a workout plan and a personal trainer or coach. The most essential component is to be self-aware and conscious of why you are where you are right now. If you are oblivious to why you overeat or avoid the gym, for example, it is very likely you will retreat to old norms after the urgency recedes or obstacles are encountered. It's human nature to turn back to familiar comforts when we run into difficulties with new approaches.

This is because underneath every behavior and habit exists a mindset and a set of beliefs. The change process I'm laying out is just as much about creating new beliefs as it is about establishing new behaviors. I move leaders through this process by building new beliefs, behaviors, and habits brick by brick.

Let's unpack the process further.

1) EXPANDING

What does it mean to "expand"? This is the starting point for the act of learning, unlearning, and relearning. Expanding is central to transforming the way that leaders lead and managers manage. Specifically, it is about revealing current thinking and expanding into new thinking.

I like to do this step as an entire leadership-team exercise for the simple reason that culture is generally composed of a collective, widely accepted set of beliefs, behaviors, and practices. In other words, such norms are held or at least reinforced by the majority of the leadership team's members. Later activities are more individualized to allow each leader to do his or her personal part to change the culture.

To "expand leaders' thinking," my team of consultants and I often conduct a multiday leadership retreat, which we call our Breakthrough Culture™ sessions. Not long ago, for example, we conducted two multiday sessions with one of our clients. The first was with the top twenty senior leaders, which included the C-suite, and a few other key executives. The second session was with the next forty leaders in the organization, comprising all of the SVPs. We did these two sessions about two weeks apart. Also, as a follow-up, a month later we did an abbreviated form of this with all VPs, over the course of ten sessions, totaling almost 300 people.

I find that if you extend these sessions more broadly than just the top executives, you are able to drive the change deeper into the organization. You also begin to see some really interesting areas of incongruity and disconnect unfold within and across these levels. That is where the opportunities for much-needed alignment among leaders become clearer.

The first part of the session involves getting the leaders to tune their heads (and hearts) to the organization's narrative. Recall that the narrative is composed of the organization's purpose, philosophy, and values outlined in the Envisioning Your Culture chapter (chapter twelve).

Initially, we take a lot of time to help leaders become clear on what it means to be a "purpose-led" company. I ask questions such as, "How would you know whether your organization was truly purpose-led? What would that look like? What attributes would you be demonstrating?" In this way, I help tease out what purpose means for that company and how it would manifest itself. If it's a company that adheres to the Balanced Scorecard, a broadly used performance management tool that many companies employ, or something similar, I might ask the leaders to reflect on what that could mean from a business/financial, customer/external, process/internal, and people/culture perspective. I might also pull best practices from other purpose-led companies, then ask the executives to answer questions such as, "What would [Google/Unilever/Burberry] do if they were you?" Or, "What would you do if you were Google?"

Next I do a deeper dive on what it means to live their values according to the organizational philosophy they've laid out. Asking questions such as, "What is the unique way that you need to bring those values to life to deliver on your purpose?" and "What is our role as leaders in leading and driving with these values and what does that look like?" help to make the discussion concrete and frame an inspirational vision of the future state.

It's important to ground leaders at this stage with sufficient substance. They need to be comfortable and certain because that comfort and certainty are about to leave them. During the next two phases, and particularly the third phase, we often run into conflicts and frustrations. People can even get testy as they are challenged to question and probe what they believe to be self-evident or real but that actually has gaps and misalignments. I believe that through this conflict the real progress of change starts to happen. This is what I consider a "nice nudge" exercise intended to challenge the current state and deconstruct it.

The work to be done here is to call out what may hold the organization back from its desired future state. The areas to explore should touch on three components of the Architecture of Culture™ that are most influenced by the narrative:

- Leadership—What are the current leadership styles, beliefs, and actions, and how might these need to shift going forward?
- Employees—What are the current employee attitudes and actions and how might these need to shift going forward?
- Business Practices—How do our current business practices guide us and how might these need to shift going forward?

The best way to deconstruct the current culture is to spend time unearthing the behaviors, rituals, artifacts, and stories that compose it. I like to ask leaders to spell out their organizational practices in areas such as how they make decisions, how delegation occurs throughout the organization, how rewards and punishments are given, how conflict is managed, and more. This gets us to the root of how the culture works.

Essentially there are two questions to answer in this part of the session: 1) What are the behaviors and artifacts from today (which are all the things you can see, hear, and feel as evidence)? This is the "what we do" component. And, 2) What are the beliefs and assumptions that guide you in doing what you do? These are the underlying and often subconscious reasons "why we do what we do."

To begin, we might brainstorm to surface the primary existing artifacts and rituals that exist within the organization—those visible structures, processes, rewards, symbols, or highly visible organizational activities that are commonplace and observable within the enterprise.

EMPLOYEES	LEADERSHIP
• Attitudes + Beliefs: What are current employees' attitudes and beliefs? What do they believe is working or not working in the organization?	• Attitudes + Beliefs: What are current leaders' attitudes and beliefs? What do they pay attention to?
• Actions + Behaviors: How do employees currently act? What are the current behaviors they have set? What are the key actions they display? Do they reflect our stated or underlying values?	• Actions + Behaviors: How do leaders currently act? What are the current behaviors or styles they have set? What are the key actions they display? Do they reflect our stated or underlying values?
• Conflict: How is conflict surfaced and handled?	• Decision-Making: How do decisions get made and communicated? Are they based on rules or values?
• Work Habits: What is the quality and quantity of work to be accomplished, remote work arrangements, length and number of workdays per week, breaks, vacations, etc.? Do they reflect the type of organization we want to create?	• Feedback: How and what feedback is given?
• Collaboration/Teamwork: How does collaboration occur and how do teams operate? How does our level of trust affect how we collaborate?	

BUSINESS PRACTICES

- Mission + Strategy: What is the current organizational strategy and mission? How are they developed, communicated, and deployed? How do they reflect the purpose and philosophy?
- Structure, Processes, + Systems: What are the key structures, processes, and systems that most drive our business? How are they currently working? What are the formal and informal business practices that most affect our culture?
- Measures + Incentives: What are the key measures and incentives within the organization? What are the metrics we talk about? How do they tie to the customer?
- Rewards: Who gets rewarded for what, and how?
- Punishments: Who gets punished for what, and how?
- Hiring + Promotion: Who gets hired? Who gets promoted?
- Communication: How does formal and informal communication happen, how is critical information shared, and with whom?
- Business Activities: What activities are key to our business? How are they important to and oriented toward our customers?

This brainstorm may become contentious because it can lead to under-discussed and even avoided topics. I've seen conversations run the gamut of sensitive concerns—from the way the office space is structured to the company dress code or the inability of employees to work remotely.

Next, it's time to discuss the underlying beliefs and assumptions. Why do we give the "badge of honor" to the top-selling manager each year? Do we view those who are "able to sell" as the heroes of our organization? Why did we ban working remotely? Is there an underlying belief that if we don't see our employees actually working, then they must not be? Do we reward activity instead of results? Do we believe people work best when they are given clear rules to cover all situations?

None of these points can be changed overnight, but they provide a concrete framing for leaders to think about how culture may need to shift moving forward. This exercise clarifies how the organization may be tripping up on its purpose and objectives, regardless of whether this purpose has been fully articulated or not. It also provides a clear view of what the company truly values, and how these values show up for leaders, managers, and employees across the enterprise.

It's unlikely that you will have taken all of your leaders and managers through this exercise. So it's important to come out of the session with clear guardrails or expectations that can be communicated and shared with people who didn't participate. It's critical that these guardrails feel real in a way that enables others to reflect on them and begin examining those boundaries or guidelines.

Here is an example of the level of detail I believe you should get to in order to provide solid guardrails or expectations for the organization. Imagine one of your values is "Give Your Best Always." The supporting guardrails that might come to represent this value and serve as a guide for what we think, believe, and expect as an organization might look something like this:

- If we see an opportunity to improve the way we serve our customers, communities, and colleagues, we say so and we help create a better solution.
- It's OK not always to have the answer; and we each take responsibility for continuous learning and self-improvement, seeking out the knowledge and resources we need to become the best we can possibly be.

- We provide the resources, environment, and flexibility for employees to give their best. Employees take responsibility for knowing what they need in order to give their best and work with their manager to reach mutually agreeable solutions.
- We won't always succeed, so we admit our mistakes, discuss our failures, and share our opportunities for improvement as we stretch to be an even better company.

These guidelines can be used to further refine your value statements. That is the definition of your values that help to make them crisp and actionable for the organization.

It's important to remember that you will want leaders to outline general moves, and not script specific moves, through these guardrails. In other words, no leader can anticipate and correct behavior in every specific instance; so guardrails are put in place to guide behavior generally. This allows everyone in the organization to appropriately translate guidance according to their own work and situation—one of the crucial first steps to develop a values-based rather than a rules-based culture.

2) EXAMINING

Self-examination is the starting point for building more self-awareness, candor, and transparency while developing the habits of introspection. These skills aren't very well developed in most of us. After all, they have not been highly valued in our society or in the business world in general. However, I believe introspection is critical to the success of Courageous Leaders and Connector Managers working today.

This work requires that we become aware of our patterns of behavior. What triggers us? What motivations lie beneath our actions? What habits and approaches do we keep repeating even though they are not serving us? Where and when are we at our best? During this phase, we must seek constructive feedback from others, while pushing past non-specific comments. We need deeper contemplation of how we step into our best self as a leader. We propel progress by concrete questioning and active listening.

You want leaders to be asking themselves and their fellow leaders questions like:

- What am I doing now?
- Why am I doing what I'm doing, as a leader?
- What is it that I believe that compels me to do it this way?
- In which ways is this serving or not serving my team and me?
- How well do I understand and know how to lead in the new "way"?
- What is the gap between what I do today and that new direction?
- What are my blind spots, and how do I know?
- How do I show up when I'm at my best, and when I'm under stress?
- What would success look like in that new world and along the way?
- What do I need to start and stop doing to get there?

This is where a mindset shift really begins. Some ways to do this are:

- Use your organization's engagement survey to delve into the role of leadership and management in creating culture; and share the results with the organization.
- Encourage leaders to have open discussions with their teams about they can better lead and how the team can work together more effectively in line with guardrails and cultural attributes; this is also a good time for the leader to share his or her personal objective to become more of a Courageous Leader or Connector Manager.
- Get a coach to observe your leadership behaviors and provide unbiased feedback on events like conversations and meetings; it may take a brave leader to volunteer for such scrutiny but it shows commitment and transparency and builds more trust.
- Ask the CEO to hold middle management chats to determine how well they understand the direction of the organization, the desired culture, and how that will enable the business's strategy, innovation, and operations; gather their recommendations on how to continue to make the direction clear and ways they will demonstrate the cultural attributes.
- Leverage 360-degree feedback to assess leaders and managers with input from reports, peers, and senior leaders; see that every person, including the CEO, is provided support in analyzing data to absorb

the sometimes painful but always helpful messages, and to build plans for better performance; consider making the feedback given to top leadership transparent.

- Instruct the leaders to write their own business eulogy to define what qualities and attributes they would want to be remembered by; have leaders discuss with their teams how they hope to be perceived and ask if there are concrete practices or styles they should work on.
- Ask leaders to write a compelling future-oriented story that includes exciting descriptions of what the leader envisions for the organization; share that with their teams to spur discussion.

Remember the point of this phase is to ask questions, listen intently, and learn more about yourself as a leader, about your team, and about your organization.

3) EXPERIENCING

It's important to develop leaders and extend their existing capabilities with new capabilities that are better aligned to what your business and your workforce needs. I've found the development of leaders is often given little attention or focus in most organizations, especially during periods of change. Typically, once leaders pronounce what the future state needs to look like, it's assumed they will just jump to that future immediately—as if they always had just the right skills, knowledge, and emotional capacity to do it but were simply waiting for the right moment. But if the new ways are counter to how they've been successful before or what they've been rewarded for in the past, this jump requires enormous focus. Everyone—not just leaders—needs continual development and support in order to step into his or her best self.

In this phase, I think it's important to create interactive and immersive experiences. A classroom-style lecture is insufficient because it won't imprint or inspire. Indeed, nothing is less effective than a group of leaders ruminating on what the attributes of the ideal leader would be. It's much more important to experience the attributes of such leadership firsthand.

In this phase it's also very important to develop the qualities of the Courageous Connector. Empathy, confidence without self-delusion, humility, collaborative ways of working, and "growing a growth mindset" (versus a fixed mindset) are all critically important for leaders today, enabling them to lead and model customer-centricity, inspire possibility, and act quickly and with certainty.

When working with leaders, we use a variety of techniques to get them to step out of their current reality and really re-imagine what they might be doing in a day or week in their work. The point is to jar them, not just incrementally move them. I find that when you want to drive something transformative and break people out of their old mindsets, it's important to leverage techniques like design-thinking or innovation methods similar to when companies are trying to develop disruptive new products or offerings. Transformation, by definition, is something that one hasn't seen or done before so it's much more nebulous in nature than simply just making an incremental step-by-step change.

I also believe that you shouldn't strive to orient everyone to the same behavior or the exact same personal-development objectives. Although you're developing a prototype of a leader for your company, each leader will do it in her own unique way by bringing her personal strengths to bear.

Here are three good ways I have found that you might create those kinds of experiences:

Creating an emotional connection to an imagined future event that creates an urgent need for them to respond
It's pretty difficult to envision something transformative while talking about it in a theoretical way, but that approach is used all the time. We talk constantly about what we will or should do in a given situation without really framing it in the proper context. We're almost always sitting in a conference room rather than grappling with the pressing opportunity firsthand. One way you can inspire and focus people to act rather than just talk is to create an imagined future event for them to solve for. I've seen companies do this in a variety of ways.

Jack Welch, former GE CEO, believed that to grow your business, you first have to destroy your business. He began the "Destroy Your Business.com" exercise back in 1999 within GE as an ambitious thought exercise to force each of its business unit leaders to give serious thought to their business's weaknesses.

After completing the Destroy Your Business (DYB) exercise, GE employees were instructed to move into the Grow Your Business (GYB) phase, using knowledge of existing (and future) weaknesses to identify new opportunities to leverage digital and online initiatives. By taking these steps, it was thought that Welch forced GE to "welcome the anxiety of competition instead of avoiding it" and helped understand the motivations of its customers better.

In general, a concrete event or scenario carries more reframing power than a series of general what-ifs.

Outlining new responses to various business situations and scenarios in order to exercise the new values

When conducting this activity with groups of leaders, we first ask them to brainstorm a list of key business practices, situations, and scenarios that represent important touch points with their leaders, peers, and teams on a daily basis, weekly basis, monthly basis, and yearly basis. Their list may include items such as: "I hold weekly project team meetings," or "I sit down with each of my team members for a one-on-one meeting," or "I represent Marketing in our strategic planning efforts." We encourage them to go and observe specific ways they might better align themselves and their teams to the values. This exercise helps them become more acutely aware of the dynamics at play because they're being asked to watch for values in action versus actively leading meetings. We also encourage them to write about what they saw in situational terms.

As a leader, this is where you must begin setting the expectation that living by the values is of the utmost importance. You are not bringing up these questions to call out or penalize anyone but to become better together. Leaders can also direct their teams to practice being solution-focused instead of simply airing grievances and complaints. I believe the way you structure conversations around solving problems is what contributes most to building accountability in organizations. In the process, you encourage a "we're all in this together" mentality.

Immersing them in new situations to build empathy and connection

Starbucks' Leadership Lab is a three-day conference-like experience that is one part leadership skills and another part product immersion. Each experience station at the conference walks all store managers through a problem-solving framework. There's a trade show, with demonstrations of new products and signs with suggestions for improving sales, such as, "Tea has the highest profit margins." The majority of experiences are meant to be educational. Several even give store managers access to top partners in the company's roasting process, blend development, and customer service. It's also about inspiring them and connecting them to the purpose and the culture of the organization in a very immersive and almost theatrical way. It's very true to Starbucks and what it is as a brand and a company. The session is said to culminate in a perfectly pristine white room with benches facing a massive Starbucks logo, inviting participants to contemplate what the company stands for—"To inspire and nurture the human spirit—one person, one cup and one neighborhood at a time."[1]

If you're thinking, *How am I going to pull off something of that magnitude*, know there are many ways to get enormous impact without the extensive labor and financial commitment shown by Starbucks. For example, during a recent leadership series we conducted for one of our Fortune 20 clients, we asked the leadership team of twenty to break into five smaller groups and each spend the afternoon getting out of the office and observing other organizations in action. Within five miles of the company's office, there was a Whole Foods, a Target, a Home Depot, a car dealership, and a whole array of other businesses. We sent them on their way, instructing them to look for the ways those employees interacted with them, as customers. When they came back, they had a whole new appreciation for customer service and were excited to share their insights with the other groups.

Some things to consider when planning for these kinds of immersive experiences:

- You want this to evoke an emotional response. It doesn't necessarily have to be practical or realistic.
- Get really clear on the message you want convey. What is the "a-ha" you want participants to have? What are you trying to build

in them? Increased empathy for the customer, relatability to the employees?

- Describe the people you want to take through this experience. Who are they? And, who do they want to be? Outline what you can infuse into this experience that helps them to practice and step into those new ways of acting.
- Define the actions you would like them to take, both during the experience and following the experience in their work.

Leverage "reverse mentoring" to build capability and empathy

Reverse mentoring partners an older, more experienced executive with a younger, less experienced newcomer. As the name suggests, the younger employee serves as the mentor. It's an approach that reinforces the idea that every single person in the organization has something to bring to the table.

Here's how the program we developed for one of our clients works: The CEO sponsored the program and initially scoped it for the top twenty executives to be paired with a Millennial counterpart for six one-hour sessions over a period of six weeks. Each executive's mentor would sit with that executive to help him or her get up to date with the latest business technologies and workplace trends. For example, the mentor might show the executive how to use Instagram, or explore why anyone would want to use Twitter to engage with a brand, or dive into a discussion on sensitive work practices like telecommuting or schedule flexibility. The program was so successful that it continued long past the initial sessions and got extended to any senior leader in the organization who wanted to participate. The organization's social-media policies softened as a direct result of the leaders' new awareness. As you can imagine, it was also very motivating for the young mentors to be provided a glimpse of executive-level management issues and a path to get to know the senior leadership team members personally.

Mentor and mentee also explored other topics such as ways to improve connection with Millennial customers and how they might improve diversity at the company. The point is that these senior leaders were willingly taking advice for running their business from young professionals. This makes reverse mentoring extremely effective at two things in parallel: breaking down misperceptions while building new capabilities.

4) INGRAINING + EMBEDDING

This phase is about building new habits and ensuring they stick. When you are accountable, you make a commitment to move from possibility to reality, *regardless* of the circumstances.

When people are pressed they will often make a few trivial commitments and check the box, so to speak. It's important not to declare victory too soon. Leaders of the most successful efforts use the credibility built by short-term wins to create momentum for tackling even bigger problems.

In this phase, I believe there are three important steps that must happen:

Making Personal Iconic Commitments

It's important to back words up with actions. Leaders have acquired new skills, built new habits, and gained confidence. We now challenge them to make commitments that are big, public, and personal. In the spirit of developing courage, we press leaders to take on something that really scares them by committing to something out of their personal comfort zone that requires vulnerability, commitment, and a leap of faith.

What kinds of actions am I talking about? You might declare that there will be 50 percent women leaders on your leadership team by next year even though you're not sure how you'll make that happen. You might pose a major business issue to your teams and ask them to solve it within the next month, without your input. What can you, as leader, do to show your commitment and conviction in a big way to the new way of leading? This is not to be done in a reckless or flippant way but in a manner that enables you to meet your objectives and moves the commitment outside of yourself.

Some key considerations for building personal iconic commitments include the following:

- Commit to a personal leadership commitment that is appropriate for your level and influence, and continue to up the ante by making another one as you make progress.
- Make sure the commitment is a stretch that's public, time-bound, and visible.
- Remember that when you make a public commitment to your peers, your team, and others, you are agreeing to stay in communication

about your progress. You must give updates sharing where you've met the objective and where you may have fallen down.

Building in Accountability Mechanisms

In order for leaders to deepen their commitments over time and share success stories and tough challenges with their peers, we often encourage them to work with an accountability partner or two. We ask them to form small groups of two to three people who commit to working with one another for a minimum ninety-day stint, having check-ins at the thirty-, sixty-, and ninety-day points. It also includes a self and team assessment at around the seventy-five-day mark for them to evaluate how they're doing. An internal coordinator can serve as a "lightweight coach" and conduct this check-in process at the start in order to make it a rhythm. I feel it's important to deep-dive at the ninety-day mark to determine whether you've achieved your objective, and are ready to make a next commitment.

Here is a framework from our work that may help you to think through yours:

	15 Days	30 Days	60 Days	Self and Team Assessment	90 Days
Intent:	Share commitment, accountability, and support	Reflection on what they did, what they noticed, how it was received	Continued reflection, results, and next-level commitment	Check in to identify how values are being demonstrated by taking actions	Sharing, celebrating, results, and next steps
Who:	Accountability Partners	Accountability Partners + Coach	Accountability Partners + Coach	Self and Team Assessment (Criteria for employee or change agent—must have witnessed you in action and the impact of your action)	Entire leadership team facilitated by two coaches
Time:	30 minutes	60 minutes	60 minutes	10–15 minutes per feedback discussion	90 minutes

	15 Days	30 Days	60 Days	Self and Team Assessment	90 Days
Key Questions to Consider:	What was your commitment? How is it connected to our purpose and values? Why is it important to you personally? What have you done or not done? What has helped keep you accountable or what can I do to support you in practicing your commitment? How can we support each other in taking action moving forward? Do you want to restate or reframe your commitment? (Reasonable to do in the cadence you have committed to)	What action(s) did you take? What did it look like in the moment? How was it received? How did you know? How did it personally feel to take this action? What did you notice about yourself that changed or shifted because you took action? Can you share some examples of other leaders living the values that could be inspirational for others? Coach to capture any potential stories that are sharable with the group	What are you noticing as you continue to take action? Has there been incremental impact over time? What would you have hoped to see as a result of your actions at this point? What have been the results (expected, exceeded, less than)? If need be, how might you change your commitment to achieve or exceed the results you were hoping for? Is there a different action you can take or an adjustment of your existing one? Is there something new you would like to start practicing?	As a leader, I am committed to (insert value or leadership principle) How have you seen me demonstrate this by (insert commitment)? What are some other ways I might demonstrate (insert value or leadership principle)?	Share the original commitments and the results (gather this information from coaches and original commitments or revised ones) Give each person 2–4 minutes to share 1 experience that had the most impact on him or her, on someone else, or that is just important to tell Wrap up—this is the difference you can make through meaningful actions that create big change. We need you to continue to take meaningful actions over the coming months and "be the change." Collect ideas for ways to sustain the leadership changes
Next Steps:	Call with coach in 15 days	Call with coach in 30 days	Self and Team Assessment	90-Day Gathering	Make your next commitment

This is obviously just one way to build in more visibility and account-ability to your process. I encourage you to find other ways to keep the culture-change process transparent, meaningful, and top of mind.

Reflecting and Introspection

As part of continuing to increase self-awareness and sustain new practices, I believe it's important to adopt exercises that force you to reflect and challenge what you're doing.

I highly recommend that leaders keep a journal for a period of time to capture thoughts and actions. A journal makes you more aware of what you're doing and where problems might be coming from. It helps to write down different triggers you notice throughout the day, such as what makes you overwhelmed and what makes you feel energized. Analyze what went right and what you might do differently next time. You may even consider spending time documenting things like food intake, water intake, or sleep, so you can notice larger trends that you might correct. If you're looking for a deeper understanding of your decision-making skills, write down what you think will happen with a decision, then wait nine or twelve months and review what you wrote. Peter Drucker called this process "feedback analysis." I think an important note here is to ask leaders to evaluate less of what they're *doing* and more of how they're *being* in certain situations throughout their day.

Mindfulness is another practice that more and more companies are embracing to increase self-awareness. For those who aren't familiar, mind-fulness basically means moment-to-moment awareness and it's a way to think in more productive and less stressful ways. Google has put a particu-lar emphasis on this in its "Search Inside Yourself" program for leaders.

I also encourage my clients to continually reflect on a broader level, asking themselves questions such as:

- What specifically is happening on a day when things go well? How do I feel and act on a great day?
- What is happening on a day when I don't do so well? How do I feel and act on a not-so-great day?
- What can I do better, and is there someone who can coach me?

5) ENROLLING OTHERS

The success of any culture change is largely dependent on how leaders lead other leaders. For organizations to thrive, senior leaders must know how to inspire and get the most from their senior managers, who in turn must drive performance and hopefully passion throughout the organization.

While it might be sufficient in a small organization to have an inspirational founder or CEO extolling the vision, it's clearly not effective or scalable in a large enterprise to have only a few of the leaders beating the drum of the new while everyone else waits around for some drummer to inspire their people.

Leaders at all levels must be encouraged and empowered to "own" the decisions on how the narrative will play out in the organizations and departments. That's why it's so important to set clear guardrails to establish commonality and a shared understanding of what that means while sketching the absolute must-do's and the absolute must-never-do's.

When it comes to leaders leading other leaders through a culture definition or change effort, we often jump immediately to how we are going to "cascade" this message. It's as if getting leaders in a room, sharing the vision, and telling them what we want them to do will inspire action and enable them to execute. I believe there are a few important considerations to keep in mind:

Enable Them to Feel It

With one of our recent clients, we created a two-hour experience that every single manager in the organization (nearly 5,000 managers) could go through to learn about their new purpose and values in action. It was inspiring, full of heartfelt videos of leaders sharing personal stories of purpose and why they work at the company. Many were so touched they wept and most were talking about the event many months after participating. Logistically it may be challenging to do something like this in person. We were able to touch every single one of these people face-to-face within a year. Although you can definitely do these kinds of events virtually, I would encourage you to give it some deep consideration before you do. When you're trying to inspire community and a shared vision, I believe it's short-changing it to do it any other way than person-to-person.

Have Your Leaders Teach Your Leaders

When leaders own and facilitate the development of the other leaders in the organization, they have real impact. One of our Fortune 20 clients recently held a leadership forum for their top 350 leaders in the organization. The CEO and his team of five led them in a two- day conversation about where they were headed as a business and how the new direction required a different culture and way of leading than what they had been doing in the past. Some of the questions they contemplated during their time together included:

- What does VUCA (volatile, uncertain, complex, and ambiguous) mean for us as an organization?
- How does VUCA affect the requirements for leadership in your role?
- How does our culture affect our ability to execute against our strategy?
- How does our culture drive leadership behaviors?
- How does our culture help/hinder the way we operate as a company?
- What does courageous leadership look like for our organization? What are some specific examples you've seen?
- How do we promote courage and develop leaders who will be courageous when it counts?

They were then asked to break into smaller groups and solve some of these challenges while laying out their own development and action plans to move their business forward. Toward the end of the session, they asked all the leaders to put forth their commitments on what their own courageous performance as a leader will look like and asked them to report back when they reconvened six months later as a leadership group.

SUSTAINING CHANGE

I hope that you now understand the critical role that leaders play in driving the transformation of their organizations. Traditional organizations are looked upon as machines that can be designed, tweaked, fine-tuned, and steered. But today's organizations are living cultures inhabited by people who bring their personalities, beliefs, and backgrounds with them to work. That is how we learn to empathize with the customer and devote passion to solving challenges in innovative ways.

Leaders can no longer merely prescribe change as though it were the latest strategy and tell others to make it so. For the new culture to take root and flourish, the leaders themselves must have the conviction and internal connection that founders might have had when they launched the organization in some garage or loft apartment. What does it take to be that kind of leader? It starts within; it is accelerated by the kind of introspection that increases self-awareness, and it leads to a kind of personal growth that inspires others to follow.

14

ALIGN: RIGHTING YOUR ORGANIZATIONAL PRACTICES

TO CREATE a "nimble, focused, and feisty" culture, it is critical that you tailor and align your organization's programs, processes, and practices. The right business practices make the difference between an organization that is positioned to pivot or unable to adapt, able to make speedy decisions or bogged down by silos, attract and empower the best talent or stifle their development and engagement.

Practices that seem to smother progress, performance, and innovation must be eradicated. Yet, alignment goes beyond making sure that your programs and practices aren't contradictory to your goals. It's just as important that such programs are also deepening your organization's purpose while encouraging your workforce to act upon the beliefs, behaviors, and values that will lift your organization to the next level.

In fact, the alignment of such practices must go beyond those programs that sit in HR. To truly align business practices with culture, people, and goals is to be holistic, integrated, and all-inclusive. Everything from communications, strategic planning, and the rules and processes that affect customer-facing employees to the less formal practices that change the enterprise climate like town hall meetings and Happy Hour Fridays must cohere in the same direction. When you bring a deeper level of consciousness, purpose, and focus to organizational programs, you enable them to serve as expansive aids rather than limiting mechanisms.

This chapter is intended to help you assess, align, eliminate, change, and discover new programs and practices that will generate a more fluid, empowered, and motivated culture. The work, resources, and mechanisms it takes to create widespread culture change certainly cannot be boiled down to one chapter, but these tools will help push your organization toward rethinking the way it structures and plans.

> "Everything must be made as simple as possible. But not simpler."
> —Albert Einstein

The major phases of the work include (1) assessing and identifying the practices and programs to align, (2) working through the alignment process and creating the proper infrastructure to support alignment, and (3) designing new actions and practices to create significant impact on your culture.

Phase	Key Activities	Key Questions to Consider
Assess	Identifying programs, processes, and practices for alignment	Which programs, processes, and practices must shift to better support the purpose? Which programs, processes, and practices must shift to create a more "nimble, focused, and feisty" culture?
Align	Working to align and redesign programs Creating a Culture Council	How must program and practice messaging and tactics shift to create greatest impact? Who are the key players to help provide guidance and remove obstacles during the alignment process?
Design	Identifying Org iconic actions Creating effective new practices	What is one major action our organization can take to prove to our customers and employees that we are committed to our purpose? What are a few new practices we can create that will lead our culture to become more "nimble, focused, and feisty"?

ASSESS

Identifying Programs, Processes, and Practices for Alignment

Aligning programs, processes, and practices to support purpose and encourage employees to act according to company values gives an organization a compelling advantage. But this alignment process can certainly take a lot of work, especially for large, complex organizations with multiple programs, dispersed workforces, and competing metrics and priorities. Every organization is also at a different level of cultural maturity; this makes it easier for some to go through rapid change, even as others struggle to implement meaningful programmatic shifts.

The good news is that you don't need to boil the entire ocean at once. Instead, you can focus on a few "waves" to bring about some meaningful change in an accelerated way. This means tackling specific programs and practices that will give you the biggest bang and build momentum. The size of your organization and your team will determine the amount of programs you can focus on at once and how many subsequent waves there will be.

There are a number of different approaches to take when identifying which programs to focus on first, depending upon your cultural maturity and complexity. The key is to find the approach that fits your situation best. Sticking to a dogmatic methodology doesn't help you navigate the politics and cultural nuances inherent within every organization. Here are a number of ways to look at it:

Option 1: Stick with the outside-in approach

In my opinion, all companies should guide their culture from their purpose. This is the path to being outrospective in nature. I believe aligning programs and practices with the purpose and the customer in mind has significant and immediate impact. Doing so allows you to identify changes that both employees and customers will see and feel. Taking an outside-in approach affects customer-facing employees, ensuring they are fully enabled to deliver on the purpose and act in line with organizational values rather than stringent rules and processes. This approach requires getting close to the customer, conducting an audit of the programs and practices that affect the customer, prioritizing changes that will have the most significant impact, and working to enact changes in a meaningful way.

In order to identify these programs, I typically recommend using these four lenses as a filter to help you determine the programs, practices, and processes that most affect a customer-facing employee's ability to deliver to the customer, and then determining the biggest and most significant gaps with which to start.

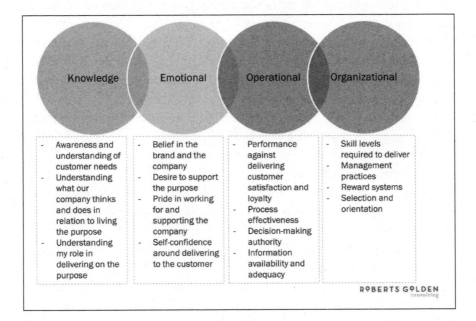

1. Do they have the **knowledge to deliver on this purpose**?
2. Are they **emotionally** vested?
3. Are they able to do it well, **operationally**?
4. Do the **organizational** practices enable and support delivering on it?

Option 2: Create awareness before the expectation of behavior shifts
During any change, it's important to help the organization and employees build awareness, capability, and muscle before beginning to assess and reward for expected changes. Real change is a process, not an event, and it requires a level of awareness and understanding of the change even before people can develop the ability and passion to act upon the change. Not to mention it's unfair to assess anyone on new performance without the ability to learn and practice it first. As an example, if your organization has always followed a traditional selling model, and you want to shift the sales

process and your sales team's behavior toward more of a consultative selling approach, you must build the clear reason "why" the decision is being made before demanding the change. You'll need to create a level of awareness for not only the reason behind the change, but also the implications and behavioral shifts necessary to make the sales team successful. It will also be helpful to paint a clear picture of what this would be like on a day-to-day level for each individual and then expand on that together in your conversations with employees. What would sales calls look like? How would each sales person handle different situations and scenarios? What process changes might need to take place to better support the sales staff? By building this level of awareness and engagement, employees are more inclined to internalize and commit to the change, rather than silently or not so silently oppose it.

This way of approaching it has implications for the way we shift and align programs. It means focusing on programs and practices that affect awareness, internalization, and engagement with the change first; then focusing on programs that affect rewards, incentives, and other ways of creating accountability soon after. Here are some ideas of programs to shift to support this cadence:

1. **Wave 1 Programs**—those that affect awareness, internalization, capability, and engagement:
   - communications, marketing & sales, finance
   - PR, community relations, customer service
   - training, leadership and talent development, recruitment and selection, new employee orientation
   - employee opinion surveys
   - diversity + inclusion programs
   - IT, R&D, strategy, supply, and distribution

2. **Wave 2 Programs**—those that affect rewards, incentives, and accountability:
   - Performance management, compensation and benefits, succession planning, 360 evaluations, awards programs

Option 3: Conduct an organizational query to identify the programs and practices that are most misaligned

For larger, more complex organizations it may be more useful to surface feedback to quickly identify pain points and areas of opportunity. To do so, conduct an organizational query to identify the programs, processes, and practices most holding you back from serving your customers. This process empowers the wisdom of the collective crowd to surface and pinpoint issues that can easily be improved to strengthen a culture.

Early on at Yahoo!, Marissa Mayer initiated a program called Process, Bureaucracy, and Jams, or "PB&J" for short, to encourage employees to share ideas on how to solve problems and boost productivity. This approach also helped surface concerns with culture and work environment but focused on solutions rather than complaints. To support the program, Mayer and her team created an online tool to collect employee concerns and votes on whether the problems were worth focusing on. Any concern reaching fifty votes would get management attention toward solving the issue. One year in, Mayer reported to solving a thousand things—some of them large and some of them small.[1]

What I appreciate about Mayer's approach is her commitment to act. She admitted to the shortcomings that were damaging the culture and empowered her people to identify and solve them. This is a bold move from a CEO and a great way to kick off a query—posing questions to employees on what they would change to strengthen the culture. There are other ways to conduct a query, of course; here are some ideas and questions to consider:

- Send a short survey to leaders throughout your organization to check which practices and programs may need to shift in order to strengthen the culture and better deliver on the company's purpose.
  - Ask three questions that tie back to creating a "nimble, focused, and feisty" culture:
    1. What programs, processes, or practices are slowing us down as an organization? (Nimble)
    2. What programs, processes, or practices are causing us to lose focus on our purpose and our customers? (Focused)
    3. What programs, processes, or practices are holding employees back from reaching their full potential? (Feisty)
- You can also move the query out broader in the organization by polling employees who are closer to the purpose and the customer, asking them the same questions you would ask leaders. Doing this will help provide a clearer line of sight into the issues employees

face on a day-to-day level, while also serving as a beneficial engagement tool helping employees to feel heard. Polling both leaders and employees separately serves as a great way to identify areas of alignment and misalignment. Many times leaders have strong, misguided assumptions on the way certain practices and policies affect employees. Getting feedback from multiple levels can provide a much-needed reality check.

- Get outside the company walls to talk with customers. Doing this helps orient you toward what they are seeing, thinking, and feeling about your company. It's a good way to gauge their perceptions, and identify any practices or barriers that are getting in the way of a great customer experience. Sometimes it's surprising to see how we show up for our customers without realizing it. If you don't have the time or budget to conduct focus groups or speak with customers directly, you can utilize surveys or scan social-media channels to assess how you're hitting home.

ALIGN

Working to Align and Redesign Programs

After identifying the programs and their cadence for alignment, it's time to work with program owners to begin the alignment process. Program alignment requires building a strong partnership and bond with program owners throughout your organization. Whether those people are in HR, corporate strategy, operations, communications, marketing, or any other function, it's important to build relationships with them to drive toward a singular focus. From my experience, it's natural for people to be suspicious of this process. They may feel like you're invading their turf and trying to change the programs they "own" and run on a daily basis. The key is to facilitate their expertise, reinforce that you are there to work alongside them, have them lead as the subject-matter experts, and provide the overarching vision of what's possible for the organization. Securing strong sponsorship on the project helps to leverage your position and provide program owners an opportunity to enact meaningful program changes. Chances are some program owners have been chomping at the bit to make adjustments to their programs. Giving them the freedom to shape the future direction and vision of the organization should help bring them on board. They're the ones who should own the changes to these programs. You, as the culture-efforts leader, should simply be shepherding.

Developing plans that successfully integrate the narrative into these practices, programs, and processes often includes two major facets:

1. Identifying ways to infuse messaging and communications within programs to align to the intended future, and
2. Shifting the tactics and strategies within these practices or programs to make a greater impact on the future state culture.

A major piece of the process is to work with the owners of these programs to help them internalize and understand how their work is currently contributing to the purpose and values, and what the "rich picture" would look like if the program was fully aligned and contributing. I like to focus on a four-step process to align programs:

1. Conduct a current state assessment
2. Develop future state recommendations
3. Identify major barriers and enablers
4. Identify next steps and action items

As a rule of thumb, I like to meet with key stakeholders to give them an overview of the process and then regroup a week or two later to check progress. The following box shows this process.

1: Current State Assessment
Purpose: Identify ways programs help or hinder the culture you want to build.

Program/Process:

Current Contributions to Purpose	Current Contributions to Values
• How does your program/process currently contribute and deliver on the purpose? • What is the evidence or tactics within your program that proves this?	• How does your program/process currently contribute to helping employees act and make decisions in accordance with the new values? • What is the evidence or tactics within your program that proves this?

Alignment to Purpose	Alignment to Values
• What are clear areas of alignment to the purpose within your program/process?	• What are clear areas of alignment to the values within your program/process?
Misalignment to Purpose	**Misalignment to Values**
• What are clear areas of misalignment to the purpose within your program/process?	• What are clear areas of misalignment to the values within your program/process?
Opportunities for Purpose	**Opportunities for Values**
• What are clear areas of opportunity to align messaging to the purpose? • What are clear areas of opportunity to align tactics to the purpose?	• What are clear areas of opportunity to align messaging to the values? • What are clear areas of opportunity to align tactics to the values?

Current Plans & Potential Barriers
- What are current plans for your program/process that may cause difficulties in aligning to the purpose and values within the next six months?
- What are other potential barriers?

- Any other notes on current state:

2: Future State Recommendations
Purpose: Identify program changes, requirements, and what success will look like.

Timing	Program Messaging *Anticipated changes for program messaging*	Program Tactics *Anticipated changes for program tactics*	The Big Move *The "big change" for your program in all three phases*	Implementation Requirements *Who owns the change?* *Financial investment required (none, minimal, significant)*	Success *What does success look like?* *How will it be measured?*
Short-Term (Quick Wins)					
Mid-Term (Momentum Builders)					
Long-Term (Big Goals)					

Sustainability
- How will you ensure that your program/process is aligned to the culture moving forward?
- How will you ensure that any future program/process changes will be aligned?

3: Alignment Barriers + Enablers
Purpose: Identify barriers and enablers to the alignment process.

Resources & Training:
- Are there specific resources you need in order to better align your program?
- Do you or team members need additional training or education to better align your program?

Complementary Programs
- Would you recommend shifts in other complementary programs that would allow your program to have more of an impact? If so, what would these programs and shifts be?
- Do you have any recommendations on other programs to align that would have a positive impact on your proposed programmatic changes?

Sponsorship
- Is there anything senior leaders could do to help sponsor you going forward? What could they do to remove barriers and enhance enablers?
- Which leaders would be most instrumental in helping you align your program?

Requests
- Are there any specific requests you have of the Culture Council going forward? (Short-term, mid-term, long-term)

4: Next Steps + Action Items
Purpose: Identify next steps and owners.

Action Items Immediate actions to be taken	Necessary Resources Resources needed for action	Timeline Resources needed for action	Owner(s) Person(s) responsible for action

It's important to shepherd, coach, and advocate for program owners along the way to make sure they don't feel stranded on an island. The core team is responsible for making sure the puzzle pieces are fitting together and that program owners feel adequately supported and "in the know." It's equally important to create an accountability structure to ensure that the alignment process is going deep enough to meet the desired change, and that program owners are staying accountable to their plans. This is when creating a Culture Council can help.

Creating a Culture Council

The purpose of a Culture Council isn't to enforce stringent rules or act as a watchful Big Brother. It's more in line with forming a government body to help guide the alignment process and plans, remove barriers and obstacles for program owners, and ensure that programs and processes are directed toward delivering on the intended future from a bird's-eye view. Because of this, Culture Council members should have a few distinct qualities:

- A cross-functional group of leaders (six to eight for larger organizations or two to four for smaller organizations)
- Influential and positioned to remove barriers and obstacles
- Empowered and available to review and approve plans
- Passionate and embodying the culture you want to create
- Strong system thinkers

After program owners have had adequate time to prepare alignment plans, it's best to have an in-person meeting to provide them with an opportunity to present their recommendations to the Culture Council. The council should serve as a cohesive review panel to assess alignment plans, provide feedback and recommendations to owners, and serve as an overall board of approval. The council is responsible for ensuring all programs are in alignment with the purpose and strategic direction of the organization, and for monitoring short-term programmatic changes.

It's best to leave the Program Alignment Kickoff Meeting with the next steps and action items identified, as well as a plan for upcoming meeting cadence. Generally, the Culture Council should be highly involved up front, meeting with the program owners at least once a month to ensure owners feel adequately supported. After the first few months, meeting frequency can be shifted, possibly to bimonthly or quarterly meetings depending upon progress.

ORGANIZATIONAL ICONIC ACTIONS

In the Purpose chapter (chapter six), I discussed "Organizational Iconic Actions," or major decisions that drive a company's sense of purpose deeper into the social stratosphere and into the heads and hearts of customers and employees. Actions like CVS' banning tobacco sales and starting stop-smoking programs to foster better health, or Gap Inc.'s starting the increasingly popular trend of raising its own minimum wage, or JPMorgan Chase's donating $100 million to Detroit over five years to help the city rebound from its financial turmoil are examples. From my experience, nothing can deepen an organization's "why" and emphasize the power of the "how" more quickly or effectively than bold actions like these. Whether you are looking to build or strengthen your culture, I highly encourage you to search for high-impact actions that bring the alignment process to the next level by coupling program and practice alignment with enterprise-wide decisions that prove an organization's commitment to its purpose.

Identifying iconic actions can be a fun, creative, and emotional process. It challenges assumptions, forces outside-the-box thinking, and tests leaders' commitment levels. The process is valuable in and of itself as it helps leaders get clear on how far they are willing to go to deliver on their purpose. The deeper impact, of course, comes when you pull off such actions to effect real change. Here are some steps to help you think through identifying opportunities for your organization:

Pull the team together
Put together a small team of six to ten people, comprising a diverse set of broad thinkers from multiple levels of your company. It's important to have a few senior leaders including the CEO to help set the tone, but also a number of creative, insightful Difference Makers. The key is to have members with a range of perspectives who are not afraid to share their views. Set the tone with a creative brainstorming session to uncover opportunities to deepen the organization's impact and alignment to purpose.

Structure the session
Once you get a date on the books, the next step is to structure a creative, thoughtful, and culturally relevant session for the team. Some thoughts on how to structure and facilitate the session:

1. Frame the Focus
   A. Let the group know that you are there to surface highly visible and high-impact actions that tie to your purpose. Provide insight into the benefits of these actions:
      - Increased customer loyalty and employee engagement
      - Positive brand-building and recognition
      - Reduced turnover
      - Long-term financial benefits
   B. Provide examples of Iconic Actions to deepen the focus—think of CVS, Gap, JPMorgan Chase, and any other examples that you think would be relevant for the group. Make sure you draw the line between the action and company's purpose to make it clear that any potential actions must be aligned with and contribute to your own company purpose.
2. Provide the brainstorming criteria: Encourage the group to think of big ideas. This session isn't about testing feasibility, it's about dreaming of the possibilities. You are looking for "Blow the Roof Off" ideas. The only criterion is that the actions tie to the purpose.
3. Break Out and Brainstorm
   A. Break the group out into two separate groups, each with a facilitator
   B. Provide each of the groups "Brainstorming Buckets" to focus on during the session. Allow groups to spend ten to fifteen minutes brainstorming ideas for each bucket. Bucket ideas:
      - Open brainstorm (any ideas welcome!)
      - What might we do in the way of our Investments/ Philanthropy?
      - How might we amp up our means of Building Local Community?
      - How can we make employees feel valued?
      - What are the ways we can make customers feel valued?
      - What are Leadership Actions that could be taken?
      - What can we do to demonstrate our commitment to Social or Environmental Issues?
      - Are there new Products or Services we might offer?
      - Future Customer Experience

C. Kick off each Brainstorming Bucket using examples of companies that are strong in the particular area to encourage outside-the-box thinking. For instance, under the Investments/Philanthropy bucket, you might ask, "If JPMorgan Chase leaders were in our shoes, what types of investments would they make?" Or for Products, you might ask, "If CVS looked at our products and services, what would it eliminate, add, or focus on to deepen our purpose?"

D. Write down *all* brainstormed ideas throughout the session. After your group has shared ideas for each category, hold a vote to surface the top two ideas from each category. Write the ten ideas on a large flip chart.

4. Reconvene & Vote

A. Once each group has two ideas for every category, bring the groups back together to share and discuss each of the ideas. After groups share and discuss their ideas, provide each person with three sticky notes, each of them representing a vote. Have all participants vote on their top three ideas by placing them next to the ideas on the flip chart.

B. Take the top ten to twelve ideas to bring into the next phase of the process.

Build the case

After these ten to twelve actions are identified, it's time to test them further by building business cases. Reach out to a few members of your organization, particularly those with strong qualitative and quantitative skills, to help you develop those business cases.

Here is a sample template to help you in building the business case:

What is the potential Organizational Iconic Action?
How does the Action tie to the purpose?
Are there significant risks or potential legal ramifications in undertaking the action (financial, safety, ethical)?

Business/Financial	Customer/External
• What are the financial implications and risks for making this decision? • What are rough estimates of costs? • Would the action lead to long-term financial benefit?	• Would the action demonstrate to our customers that we are committed to them? • Does the action clearly benefit our customers and potential customers? • Can the action be communicated externally? Would the impact be significant if communicated? • Would the action clearly link our brand with our purpose?
Process/Internal	**People/Culture**
• Is the action feasible? • Who in the organization would be responsible for creating, communicating, and executing the action? • Would the action require Board approval? • Would the action require new practices, programs, and procedures or major shifts or changes to them?	• Would the action contribute to our employees feeling more connected to our organization? • Would the action demonstrate to our people that we are committed to our purpose? • Would the action demonstrate a shift in our culture? • Would the action be a reason for employees to stay or new employees to join our organization?
Suggestion/Recommendation from Team Member:	

Swim with the sharks

After the business cases have been built for each of the ideas, it's helpful to structure a business-pitch session. Think ABC's hit TV show *Shark Tank*, or any traditional startup pitch to potential investors. Have the project team pitch a business case for each Iconic Action to the final decision-makers. (These final decision-makers will likely be your company's senior executives, but if your leaders are willing to let the project team be part of the decision-making body, that is highly encouraged.) This process allows for a little levity leading up to the big decision, while also vetting all sides of the argument. Take the time to discuss each idea thoroughly, and assess the potential positive and negative impacts. Provide each decision-maker with twenty dollars of Monopoly Money to use to cast their votes at the end of the process, dividing their funds among any of the ideas as they see fit. The idea (or ideas) that attracts the most money is deemed the winner. Aim to walk out of the session with a "go" decision on one or two of these Iconic Actions.

Plan. Execute. Communicate. Celebrate.
Once the "go" decisions have been made, it's time to carefully plan. Identify the key stakeholders and functions that will be critical to pulling off the actions. Hold planning sessions to identify the necessary resources and best timing. Work with your communications and marketing teams to develop a strategy for internal and external messaging. With plans in place, set a date to pull the trigger. Make sure you are fully ready when the decision is executed. Organizational Iconic Actions pull a lot weight and credibility if done right, serving as proof that the organization is fully dedicated to delivering on its purpose. It's important to provide the proper amount of attention to these actions, taking the time to celebrate, communicate, and discuss them as an organization. Actions deeply rooted in purpose provide the opportunity to build momentum for an organization—spurring a natural chain of events within practices and individual actions that can help create a noble movement.

Creating High-Impact Practices

While Organizational Iconic Actions are outward-facing and -focused, much of the alignment process centers on internal programs that aren't necessarily visible to the outside world. Discovering high-impact internal practices to shift a culture toward becoming more nimble, focused, and feisty oftentimes takes the same creativity, dedication, and outside-the-box thinking as outward-directed actions. These new, innovative practices can have a profound influence on a culture, signaling to employees that the organization is structuring and making changes to provide employees greater opportunities to make an impact.

New practices should stem from your organizational narrative—meaning that they should satisfy at least one of the following:

- Provide opportunities for employees and leaders to deliver on the purpose and bring more purpose to their own work,
- Deepen and strengthen your organizational philosophy and mindsets; or
- Encourage decisions and actions that are aligned to the values.

Often during the Program Alignment Process, owners focus on opportunities to align existing processes and practices and overlook the possibility of creating new practices. Many of the creative practices that we've highlighted throughout the book don't necessarily have a clear "owner," which means that companies must actively ideate and pursue these practices.

Creating new practices requires commitment from those responsible for leading the organization through change. Senior leaders and those supporting the change need to embrace the idea of exploration and transformation.

As a framework, think of just a few of the practices we've discussed throughout the book and some key questions to ask when identifying new practices. I've grouped them by category (Nimble, Focused, Feisty) on the next several pages.

NIMBLE

Position to Pivot

- Cisco created a "Spin-In" process in which teams of engineers and developers work on specific projects and "launch" as if they are a startup.
- GE started FastWorks—a program geared toward operating more like a startup—and trained nearly 300 coaches across the business to drive the program forward.
- GE also launched the "Power of the Pivot" award to recognize those who are willing to explore, innovate, and pivot to new opportunities.

Co-Create and Collaborate

- Pixar set up small incubation teams to bring ideas to a point where they can be "sold" to top leadership. When a green light is given, a "brain trust" of senior and experienced leaders supports the production team to provide candid feedback and ideas, and the production team isn't required to change anything based on the feedback; this gives them a lot of autonomy.
- Thomson Reuters crowdsources ideas through internal competitions across the organization to find solutions to both big and small problems.

Structure for Speed

- HCL Technologies and Nordstrom "Invert the Pyramid" to provide their customer-facing employees the proper flexibility and support to make decisions that are in the best interest of the customer.
- Ritz-Carlton employees are authorized to spend up to $2,000 per incident on a customer at their own discretion to align with their motto of "Ladies and gentlemen serving ladies and gentlemen."
- Whole Foods has self-directed teams who meet regularly to discuss issues.

Key Questions to Ask

1. How can we encourage collaboration and drive decisions throughout our organization?
2. How can we reward and empower employees to make quicker and more self-guided decisions to best serve our customers?
3. What programs, processes, or structures can we eliminate or replace in order to become more nimble and agile?
4. How can we structure our teams and organization to be more flexible?

FOCUSED

Lead with Purpose

- CVS, along with banning the sale of tobacco products, changed its name from CVS Caremark to CVS Health, launched a smoking-cessation program, and created a technology-development center to build more customer-centric experiences.
- Roche infused the voice of the patient into its innovation and product development.
- Unilever ensures that an "authentic purpose" is at the core of its 400+ brands.

Keep the Customer Close

- Burberry shifted its focus toward the Millennial consumer, thereby driving its internal and external strategies.
- Old Navy talks about "Mike, Jenny, and the kids" constantly to remind leaders and employees of their target customers.
- John Deere offers an Executive Connect Program in which finance leaders work with their customers on a farm for a day.

Key Questions to Ask

1. How can we drive our purpose deeper through our products, people, and practices?
2. How can we design and refine our products and services to better serve our customers?
3. How can we shift our internal and external strategies to narrow in on our target customer?
4. How can we offer our non-customer-facing employees and leaders an opportunity to connect with customers?

FEISTY

Enable a Workforce That Is Bold and Plays Big

- Salesforce.com has a "Build Your Own Dream Team" event where potential job candidates are encouraged to bring a group of friends to a social hiring event.
- Many organizations utilize reverse mentoring, in which minorities or Millennials mentor top executives about skills or perspectives that they might be lacking.
- LinkedIn offers InDay events, where one Friday a month employees are allowed to work on projects and personal interests outside the responsibilities of their jobs.
- Novartis launched an online recognition program that allows employees to award points and prizes to other employees across the organization.

Key Questions to Ask

1. How can we clarify and drive the behaviors we expect of our people through the way we hire, fire, and promote? How can we create these practices to better represent the culture we want to create?
2. How can we drive more diversity of perspective throughout the organization?
3. What are creative ways to motivate our workforce outside of financial incentives?
4. How can we align and expand our employees' roles and responsibilities with their personal passions and purpose?
5. How can we celebrate and recognize our people in authentic, meaningful ways?

ALIGNMENT RECAP

Working to align organizational programs, practices, and processes is an emotionally trying and challenging process. It takes a strong commitment from stakeholders across the organization to shift programs that may be creating obstacles to the organization's desired future; it also takes outside-the-box thinking to drive the company's vision even further. But the work of alignment serves as evidence that the organization is committed to doing something different. While the process is challenging, it should also be fun and creative; it's about balancing small changes with more effective actions to propel the organization forward. Inevitably, however, the momentum begins to grow and internal movement begins to take place.

15

ENGAGE: SPARKING A MOVEMENT WITHIN YOUR PEOPLE

ENGAGEMENT IS THE LINCHPIN of culture change. When you engage your people, entrusting them to create and shape the culture you want, you encourage a movement to grow. This is especially the case when the work of Engage is done in concert with that of Lead and Align.

What do I mean by a movement? Let me explain first what I don't mean. For too long, we have approached engaging people or change management as an activity that is shallow. For example, we might get a few people together to form a project team and spend an afternoon thinking about what's best for our employees (rather than asking or involving them). Then, with that same team, we might proceed to create elaborate strategies and plans that drive top-down methods to get them to buy in to said change. But no matter how you look at the idea of "buy in," it still comes down to one person getting another person to accept his or her ideas. The premise requires a kind of coercion and salesmanship to best "position" what it is you want people to do. I believe there's a better way—giving people ownership. If you look at any successful movement through history, you will find that the people involved had a shared sense of purpose and conviction, and they felt compelled by that emotional investment and empowered to act by the trust put in them by leaders.

Are you familiar with the concept of push versus pull? Historically, much of what we have done in our organizations (or educational systems, or governments, or just about any institution, for that matter) has been predicated on the concept of "push." Our marketing programs, our social-media efforts, our employee communications, our leadership dictums, our change-management efforts (ahem) were built primarily to "speak at" people versus engage with them in a meaningful way. This notion of push treats everyone as a consumer or recipient of whatever it is that you're trying to "sell." Push programs deliberately try to limit choice and variance as much as possible. This approach encourages making everything a "one size fits all" solution. Pull, in contrast, considers individuals to be creators and active participants in the change, and provides them with the tools, resources, information necessary for them to "have it their way" and make the change personally meaningful.

Becoming an NFF organization requires this important shift in how you engage with your people. Customers are no longer willing to be passive recipients of what we decide to dish out to them; the same goes with our Difference Maker employees. This new dynamic transforms the act of communicating and learning from a passive, consumer-style activity to a much more active endeavor in which everyone involved is a co-creator.

In order to engage with employees more directly, it might be helpful to have a frame for thinking about what you're trying to "pull" others through. That is the path to embracing and actively participating as a co-creator in the culture. Below is my version of a "change curve." This is the path that people progress along while they're making change. While the point is to evoke each of your employees' sense of individual action and advocacy over time, that sense can't exist without a foundation of awareness, attitude, and ability. In this chapter I describe how to create this pull effect while taking employees along the path. Remember that it will take time and sustained energy to move people. Even inspiration doesn't have a lasting effect if it's not built upon and consistently demonstrated over time.

This movement must be anchored by the work you do to influence and connect others by creating conversation throughout the organization. For example, forums can be used to engage employees while inspiring them

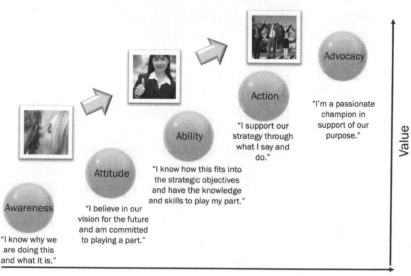

Time

and creating clarity around action. The secret is to give people permission, or the *pull*, to act on their own volition.

In this chapter, I'll talk about five important considerations for accomplishing this:

- Know your people
- Bring your narrative to life through storytelling
- Align people's work and embed specific behaviors
- Create a ripple effect through leveraging "networks"
- Create engaging and integrated experiences tied to your narrative

1) KNOW YOUR PEOPLE (ANALYZING YOUR STAKEHOLDERS)

The first step in the journey is to truly understand your employees so you know what actually "pulls" them rather than making sweeping assumptions like "our people are motivated only by money" or "our people are motivated by climbing the corporate ladder." Your objective is to understand who your people are, what makes them tick, what their concerns are, and where they're willing to go with you. Another objective is to identify the informal influencers within the organization who may be able to act as what I call "cultural frontrunners." I'll share more about that later in this chapter.

This type of "research" is different from the employee conversations and surveying I suggested in the "Envisioning Culture" phase. That work was about getting employees' perspectives about your culture, values, and organization. The work in this chapter is about getting to know your employees, who they are, and what activates their urge to act over their urge to comply.

Here are some of the key questions that are important to explore:

1. What do you value as an individual?
2. How would you describe yourself?
3. What motivates you?
4. What does a walk in your shoes look like?
5. What gets you out of bed in the morning?
6. Who or what influences your behavior?
7. What are your goals and aspirations?
8. What are your life priorities?

Let me share a few of the methods I recommend to uncover answers to these questions.

Surveys

Conducting a survey across a large sample of your employees is a good way to understand, at a collective level, the different types of people you have in your organization. With a survey you can manage engagement and communications more effectively.

To that end, once you collect the data, I highly encourage you to create "personas" from what you've uncovered in order to guide the way you will communicate with, engage with, and influence different types of people on a go-forward basis. A persona is essentially an informed summary of the mindset, needs, and goals that are held by your stakeholders, which in this case are your employees. They are fictional characterizations that are drawn from the actual research data. The best personas are typically composed of illustrations and descriptive text of the types of personas. From the data, you should be able to ascertain types by such broad characteristics as personal motivation, generational breakdown, etc., depending on what seems most meaningful and helpful. Putting a face to your findings makes your insights visible and usable by a broader set of people. This, in turn, creates more consistency in understanding across your organization.

You can find many examples of how to create personas from a wide array of books on the topic of design-thinking or human-centered design. I've essentially used that approach in the chapter on Difference Makers where I described the key set of qualities and attributes of a successful new-era worker. Even though I have generalized, this shouldn't prevent me from understanding these workers' uniqueness as individuals, including their strengths, views, motivators, and more. Coloring too broadly with one brush is a trap to avoid if you want to create real resonance with your people.

Polls

I think frequent polls are a good way to build deeper and more consistent conversation and trust in the organization. Of course to build this trust you have to commit to taking action on the data you're getting, but even conducting polls demonstrates to employees that you're interested in their input on an ongoing basis. With new technology tools such as Waggl, employees can easily be involved as part of the process. They can comment and also rate their peers' answers. Not only does polling help you get to know your employees, but it also creates conversation and engagement in the organization at the same time. Also, be specific. Consider what would happen if you were to pose a poll question to your employees such as, "In which ways do you feel proud and motivated by our organization's purpose?" The ensuing conversation would be very different than if you were to ask employees to rate how proud they feel about your purpose.

Manager Conversations and/or Team Conversations

It's always very powerful to have every one of your managers facilitate a discussion with each of their team members. It's a great way for managers to build the type of connections that I referred to in the Courageous Connector chapter and get more to the heart of what matters to their people. In fact, this is one of the most critical things you can ask your managers to do so they can help guide their team members to operate at their very best. Another good way to facilitate conversation is over a team meeting where you use questions as prompts for everyone to learn more about who their team members are and what matters to them. I find it's a great way to create more cohesion and connection among team members, which ultimately leads to better collaboration.

Observation

Immerse yourself in situations that your people experience. Observe what they're doing, how they are doing it, and what prompts their behavior. You'll find that careful observation provides valuable insight that you won't be able to get through conversations or surveys. Often people are likely to say or do things they're not aware of or wouldn't be able to express, even if prompted. The opportunity to watch and listen without interfering enables you to capture natural behavior. Pay close attention to things like tasks, how employees adjust depending on what they encounter, where they seem to light up or turn off, what they rely on to do their jobs, and more.

2) BRING YOUR NARRATIVE TO LIFE THROUGH STORYTELLING

Stories are fundamental to the "Engage" work you will do as an organization. Because stories are hard-wired into our psyche, they're often one of the most powerful ways to start to shift your culture. People have been passing information along through storytelling for as long as humans have had a rich language to draw from. Stories are a great way to connect people with ideas. A well-told story—focused on sharing pertinent details that express surprising meaning and underlying emotions—hits the head and the heart simultaneously.

There are two key considerations about storytelling I've found in my work. First, I believe a large percentage of the stories you surface should come directly from your employees. That's what's meaningful to them and will resonate with other employees best. Second, you need a multipronged approach for disseminating these stories across your organization.

There are many ways to go out and scour your organization for stories. You can hold a contest, facilitate the story-sharing process as a video series in which you interview employees, and even dig into your internal social network to find stories that people have posted. The most important consideration is that you're looking for stories of your purpose and values in action, not just any feel-good story. One of our clients was focusing a majority of its stories promoting employee community-service days. Although that can be a great message, our client was able to realize that it would be much more important to highlight stories of employees living the company's values in serving customers. This approach helped to cement that their organization was very focused on customer centricity.

Stories will show where your purpose and values are coming to life in your organization. They should describe what it looks like, in tangible detail, when someone is living your purpose and values, or when he is not.

On that latter point, one of our clients has been inadvertently showcasing stories of teams coming together to solve an urgent issue by staying at work for three days in a row. The problem was that these were the same team members who had actually created the problem. This perpetuated the belief that leadership rewarded intervention more than it valued the collaboration needed to get to the right solution in the first place. We helped our client go back out with another version of the story that fixed the mixed message. It can be very helpful to share stories rich with behaviors that uphold as well as deviate from your organizational values. This is a clear way to convey the behaviors and attitudes that matter.

Some additional considerations for story surfacing and sharing are:

- Video your leaders or have them present to employees in small groups, sharing their thoughts on the organization's philosophy with personal stories that illustrate it. The COO from one of our Fortune 50 clients once shared a very heartfelt story of his aging mother and how that connected him to the purpose of his company in the way it served elderly people in their time of need. Such stories often stand in stark contrast to the messages that leaders typically send about business objectives and results. Having them describe the organizational philosophy (the beliefs behind why and how we do what we do as an organization) casts leaders in a very human light and helps create more connection to them and the brand.
- Communicate stories of how you've aligned your organizational programs, practices, and processes with your purpose and values. For example, have you recently altered your performance

management to make it more aligned with what you say you value? Describe the impetus for that shift, the decisions made to get there, and any trade-offs involved. Such illustration helps everyone understand the struggle to balance difficult choices made as a company.

- Have employees share their stories of other employees over video, on your intranet, in hallway gatherings, in staff meetings, and in town halls. At Ritz-Carlton hotels, employees widely share stories about doormen, cleaning and maintenance staff, and other employees going above and beyond for customers or for one another.

- Find and correct false stories that are out there in the organization. Perhaps there is folklore about prior leadership beliefs that no longer applies. In one of our client organizations there were so many inaccurate legacy stories floating around that we had leadership do a global road show in the style of the "Mythbusters" television show. The leaders talked to employees about what they stood for and then played a game of "myth or truth." It was a fun, light-hearted way to set the record straight on what the organization stood for and the way that leadership would lead.

- Try setting up "story stations" in your respective functions, geographies, or locations. You can use an iPhone or video recorder to enable employees to capture sixty-second clips of themselves answering a few questions posed to them, then have them posted to a social network or sent back to their respective leaders to share. Ask them to answer questions such as, "Tell us about the last time you…" Or, "What was the best interaction you had with a customer? What did you do to solve the customer's need?"

Stories are the best indicators of your culture in action. They tend to be tangible in a way that helps people answer questions about what the culture at the company is like. Stories that are on-message and authentic to the culture you are aiming to create also help to build more cohesive, connected teams.

What stories could your employees tell that would show your culture in action?

3) ALIGN PEOPLE'S WORK
AND EMBED SPECIFIC BEHAVIORS

Culture efforts are often perceived as airy-fairy and disconnected from the actual work of an organization because they're missing alignment between people's work and specific behaviors. To correct this misperception, there are two things in particular I would recommend as must-do practices: create clarity of right action and create linkage to your employees' jobs and passions.

Create Clarity of Right Action

Often our culture efforts consist of communicating something to our employees like, "We need to be more innovative." To me, this is about as helpful as a USDA campaign that asks the American public to eat more healthfully. What does that even mean? It's non-specific, vague, and doesn't point to any key attitude, behaviors, or steps one would need to take. In other words, it's not giving people any guardrails for action. It also doesn't provide any forum to generate possibilities of what that term may mean, reinforcing the disconnect in how people might embrace and apply the imperative in their day-to-day lives.

My suggestion is to make sure that, by level and function, a few critical behaviors are established to support your guardrails and provide a linkage to what behaviors are expected. Then you are able to take those principles to employees to have them co-create what the principles will actually look like (and won't look like) when played out in their specific situation. Being vague or obtuse will hamper culture change as much as being dictatorial or overbearing. You want to create independence of thought and action in line with values, not strip your people of their ability to own and internalize what's right.

This approach gives employees the "pull" we discussed that puts them in the driver's seat for taking it to the next level and applying it.

Here's an example of how that can be applied to an organizational value around customer focus. I recommend that your guardrails be centered on laying out the critical behaviors you expect for each of your values.

Example organizational value Customer Focus			
Level in the organization	**Critical behavior**	**What it looks like**	**What it doesn't look like**
		This is where you would ask the leaders, managers, and employees to help define what this particular value would look like for their and others' level	
Senior leadership	To connect and take action: Empower front-line employees through two-way conversations describing their impact on customers, collecting their feedback, and following up on their ideas	• Share a customer story when explaining the impact an individual has on the customer journey and the company as a whole • Request that employees reveal complaints, issues, and improvement ideas • Implement ideas that will deliver high impact or give feedback as to why action will not be taken on an idea	• Solely talk about performance in terms of metrics • "Talk at" people without ever asking for their opinion, advice, or experiences • Gain insights only from talking with managers while avoiding the front line
Management	Enable employees: Ask and convey to employees how their decisions affect customers and how they are improving the customer experience to empower them, then share broadly	• Discuss customers first in every interaction • Publicly share stories to show how each employee's tasks enhance or hamper a customer's experience • Privately provide feedback and ask employees who diminish the customer experience what they can do differently	• Only discuss and review specific tasks and performance metrics • Encourage workarounds and heroics as the only way to get things done • Point the blame at someone else when issues occur or a consumer is not satisfied

Employees	Customer first: Put yourself in customer's shoes by asking "how does this affect the customer" and then empower yourself to do what is right for the customer	• First ask how the customer and his experience is affected • Think through and provide solutions to resolve the customer's issue the first time • Connect on a personal level and put yourself in the customer's situation	• Provide the easiest or a good-enough answer to pass the customer on, not the most viable one • Make the customer have to call or come back more than once • Treat each customer as an issue instead of a person

Your employees have the opportunity to weigh in on the "what it looks like" and the "what it doesn't look like" part. They also have the clear expectations but flexible parameters to decide how this particular value should come to life in terms of behaviors, practices, and attitudes for their respective functional areas and roles.

Create Linkage to Their Jobs and Passions

Getting to know who your employees are at a personal, individual level is likely a stretch for your organization, particularly if it's large. Intimacy is not usually a priority for most enterprises. In the past, we've sought only to understand how employees fit into the scheme of executing on our objectives, rather than how we help to execute on theirs. New-era companies think differently about this. They know it's more about enabling a give-give partnership than establishing a give-take relationship.

It's probably no surprise to you, however, that the design of employees' jobs can significantly shape how they find meaning and fulfillment in their work and even how well they do their work. Typically in most organizations, we think about a "job to be done" and outline a set of objectives, criteria, and tasks to be completed, and we set about hiring someone to fulfill precisely that—down to every single bullet item. At the University of Michigan, however, a professor has defined a new way of connecting a person's individual strengths and passions to the fulfillment of the organization's goals. It's called job-crafting, and it is a way to think about job design that puts employees in control of cultivating meaning in their work.

Old-era thinking says the best way to find more meaningful work is to find a new job. But the theory behind job-crafting points to something else—you can change the job you're in to better meet your needs. Employees can craft their roles through their tasks, their relationships, and their mindsets.

Task-crafting is about redesigning the tasks in a job. The relational aspect is about changing your relationships with coworkers, clients, and others in your environment. And mindsets are about changing the way employees perceive the tasks and relationships that make up their jobs. For example, a ticket agent could come to see her job as an essential part of providing people with entertainment, not just processing orders.

Some of the steps to do job-crafting include:

- Documenting and deconstructing the current job on a daily, weekly, and monthly basis, noticing where employees are spending their time and energy
- Concentrating on where changes might increase engagement by identifying motives, strengths, and passions—and creating a new diagram of how that role would better look to meet both individual and organizational purpose
- Considering the challenges in making this a reality by building a plan

On the next page is a worksheet that you may use to help your employees contemplate the intersection of their work and their passions, enabling such conversations to get rolling.

How do you currently spend your time at work?	What do you value? What motivates you?	How do you want to spend your time at work? (List main activities)
Most time	What are your interests? What do you like doing?	Most time
Medium time		Medium time
Least time	What are your strengths? What are you good at?	Least time
What's the smallest, quickest next step that you might take?		

If your managers have taken the steps to get to know their employees on an individual basis, this work will be a logical next step to help team members work and operate at their best. In my opinion, there is no point in asking the questions about who your employees are when they're at their best, what motivates them, and so on, if you're not going to use that information in the design of how you manage, communicate, and set roles and responsibilities.

There's a helpful set of tools and resources at www.jobcrafting.org.

4) CREATE A RIPPLE EFFECT THROUGH "NETWORKS"

Networks can flourish spontaneously in any setting but often they operate under the surface, making it hard to recognize and tap into them. Most large corporations have hundreds of informal networks, such as peer groups, communities of practice, employee resource groups, councils, or even more informal networks. Have you heard about the practice of social-network analysis (SNA) or organizational-network analysis (ONA)? I was introduced to this work some years back by Rob Cross, a professor at the University of Virginia. The SNA/ONA process maps and measures flows between people or things in a network, called nodes, as well as the ties that make up the relationships and interactions that connect those nodes.

It's fascinating to apply this analysis to an organization. How people actually operate and get things done in an organization has very little to do with formal organizational structure. In other words, organizational charts don't explain how the real work gets accomplished. In fact, often the formal organizational structure gets in the way. This approach is a way of identifying informal leaders, meaning people whom others go to because they may have an understanding of how things work around the company or why things are the way they are. These informal leaders may be people others listen to because they are deemed to be much more trustworthy and honest than their senior leaders.

Even without an intensive SNA exercise, asking the right questions of your employees gives you an opportunity to better understand who the "go-to" people are in the organization, as perceived by their peers. Informal influencers are highly respected individuals who can help your colleagues engage in your culture work. They help create "pull" rather than push.

When it comes to tapping into such people, it helps to leverage them as cultural frontrunners. Informal influencers shouldn't be relied on as mouthpieces for the change; rather they should be thought partners for the road ahead. Informal leaders' influence and authority would quickly dwindle if they were to appear to be doing the bidding of management. It's important to recruit and onboard these influencers to cut through the issues that are holding the culture back and drive forward the new ways that are going to make a big impact.

How do you "recruit" them? First you identify who they are by asking your people who is most influential to them while also asking leaders who they think personify the desired culture. From there such people should receive invitation letters describing the efforts, why they were nominated, and how the company wants them to help. Their participation should be voluntary. If they feel coerced, there won't be a good outcome. If they're able to opt in, then goodwill is created and trust is established. Most influencers, I've found, are eager to help and appreciate being involved. In the culture-transformation efforts we lead for clients, we leverage cultural frontrunners as one important factor for leading change in the organization. Throughout the culture-change process, they're brought together, asked for their ideas, prompted to take action, and given a lot of latitude to determine ways to get their peer groups inspired and actively involved in driving the purpose and cultural vision.

Leveraging Social Collaboration Technologies to Tap into Shared Purpose and Access Previously Hard-to-Reach Audiences

Over the last decade, new social-networking technologies have infiltrated our personal lives and businesses. While humans continually innovate and evolve new ways to communicate, these tools are particularly significant in tapping into the power of pull. They can help galvanize shared vision and action across large numbers of people or groups that are geographically far-flung, and contribute greatly to the momentum of change.

I referenced these tools earlier in the book. Remember how Sam Palmisano and his leadership team at IBM did their Values Jam? Undertaking something like this can be a powerful way to show employees that culture is created by them through their active involvement.

At one of our Fortune 100 retail clients, the CEO wanted to get more involved with employees to demonstrate the kind of open, candid culture of feedback he hoped to establish. Doing so was challenging, however, from a geographic and time standpoint. So, we encouraged him to create his own online community groups to talk directly with people instead. His All-Star Group, for example, is a select group of ten employees invited to be part of his virtual "sounding board" to solicit ideas and provide feedback on a quarterly basis. This group allows a store associate in Seattle, a district manager in Dallas, a corporate marketing associate at headquarters, and an IT engineer in Bangalore to interact together and provide their two cents to one another and their CEO. This CEO also listens carefully to the contributions that associates are making each day in the community and is an active commenter and contributor. Such efforts translate into tremendous employee loyalty and enthusiasm and help all employees benefit from the CEO's contributions and participation.

Networking also helps where standard communications can't. In the summer of 2007, for example, Richard Schulze, chairman of Best Buy, went to his board of directors with an unusual problem. Employees earning less than $80,000 weren't buying into the company's retirement plan. Only 18 percent had a 401k plan, a percentage sure to attract unwelcome questions from the IRS.

The majority of Best Buy's employees are between the ages of sixteen and twenty-four, so as you can imagine generally they were turned off by anything with the word "retirement" in its title. Instead of just shoving more HR-speak and corporate communication down their throats about the importance of signing up and investing in their future, Best Buy worked to adopt the language and culture of these Millennials.

They put up a call on their internal social-networking site, "Blue Shirt Nation," asking employees to make five- to seven-minute videos translating the new 401k into something that was meaningful to them, easy to understand and compelling to their peers. The winning Starsky and Hutch–style video helped participation in the 401k plan jump from 18 to 47 percent.

5) CREATE ENGAGING EXPERIENCES TIED TO YOUR NARRATIVE

Engaging experiences can be important catalysts for creating breakthroughs in your culture. In my definition, an experience is active participation in an event that leads to mastery, knowledge, or emotion. In other words, involvement or exposure should lead to learning by actually feeling and doing something versus just hearing about something. This approach is exponentially more powerful than having something communicated to employees during a town hall meeting and much more meaningful than a motivational speech to all your employees. Being part of an experience creates beliefs that, when channeled properly, create commitment and action. Remember how I described the Leadership Lab that Starbucks does for its managers? Bringing tens of thousands of their people together to spread cultural gospel also creates community and deeper knowledge.

When we help our clients to create experiences, we believe it's important they meet these requirements. Forums should:

- Be shaped to get people to rally around the purpose—to really own it, shape, and live it, versus just hear or learn about it
- Create shared context by taking the organizational values and creating alignment, meaning, and zealous commitment to them

- Be hopeful, inspirational, fun, and work to mobilize resources to find solutions and take action

You can look at experiences in many different ways. It's important to test whether or not you're giving people the opportunity to immerse and learn and adopt new beliefs through actually doing something. Let me share a few examples to give you an idea:

A New Employee Experience to Immerse in the Culture Quickly

One of our clients, a large, global apparel retailer, was having two primary issues when it came to hiring and onboarding new employees. The first was unusually rapid employee churn (as in, many new hires were no-shows after the first few days of employment), and the second was that new employees were either not a good cultural fit or were taking a long while to get the culture ingrained.

By auditing the company's organizational practices and programs, we saw that the new-employee orientation (NEO)—which was the initial impression and representation of the brand to these new associates—was lackluster, uninspiring, and disconnected from what new employees needed to be able to do immediately in their roles, and didn't surface what made the company's culture special in an engaging way. The existing NEO seemed like a 1950s "instructor with a manual" approach. To top it off, this old-school approach was being provided to what was largely an audience of Millennials, who were their most frequent recruits. My team's role was to facilitate the numerous stakeholders (leadership, store operations, training and development, HR, marketing, representative store managers, and a group of new employees) to collaboratively conceptualize a new employee experience that was interactive, rich with storytelling and sharing, and immersive. The new multiday employee experience would be told through a magazine, as if the new associates were journalists reporting on everything they were learning about the brand. It was rich with immersive experiences that had never been part of the previous NEO. For example, we incorporated a fun "Fitologist" training so that associates could try on all the different types of jeans to find their best fit, enabling them to consult with customers in the same way. As part of this, the new employees did a mini fashion show displaying and describing the qualities of the jeans to the other associates. Next, we developed a 30/60/90 day plan for store managers and training managers to leverage with these new associates. At thirty days, new employees had a "walk-along" with their store manager so they could get more guidance and insight in real-time on creating just the right customer experience. At ninety days, the new employees came back together for a session to share stories and lessons learned from their first three months. These are the kinds of things that imprint a culture and demonstrate to employees what the organization stands for and cares about.

An Experience to Create Community and Connection to the Values

To spark community and mobilize people around a "culture of helping" at one of our Fortune 100 clients, we sent out a call to action to employees to join an impromptu "flash mob wave" around the United States. The recently popular song lyrics from "Happy" by Pharrell Williams were turned to "Helping." Every team, function, and geography was instructed on the dance moves, and told to change the last line to describe the unique commitment they were making to help their colleagues and customers. There was huge participation and people talked about it for months. It helped to spark community, showed that the organization was about having fun while working hard, and gave organizational values more personal meaning and substance.

Creating Connection with Your Purpose and Values

In our work, we're constantly trying to determine how employees can engage with an organization's purpose and values in heartfelt, emotion-evoking ways. At one of our clients, we recently sent the top sixty leaders in the company on the road to visit every single one of the company sites and locations. Those leaders weren't tasked to go out and do a typical "road show" or town hall meeting but rather a session jointly facilitated with the regional leadership and management teams to help bring the organization's narrative to life in a meaningful way for employees. We picked sixty leaders, a fairly sizable group, to ensure that all locations could participate within two months. That strategy helped to reinforce that it was the responsibility of all leaders to get out there and model the purpose. And employees had the chance to see a new leader whom they may have never seen before.

Each of these three-hour sessions with employees was designed to uncover bright spots (where the desired culture was already showing up in the organization) and surface barriers (the biggest roadblocks). Part of it was done through an immersive storytelling session in which employees in smaller groups shared what purpose meant to them and how they created emotional connection with their customers. At all of the sessions, most of the stories were captured in real-time through videos. At one of the larger sessions, a twenty-foot mural was drawn by a graphic recorder in real-time. We coupled the mural with the stories surfaced from across the entire organization to create a video and story collage that inspired and engaged the company's thousands of employees.

BRINGING CULTURE TO LIFE

When it comes to culture change, it's easy to see large organizations as monolithic and made up of largely anonymous groups and forces. But we all know that the people we work with make the difference in how we think about an organization, the good times we share, the challenges we meet together, and the sense of purpose, community, and meaning we create. Engagement is a way of activating those feelings strategically and deliberately in order to effect the change you are seeking to make. In the process, I have seen over and over how it can bring the people of an organization together, renewing their sense of belonging and emotional connection with their coworkers, leaders, and customers. It's the glue that binds us together even as it provides us with the energy that makes the work worthwhile.

CONCLUSION

THE END OF HOW AND THE START OF WHY NOT

IF YOU'VE EVER WORKED for a company when a new CFO comes on board, you may know the feeling. Something big and fundamental is likely going to change. Such was the case at Google—the biggest, most freewheeling of Silicon Valley cultures—when Ruth Porat, former Morgan Stanley CFO and thirty-year veteran of Wall Street, was hired in May 2015 with a $70 million pay package. Wall Street was practically giddy with the news. Finally, financial discipline would be instilled. Some of those crazy moon-shot projects would be shelved. Google would have to deliver consistent performance and shareholder returns more in line with an ordinary company.[1]

Not so fast. A few months later, Google showed how little it cared for ordinary thinking. If anything, Porat's hiring and the disciplines she instilled fortified the company for a new beginning rather than an ending. Google CEO Larry Page announced in stunning fashion that Google would reorganize in August 2015. Google itself would be one subsidiary of a larger holding company called Alphabet. This was done not to kill all those moon shots and side businesses but to give them even more autonomy and agility. As Timothy Lee noted on Vox, "Page and Brin believe that these projects have become too diverse and sprawling for a single operating company to manage all of them effectively. Different projects require different types of leaders, different company cultures, and different types of resources." Or, as Page himself put it, "'We've long believed that over time companies tend to get comfortable doing the same thing, just making incremental changes. But in the technology industry, where revolutionary ideas drive the next big growth areas, you need to be a bit uncomfortable to stay relevant."[2]

To me, this news also said something very clearly: Google knows that to stay "nimble, focused, and feisty," it must ensure that its culture—or cultures—can sustain and amplify that kind of energy.

Right now, that is the winning play: companies that deliberately foster and leverage their culture as a strategic tool to be nimble, focused, and feisty are leading in the new economy. Will that work forever? Given the VUCA forces that show no signs of loosening their grip on the global market, I don't see the supremacy of NFF cultures ending soon. Regardless of what does show up around the next corner, however, I believe that culture-savvy organizations like Google will react more quickly and appropriately to continue to succeed. Such organizations are, in a very real sense, built to thrive.

I started this book talking about GE. Despite many decades of success, GE continues to reinvent itself actively: right now, it's instilling a renewed culture of innovation focusing more deliberately on customers. I've spent a lot of time praising Netflix, and I've enjoyed how it continues to focus on culture internally—by adopting some of the most progressive people-practices of any company in operation today—while innovating externally, taking on entrenched competitors in cable TV to secure its own future and better meet customer demand.

My point is not to say that these successful companies will always be leading from the front. My point is that they want to be at the front so they work constantly on the culture that gets them there. Culture is the longest and most valuable play any organization or business can make. Period. It's the code that gets passed from year to year, from person to person, that builds the fabric, resiliency, adaptability, and soul of an organization, guiding everyone on how to think, act, and make decisions so that the business is positioned and equipped to thrive.

Why else would a company like Apple refuse to rest on its laurels? Culture has been a big part of Apple's phenomenal success in its second iteration. Yet, Apple under Tim Cook continues to evolve and enrich that culture to keep the company renewed and invigorated.

Most recently, Cook recruited and ultimately lured Angela Ahrendts to run Apple's retail and online operations. Yes, that Angela Ahrendts, the leader I mentioned in chapter seven who transformed Burberry as its CEO.

A recent in-depth *Fortune* article, "What the Heck Is Angela Ahrendts doing at Apple?"[3] reveals a lot about Apple's evolving philosophy.

Cook didn't just hire Ahrendts for her retail savvy—after all, Apple's stores are the most profitable in the world—but rather for her leadership. He brought her on because even though Apple is a company where transformative hits have become routine, the leaders know they are not immune to the complacency that has felled many legendary companies before.

This is what it means to build a culture that is your source for growth, resiliency, and adaptability—a constant "why not" in a world that continues to operate in "what." The latter breed of companies focuses primarily on out-producing, out-supply-chaining, and out-operationalizing their competition, but will never beat an Apple that way.

Cook and Ahrendts have big plans. They're still mum on how it will all unfold but they are dreaming of ways that the company can continue to dominate and act as an even greater force for social change through their retail stores. Apple has always intended for those stores to be community centers and to expand from serving existing and potential customers to creating opportunities for underserved minorities and women. Cook believes that Ahrendts can get this right. Please note that Cook, himself, did not get this right the first time. Before Ahrendts, Cook hired John Browett, but realized quickly he wasn't a "cultural fit." Browett was used to running chains with thinner margins and he inflamed Apple's staff by cutting hours and benefits. Sound like a potential Blockbuster Video/ James Keyes kinda moment? Yet, because Apple is "nimble, focused, and feisty," Cook didn't let that happen. He adjusted quickly and moved on. Ahrendts has already improved morale with communication, new career-development paths, and good old empathy.

The lesson is that culture is always a work in progress. That's the good news and the bad news. As a leader, you are gifted with the opportunity to constantly shape your culture and nurture it, but you also have to constantly spend energy and resources doing so. Is it worthwhile? I believe so. At its simplest, culture can either be a backpack full of rocks weighing you down, or a jetpack that keeps you moving and pivoting as it lifts you up and propels you forward.

I hope this book has shown you how to strap that jetpack on and begin to soar.

NOTES

Introduction: Why How Beats What

1 "Fortune 500 firms in 1955 vs. 2014; 88% are gone, and we're all better off because of that dynamic 'creative destruction'" by Mark J. Perry, *American Enterprise Institute*, Aug. 2014. http://www.aei.org/publication/fortune-500-firms-in-1955-vs-2014-89-are-gone-and-were-all-better-off- because-of-that-dynamic-creative-destruction

2 "The Profit Power of Corporate Culture" by Sean Silverthorne, *Harvard Business School Working Knowledge*, Sept. 2011. http://hbswk.hbs.edu/item/6818.html

3 "Tom Peters True Confessions," by Tom Peters, *Fast Company*, Nov. 2001. http://www.fastcompany.com/44077/tom-peterss-true-confessions.

4 "Jack Welsh Tackles Immelt's Tenure, Hillary's Bid and Ted Cruz's Chances" by Gregg Greenberg, *The Street*, April 2015. http://www.thestreet.com/story/13112115/1/jack-welch-tackles-immelts-tenure-hillarys- bid-and-ted-cruzs-chances.html

5 "Jeffrey Immelt is Putting His Own Stamp on Jack Welch's G.E." by Steve Lohr, *The New York Times*, April 2015. http://www.nytimes.com/2015/04/14/business/jeffrey-immelt-with-new-challenges-refashions- jack-welchs-ge.html?_r=0

6 "GE's Culture Challenge After Welch and Immelt" by Raghu Krishnamoorthy, *Harvard Business Review*, January 2015. https://hbr.org/2015/01/ges-culture-challenge-after-welch-and-immelt

7 Ibid

8 *How Google Works*, by Eric Schmidt and Jonathan Rosenberg, Grand Central Publishing, 2014. p. 28

9 Ibid, p.62

Chapter 1: How Culture Makes or Breaks You

1 "How I Did It: Blockbuster's Former CEO on Sparring with an Activist Shareholder" by John Antioco, *Harvard Business Review*, April 2011. https://hbr.org/2011/04/how-i-did-it-blockbusters-former-ceo-on- sparring-with-an-activist-shareholder

2 "When Blockbuster Forgot What Business They Were In," by Dain Dunston, *DainDunston.com*. http://daindunston.com/when-blockbuster-forgot-what-business-they-were-in/

3 R. Duane Ireland, Robert Hoskisson, and Michael Hitt, *Understanding Business Strategy: Concepts and Cases, Second Edition* South-Western College Publishers (2008) p.C-30 and C-31

4 Ibid.

5 "Blockbuster: The Customer Owns Your Purpose" by Dain Dunston, *DainDunston.com*.http://daindunston.com/blockbuster-the-customer-owns-your-purpose

6 "Snoozing and Losing: A Blockbuster Failure" by MG Siegler, *Tech Crunch*, April 2011. http://techcrunch.com/2011/04/06/make-it-a-blockbuster-night

7 "My Thoughts on the Demise of Blockbuster" by Bob Duncan, *Bobby Dunx (blog)*, November 2013. https://bobbydunx.wordpress.com/2013/11/17/my-thoughts-on-the-demise-of-blockbuster

8 "Why Blockbuster Failed Personal Experience," *Leatherwing* Media, October 2015.

9 "How Netflix Reinvented HR" by Patty McCord, *Harvard Business Review,* Jan./Feb. 2014. https://hbr.org/2014/01/how-netflix-reinvented-hr

10 "Nike: The No. 1 Most Innovative Company" by Whitney Pastorek, *Fast Company,* Feb. 2013. http://www.fastcompany.com/most-innovative-companies/2013/nike

11 "Hitting the Mark: Ensuring Your Omnichannel Strategies Cater to Today's Shopper" by Meyar Sheik, *Certona.* http://www.certona.com/newsroom/hitting-the-mark-ensuring-your-omnichannel-strategies-cater- to-today-s-shopper

12 "Big Demands and High Expectations: The Deloitte Millennial Survey," *Deloitte,* Jan. 2014. http://www2.deloitte.com/content/dam/Deloitte/global/Documents/About-Deloitte/2014_MillennialSurvey_ExecutiveSummary_FINAL.pdf

13 "Why Millennials Are Ending the 9 To 5" by Kate Taylor, *Forbes,* Aug. 2013. http://www.forbes.com/sites/katetaylor/2013/08/23/why-millennials-are-ending-the-9-to-5

14 "Organizational Culture Matters on the Bottom Line: Evidence from the High-Tech Industry" by Jennifer Chatman, Hass School of Business, University of California Berkeley, Sept. 20, 2012. http://newsroom.haas.berkeley.edu/research-news/my-research-organizational-culture-matters-bottom-line-evidence-high-tech-industry

15 "Engineering Culture at Airbnb," by Mike Curtis, *Airbnb,* June 2014. http://nerds.airbnb.com/engineering-culture-airbnb

16 "The Rise and Inglorious Fall of Myspace" by Felix Gillette, *Bloomberg Businessweek,* June 2011. http://www.bloomberg.com/bw/magazine/content/11_27/b4235053917570.htm

17 $99,970,000,000 Is the Difference Between These 3 Decisions" by Nick Hughes, *Business Insider,* June 2011. http://www.businessinsider.com/999970000000-is-the-difference-between-these-3-decisions-2011-6

18 "Silicon Valley's Most Important Document Ever" by Janko Roettgers, *Gigaom,* Jan. 2013. https://gigaom.com/2013/01/29/netflix-company-culture

19 "How Netflix Reinvented HR" by Patty McCord, *Harvard Business Review, Jan./Feb. 2014.* https://hbr.org/2014/01/how-netflix-reinvented-hr

Chapter 2: A Different Mindset

1 "The Problem with the Founder's Letter" by Kevin Kelleher, *Fortune,* Feb. 2012. http://fortune.com/2012/02/03/the-problem-with-the-founders-letter

2 *How Google Works,* by Eric Schmidt and Jonathan Rosenberg, Grand Central Publishing, 2014. p. 23

3 Ibid, p. 5

4 Ibid, p. 20

5 Ibid, p. 166

6 http://www.brainyquote.com/quotes/quotes/m/marioandre109743.html

7 "Zuckerberg Claims 'We Don't Build Services to Make Money'" by Larry Magid, *Forbes,* Feb. 2012. http://www.forbes.com/sites/larrymagid/2012/02/01/zuckerberg-claims-we-dont-build-services-to-make- money/

8 "Amazon Profits Fall 45 Percent, Still the Most Amazing Company in the World" by Matthew Yglesias, *Slate,* Jan. 29. http://www.slate.com/blogs/moneybox/2013/01/29/amazon_q4_profits_fall_45_percent.html

9 "Jeff Bezos Explains Amazon's Strategy for World Domination" by Matthew Yglesias, *Slate,* April 2013. http://www.slate.com/blogs/moneybox/2013/04/12/amazon_as_corporate_charity_jeff_bezos_says_there_s_a_method_to_the_madness.html

10 "Amazon Profits Fall 45 Percent, Still the Most Amazing Company in the World" by Matthew Yglesias, *Slate,* Jan. 29. http://www.slate.com/blogs/moneybox/2013/01/29/amazon_q4_profits_fall_45_percent.html

11 *How Google Works,* by Eric Schmidt and Jonathan Rosenberg, Grand Central Publishing, 2014. p. 5

12 Ibid, p. 214

13 Ibid, p. 223

14 Ibid, p. 224

15 Ibid, p. 224

16 "How Companies Can Profit from a "Growth Mindset," *Harvard Business Review,* Nov. 2014. https://hbr.org/2014/11/how-companies-can-profit-from-a-growth-mindset

17 "Detroit's Dilemma" by Will Oremus, *Slate,* July 2014. http://www.slate.com/blogs/future_ tense/2014/07/01/detroit_vs_google_self_driving_cars_and_the_innova tor_s_dilemma.html
18 Ibid.
19 "Microsoft (Yes, Microsoft) Has a Far-Out Vision" by Nick Wingfield, *The New York Times,* April 2015. http://mobile.nytimes.com/2015/05/03/technology/microsoft-yes-microsoft-has-a- far-out-vision.html?_r=0
20 Ibid.

Chapter 3: They Position to Pivot

1 "Nokia's New Chief Faces Culture of Complacency" by Kevin J. O'Brien, *The New York Times,* Sept. 2010. http://www.nytimes.com/2010/09/27/technology/27nokia. html?pagewanted=all&_r=0
2 "Nokia," *Wikipedia.* http://en.wikipedia.org/wiki/Nokia
3 "Pivot, Don't Jump To a New Vision," by Eric Ries, *Startup Lessons Learned (Blog),* June 2009. http://www.startuplessonslearned.com/2009/06/pivot-dont-jump-to-new-vision.html
4 Ibid.
5 Ibid.
6 "Build a Change Platform, Not a Change Program" by Gary Hamel and Michele Zanini, *McKinsey & Company,"* October 2014. http://www.mckinsey.com/insights/organization/ build_a_change_platform_not_a_change_program
7 "Cisco's CEO on Staying Ahead of Technology Shifts" by John Chambers, *Harvard Business Review,* May 2015. https://hbr.org/2015/05/ciscos-ceo-on-staying-ahead-of-technology-shifts
8 "Behind GE's Vision For the Industrial Internet of Things" by Jon Gertner, *Fast Company,* June 2014. http://www.fastcompany.com/3031272/can-jeff-immelt-really-make-the-world-1-better
9 "How GE Teaches Teams to Lead Change" by Steven Prokesch, *Harvard Business Review,* Jan. 2009. https://hbr.org/2009/01/how-ge-teaches-teams-to-lead-change
10 "The Immelt Revolution" by Diane Brady, *Bloomberg,* Marcy 2005. http://www.bloomberg. com/bw/stories/2005-03-27/the-immelt-revolution
11 "The Biggest Startup: Eric Ries and GE Team Up to Transform Manufacturing" by Thomas Kellner, *GE Reports,* Dec. 2013. http://www.gereports.com/post/82723688100/the-biggest- startup-eric-ries-and-ge-team-up-to
12 "General Electric Wants to Act Like a Startup" by Rick Clough, *Bloomberg,* Aug. 2014. http://www.businessweek.com/articles/2014-08-07/ge-taps-lean-startup-ideas-for-faster- cheaper-product- rollout
13 "The Open Secret of Success" by James Surowiecki, *The New Yorker,* May 2008. http://www. newyorker.com/magazine/2008/05/12/the-open-secret-of-success
14 "Lessons from Toyota's Long Drive" by Thomas A. Stewart and Anand P. Raman, *Harvard Business Review,* July/Aug. 2007. https://hbr.org/2007/07/lessons-from-toyotas-long-drive/es
15 "The Open Secret of Success" by James Surowiecki, *The New Yorker,* May 2008. http://www. newyorker.com/magazine/2008/05/12/the-open-secret-of-success
16 "Toyota: The Birth of the Prius" by Alex Taylor III, *CNN Money,* Feb. 2006. http://money. cnn.com/2006/02/17/news/companies/mostadmired_fortune_toyota
17 "Toyota Celebrates 10 Years of Prius," *Toyota,* July 2010. http://toyotanews.pressroom.toyota. com/article_display.cfm?article_id=2033
18 "Worldwide Sales of Toyota Hybrids Top 6 Million Units," *Toyota,* Jan. 2014. http://corporatenews. pressroom.toyota.com/releases/worldwide+toyota+hybrid+sales+top+6+million.htm
19 "Atoms can be in two places at the same time," Universität Bonn, *Science Daily,* Jan. 2015 http://www.sciencedaily.com/releases/2015/01/150120085919.htm
20 "11 Rules for Creating Value in the #SocialEra" by Nilofer Merchant, *NiloferMerchant.com.* http://nilofermerchant.com/library/socialera

Chapter 4: They Structure for Speed

1 "The Thought Leader Interview: Vineet Nayar" by Art Kleiner and Vikas Sehgal, *Strategy+Business,* Oct. 2010. http://www.strategy-business.com/article/10410
2 "Linda A. Hill on the Creative Power of the Many" by Jen Swetzoff, *Strategy+Business,* March 2015. http://www.strategy-business.com/article/00315

3 "Building Organizations That Work" by Susan Greenberg. *Stadford Business*, Aug. 2012. https://www.gsb.stanford.edu/insights/building-organizations-work

4 "Elliot Jaques Levels With You" by Art Kleiner, *Strategy+Business*, Jan. 2001. http://www.strategy-business.com/article/10938?gko=f119b

5 "How Companies Can Learn to Make Faster Decisions" by Eric Winquist, *Harvard Business Review*, Sept. 2014. https://hbr.org/2014/09/how-space-x-learned-to-make-faster-decisions

6 "The Evolution of Decision Making: How Leading Organizations Are Adopting a Data-Driven Culture," *Harvard Business Review*. https://hbr.org/resources/pdfs/tools/17568_HBR_SAS%20Report_webview.pdf

7 "How Ritz-Carlton Stays at the Top" by Robert Reiss, *Forbes*, Oct. 2009. http://www.forbes.com/2009/10/30/simon-cooper-ritz-leadership-ceonetwork-hotels.html

8 "The Secrets of Generation Flux" by Robert Safian, *Fast Compnay*, Oct. 2012. http://www.fastcompany.com/3001734/secrets-generation-flux

9 "Great Intrapreneurs in Business History" by Jake Swearingen, *CBS Money Watch*, June 2008. http://www.cbsnews.com/news/great-intrapreneurs-in-business-history

10 "Whole Foods Case Study: A Benchmark Model of Management for Hospitality" by Arturo Cuenllas, *Hospitality Net*, Feb. 2013. http://www.hospitalitynet.org/news/4059396.html

11 "Whole Foods—A Discipline Democracy," *Freibergs*. http://www.freibergs.com/resources/articles/accountability/whole-foods-a-disciplined-democracy

12 "Inside GitHub's Super-Lean Management Strategy—And How It Drives Innovation" by Chris Dannen, *Fast Company*, Oct. 2013. http://m.fastcompany.com/3020181/open-company/inside-githubs-super-lean- management-strategy-and-how-it-drives-innovation

13 "Red Hat CEO: How I traded Top-Down Mandates for 'Open' Decision-Making" by Heather Clancy, *Fortune*, June 2015. http://fortune.com/2015/06/06/red-hat-ceo-open-organization

14 "This U.K. Company Offered Its Employees Unlimited Vacation Time. It Was a Total Failure" by Jessica Stillman, *Slate*, July 2015. http://www.slate.com/blogs/moneybox/2015/07/14/unlimited_vacation_time_this_company_tried_it_and_it_was_a_total_failure.html

Chapter 5: They Solve Problems by Co-Creating and Collaborating

1 "Apollo 13: A Dying Ship and a Crew Fighting for Life" by Nick Greene, *About*, Oct. 2015. http://space.about.com/od/spaceexplorationhistory/a/apollo13_2.htm

2 "Apollo 13: Facts About NASA's Near-Disaster" by Elizabeth Howell, *Space.com*, Aug. 2012. http://www.space.com/17250-apollo-13-facts.html

3 "Jim Collins on Tough Calls" by Jerry Useem, *Fortune*, June 2005. http://archive.fortune.com/magazines/fortune/fortune_archive/2005/06/27/8263408/index.htm

4 2007, the Economist Intelligence Unit published a paper entitled, Collaboration: Transforming the way business works

5 "Eight Ways to Build Collaborative Teams" by Lynda Gratton and Tamara J. Erickson, *Harvard Business Review*, Nov. 2007. https://hbr.org/2007/11/eight-ways-to-build-collaborative-teams

6 "The Wisdom of Crowds," *All About Psychology*. http://www.all-about-psychology.com/the-wisdom-of- crowds.html

7 "Rethinking Group Projects with "Who Wants to Be a Millionaire?" by Brian Robben, *Take Your Success*, Feb. 2015. http://www.takeyoursuccess.com/rethinking-college-group-projects-with-who-wants-to-be-a- millionaire

8 "Thomson Reuters Uncovers Internal Engineering Talent with Crowdsourcing" by Nicole Laskowsk, *Tech Target*, April 2014. http://searchcio.techtarget.com/opinion/Thomson-Reuters-flushes-out-internal- engineering-talent-with-crowdsourcing

9 "Ask Your Customers for Predictions, Not Preferences" by Julie Wittes Schlack, *Harvard Business Review*, Jan. 2015. https://hbr.org/2015/01/ask-your-customers-for-predictions-not-preferences

10 Ibid.

11 "Collaborative Relationships, A Mammoth Achievement!" by Neil A. Walker, *PPM Practitioner (Blog)*, March 2013. https://ppmpractitioner.wordpress.com/2013/03/10/collaborative-relationships

12 "How Pixar Helped Jobs build a More Collaborative Apple" by Luke Dormehl, *Cult of Mac*, March 2015. http://www.cultofmac.com/315770/how-pixar-helped-jobs-build-a-more-collaborative-apple

Chapter 6: They Lead with Purpose

1 "History of Kaiser Permanente," *Kaiser Permanente.* http://share.kaiserpermanente.org/article/history-of- kaiser-permanente http://kaiserpermanentehistory.org/wp-content/uploads/2015/03/GaintnerKPShortHistory.pdf

2 "Fast Facts About Kaiser Permanente," *Kaiser Permanente,* March 2016. http://share.kaiserpermanente.org/article/fast-facts-about-kaiser-permanente

3 http://faculty.washington.edu/janegf/buildingvision.html

4 "Netflix Adds a Record 3.3 Million New Subscribers, Continuing a Blowout Year" by Ben Popper, *The Verge,* July 2015. http://www.theverge.com/2015/7/15/8974557/netflix-q2-2015-earnings-record- subscriber-growth

5 "Purpose is Good. Shared Purpose Is Better" by Mark Bonchek, *Harvard Business Review,* March 2013. https://hbr.org/2013/03/purpose-is-good-shared-purpose

6 http://www.cvshealth.com/newsroom/press-releases/pharmacy-services-corporate-info-events/cvs-caremark-stop-selling-tobacco

7 "Why Did CVS Stop Selling Cigarettes? Because It Wants to Be taken Seriously as a Health Care Company." by Jordan Weissmann, *Slate,* Sept. 2014. http://www.slate.com/blogs/moneybox/2014/09/03/cvs_stops_selling_cigarettes_it_wants_to_be_taken_ser iously_as_a_healthcare.html

8 "CVS Health: Financial Incentives Help Smokers Quit" by Mike Hower, *Sustainable Brands,* May 2015. http://www.sustainablebrands.com/news_and_views/behavior_change/mike_hower/cvs_health_finds_finan cial_incentives_help_people_quit_smo

9 "Pharmacy Giant CVS Health Will Open Digital Innovation Lab in Boston" by Scott Kirsner, *Beta Boston,* Nov. 2014. http://www.betaboston.com/news/2014/11/17/pharmacy-giant-cvs-health-will-open-digital- innovation-lab-in-boston

10 "CVS Revenues Up After Cigarette Sales Ban" by Laura Sampler, *Time,* Nov. 2014. http://time.com/3557120/cvs-revenues-increase-after-cigarette-ban

11 "Gap Raising Its Minimum Pay" by Chris Isidore, *CNN Money,* Feb. 2014. http://money.cnn.com/2014/02/20/news/companies/gap-minimum-wage

12 "13 Companies That Aren't Waiting for Congress to Raise the Minimum Wage" by Jenny Che, *The Huffington Post,* April 2015. http://www.huffingtonpost.com/2015/04/02/companies-minimum- wage_n_6991672.html

13 "Sans Artificial: General Mills Scrambles To Reformulate Lucky Charms" by Allison Aubrey, *NPR,* June 2015. http://www.npr.org/sections/thesalt/2015/06/22/416486286/sans-artificial-general-mills- scrambles-to-reformulate-lucky-charms

14 "Why I Started Crohnology," *Crohnology.com,* 2016. https://crohnology.com/about

15 "Empathy and Drug Development – Listening to Sheila Babnis" by Julie Anixter, *Innovation Excellence,* Feb. 2015. http://www.innovationexcellence.com/blog/2015/02/10/empathy-and-drug-development- listening-to-sheila-babnis

16 "Innovation Starts with the Heart, Not the Head" by Gary Hamel, *Harvard Business Review,* June 2015. https://hbr.org/2015/06/you-innovate-with-your-heart-not-your-head

17 "Interview: Unilever's Paul Polman on Diversity, Purpose and Profits" by Jo Confino, *The Guardian,* Oct. 2013. http://www.theguardian.com/sustainable-business/unilver-ceo-paul-polman-purpose-profits

18 "Unilever's Corporate Challenge: Fine Purpose or Perish" by Phillip Haid, *Financial Post,* May 2014. http://business.financialpost.com/entrepreneur/unilevers-corporate-challenge-find-purpose-or-perish

19 "Unilever Boss Paul Polman Slams Capitalist Obsession With Profit" by Rebecca Burn-Callander, *The Telegraph,* Jan. 2015. http://www.telegraph.co.uk/finance/newsbysector/epic/ulvr/11372550/Unilever-boss- Paul-Polman-slams-capitalist-obsession-with-profit.html

20 "Six Reasons Companies Should Embrace CSR" by James Epstein-Reeves, *Forbes,* Feb. 2012. http://www.forbes.com/sites/csr/2012/02/21/six-reasons-companies-should-embrace-csr

Chapter 7: They Keep the Customer Close

1 "CEO Talk: Angela Ahrendts on Burberry's Connected Culture" by Imran Amed, *Business of Fashion,* Sept. 2013. http://www.businessoffashion.com/2013/09/burberry-angela-ahrendts.html

2 Ibid

3   "Burberry's CEO on Turning an Aging British Icon Into a Global Luxury Brand" by Angela Ahrendts, *Harvard Business Review*, Jan./Feb. 2013. https://hbr.org/2013/01/burberrys-ceo-on-turning-an-aging-british-icon-into-a-global-luxury-brand

4   "In Sports or Business, Always Prepare for the Next Play" by Adam Bryant, *The New York Times*, Nov. 2010. http://www.nytimes.com/2012/11/11/business/jeff-weiner-of-linkedin-on-the-next-play-philosophy.html?pagewanted=all&_r=1

5   Drucker, P. *Management: Tasks, Responsibilities and Practices*, Heinemann, 1973.

6   "10 Minutes On Building the Customer-Centered Organization," *PricewaterhousCoopers*, 2013. http://www.pwc.com/en_US/us/10minutes/assets/pwc-customer-centered-organization.pdf

7   "Tesla Won't Produce the Model X Until It's Sufficiently Awesome," *Fuel Freedom Foundation*, Nov. 2014. http://www.fuelfreedom.org/this-is-why-tesla-is-delaying-its-suv-the-model-x/

8   "GM CEO Mary Barra Knows Big Changes Are Coming to Autos. Here's How She Intends to Lead, Not React" by Daniel Roth, *LinkedIn Pulse*, June 2015. https://www.linkedin.com/pulse/gm-ceo-mary-barra-knows-big-changes-coming-autos-heres-daniel-roth

9   "Myth Busted: Steve Jobs Did Listen to Customers," by Drew Hansen, *Forbes*, Dec. 2013. http://www.forbes.com/sites/drewhansen/2013/12/19/myth-busted-steve-jobs-did-listen-to-customers

10 The Gartner Supply Chain Top 25" by Stan Aronow, *Gartner*, 2015. http://www.gartner.com/technology/supply-chain/top25.jsp

11 "Big Data: How Netflix Uses It to Drive Business Success" by Bernard Marr, *Smart Data Collective*, April 2015. http://www.smartdatacollective.com/bernardmarr/312146/big-data-how-netflix-uses-it-drive-business-success

12 "The Case of the Ornamental Anthropologist" by Jacob Brogan, *Slate*, May 2015. http://www.slate.com/articles/technology/future_tense/2015/05/netflix_tries_to_put_a_human_face_on_big_data_with_its_own_anthropologist.2.html

13 https://pr.netflix.com/WebClient/getNewsSummary.do?newsId=496

14 "Gap's Old Navy Targets 'Jenny' to Revive Sales" by Andria Cheng, *Market Watch*, Oct. 2008. http://www.marketwatch.com/story/gaps-old-navy-targets-jenny-in-new-growth-strategy

15 "Jeff Bezos Reveals His No. 1 Leadership Secret" by George Anders, *Forbes*, April 2012. http://www.forbes.com/forbes/2012/0423/ceo-compensation-12-amazon-technology-jeff-bezos-gets-it.html

16 "Combining Purpose with Profits" by Julian Birkinshaw, Nicolai J. Foss and Siegwart Lindenberg, *MIT Sloan Management Review*, Feb. 2014. http://sloanreview.mit.edu/article/combining-purpose-with-profits

17 http://www.gene.com/about-us/awards-recognition

18 "Inside Amazon's Idea Machine: How Bezos Decodes Customers," by George Anders, *Forbes*, April 2012. http://www.forbes.com/sites/georgeanders/2012/04/04/inside-amazon

19 John Deere: Our Guiding Principles," *John Deere*, Sept. 2012. http://investor.deere.com/files/doc_downloads/guiding_principles/guidingprinciples_english.pdf

20 "John Deere – Not Your Father's Tractor Company" by Jim Tincher, *Heart of the Customer*, May 2015. http://www.heartofthecustomer.com/john-deere-not-your-fathers-tractor-company

21 "Company Goals: Do Your Employees Have a 'Line of Sight' to Them?" by Jacque Vilet, *TLNT*, June 2012. http://www.tlnt.com/2012/06/07/company-goals-do-your-employees-have-a-line-of-sight-to-them

22 "The Aligned Organization," *McKinsey & Company*. http://www.mckinsey.com/~/media/mckinsey/dotcom/client_service/operations/lean%20management%20c ompendium/pdfs-lean%20management%20enterprise/4_the%20aligned%20organization.ashx

23 https://www.youtube.com/watch?v=55cKZwCBSiE

Chapter 8: Their Leaders Are Courageous Connectors

1   "A Leader's Framework for Decision Making" by David J. Snowden and Mary E. Boone, *Harvard Business Review*, Nov. 2007.https://hbr.org/2007/11/a-leaders-framework-for-decision-making

2   "Management Is (Still) Not Leadership" by John P. Kotter, *Harvard Business Review*, Jan. 2013. https://hbr.org/2013/01/management-is-still-not-leadership

3   Ibid.

4   *The Future of Work: How the New Order of Business Will Shape Your Orgazization, Your Management Style and Your Life*, by Thomas W. Marlone, Harvard Business Review Press, April 2004.

5   "Tim Cook Erupts After Shareholder Asks Him to Focus Only on Profit" by Kyle Russell, *Business Insider,* Feb. 2014. http://www.businessinsider.com/tim-cook-versus-a-conservative-think-tank-2014-2

6   "Why Zappos Offers New Hires $2,000 to Quit" by Keith R. McFarland, *Bloomberg,* Sept. 2008. http://www.bloomberg.com/bw/stories/2008-09-16/why-zappos-offers-new-hires-2-000-to- quitbusinessweek-business-news-stock-market-and-financial-advice

7   "The HBR Interview: 'We Had to Own the Mistakes'" by Adi Ignatius, *Harvard Business Review,* July/Aug. 2010. https://hbr.org/2010/07/the-hbr-interview-we-had-to-own-the-mistakes

8   "The Best Leaders Are Humble Leaders" by Jeanine Prime and Elizabeth Salib, *Forbes,* May 2014. https://hbr.org/2014/05/the-best-leaders-are-humble-leaders

9   "5 Time-Tested Success Tips from Amazon Founder Jeff Bezos" by John Greathouse, *Forbes,* April 2013. http://www.forbes.com/sites/johngreathouse/2013/04/30/5-time-tested-success-tips-from-amazon-founder- jeff-bezos

10 "The Best Leaders Are Humble Leaders" by Jeanine Prime and Elizabeth Salib, *Forbes,* May 2014. https://hbr.org/2014/05/the-best-leaders-are-humble-leaders

11 "Nilofer Merchant – How the Air Sandwich Can Kill Your Business" by Alexandra Levit, *QuickBase,* Jan. 2015. http://quickbase.intuit.com/blog/2015/01/09/nilofer-merchant-how-the-air-sandwich-can-kill- your-business/#sthash.ZKu6aYB1.dpuf

12 "Time to Fix Patents," *The Economist,* Aug. 2015. http://www.economist.com/news/leaders/21660522- ideas-fuel-economy-todays-patent-systems-are-rotten-way-rewarding-them-time-fix

13 "Managing Collaboration at the Point of Execution: Improving Team Effectiveness with a Network Perspective" by Rob Cross, Kate Ehrlich, Ross Dawson, and John Helferich, *IBM.* http://www.watson.ibm.com/cambridge/Technical_Reports/2008/CMR%20Teams%20and%20Collaboration%20Final.pdf

14 "Jonathan Bendor: Why Criticism is Good for Innovation" by Theresa Johnston," *Stanford Business,* June 2015. http://www.gsb.stanford.edu/insights/jonathan-bendor-why-criticism-good-innovation

Chapter 9: Their People Are Difference Makers

1   "Connect Team Members' Work to Their Personal Dreams" by Matt Tenney, *The Huffington Post,* Aug. 2015. http://www.huffingtonpost.com/matt-tenney/connect-team-members-work_b_7971264.html

2   http://studentleadership.com/wp-content/uploads/2013/06/SLP006.pdf

3   "Unlocking the passion of the Explorer," by John Hagel III, John Seely Brown, and Tamara Samoylova, *Deloitte University Press,* Sept. 2013. http://dupress.com/articles/unlocking-the-passion-of-the-explorer/

4   "What the Millennials Are Teaching the Rest of the World" by Raghu Krishnamoorthy, *LinkedIn Pulse,* May 2015. https://www.linkedin.com/pulse/what-millennials-teaching-rest-world-raghu- krishnamoorthy?trk=hp-feed-article-title

5   "Autodesk – 120 Million Reasons Why the Future Lies with Makers" by Haydn Shaughnessy, *Forbes,* June 2013. http://www.forbes.com/sites/haydnshaughnessy/2013/06/17/autodesk-120-million-reasons-why-the-future-lies-with-makers

Chapter 10: They Enable a Workforce That Is Bold and Plays Big

1   "The Execution Trap" by Roger L. Martin, *Harvard Business Review,* July/Aug. 2010. https://hbr.org/2010/07/the-execution-trap

2   "Why We Love to Hate HR...and What HR Can Do About It" by Peter Cappelli, *Harvard Business Review,* July/Aug. 2015. https://hbr.org/2015/07/why-we-love-to-hate-hr-and-what-hr-can-do-about-it

3   "The Cheesecake Factory Has a Bright Future" by Natalie O'Reilly, *Fool.com,* Oct. 2013. http://www.fool.com/investing/general/2013/10/24/the-cheesecake-factory-has-a-bright-future.aspx

4   "Big Med" by Atul Gawande, *The New Yorker,* Aug. 2012. http://www.newyorker.com/magazine/2012/08/13/big-med

5   "Mechanize Your Hiring Process to Make Better Decisions," *First Found.* http://firstround.com/review/Mechanize-Your-Hiring-Process-to-Make-Better-Decisions

6 "Top 10 Corporate Interview Processes for Hires that Fit" by Lexie Forman-Ortiz, *Smart Recruiters,* March 2013. https://www.smartrecruiters.com/blog/top-10-corporate-interview-processes-for-hires-that-fit

7 "The 5 Best Hiring Quotes" by David Smooke, *Smart Recruiters,* March 2012. https://www.smartrecruiters.com/blog/the-5-best-hiring-quotes

8 "How the Wrong People Get Promoted and How to Change It" by Mark C. Crowley, *Fast Company,* April 2015. http://www.fastcompany.com/3045453/hit-the-ground-running/how-the-wrong-people-get-promoted-and-how-to-change-it

9 "Inside Google's Insanely Popular Emotional-Intelligence Course" by Vivian Giang, *Fast Company,* March 2015. http://www.fastcompany.com/3044157/the-future-of-work/inside-googles-insanely-popular- emotional-intelligence-course

10 "Can the Brilliant Jerk Be Managed Effectively?" by James Heskett, *Harvard Business School Working Knowledge,* December 2014, http://hbswk.hbs.edu/item/7682.html and Jack Welch, Jack: Straight from the Gut (New York: Warner Books, 2001), especially pp. 185-204.

11 "The 2015 Deloitte Millennial Survey," Deloitte, Jan. 2015. http://www2.deloitte.com/content/dam/Deloitte/global/Documents/About-Deloitte/gx-wef-2015-millennial-survey-executivesummary.pdf

12 "New Research Unlocks the Secret of Employee Recognition" by Josh Bersin, *Forbes,* June 2012. http://www.forbes.com/sites/joshbersin/2012/06/13/new-research-unlocks-the-secret-of-employee- recognition

13 "11 Non-Traditional Ways to Reward Innovative Employees" by Lisa Bodell, *Ere Media,* December 2014. http://www.eremedia.com/tlnt/11-non-traditional-ways-to-reward-innovative-employees-2/

14 "Catch People in the Act of Doing Things Right" by Bill Taylor, *Harvard Business Review,* Oct. 2012. https://hbr.org/2012/10/catch-people-in-the-act-of-doing-things-right

15 "Why Employee Ranking Can Backfire" by Phillis Korkki, *The New York Times,* July 2015. http://www.nytimes.com/2015/07/12/business/why-employee-ranking-can-backfire.html?_r=2

16 "How GE Renews Performance Management: From Stack Ranking to Continuous Feedback" by Steffen Maier, *LinkedIn Pulse,* Aug. 2015. https://www.linkedin.com/pulse/how-ge-renews-performance- management-from-stack-ranking-steffen-maier

17 "P&G Recognized for Excellence in Leadership Develompent," Procter & Gamble News, Jan. 2015. http://news.pg.com/blog/leadership/ceo-mag

18 "O.K., Google, Take a Deep Breath" by Caitlin Kelly, *The New York Times,* April 2012. http://www.nytimes.com/2012/04/29/technology/google-course-asks-employees-to-take-a-deep-breath.html?pagewanted=all&_r=0 "To Raise Productivity, Let More Employees Work From Home" by Nicholas Bloom, *Harvard Business*

19 *Review,* Jan./Feb. 2014. https://hbr.org/2014/01/to-raise-productivity-let-more-employees-work-from-home

Chapter 11: Architecting Culture: A Framework for Building Your Culture

1 "Your Company's Purpose Is Not Its Vision, Mission, or Values" by Graham Kenny, *Harvard Business Review,* Sept. 2014. https://hbr.org/2014/09/your-companys-purpose-is-not-its-vision-mission-or-values

2 "Ten Things We Know to Be True," *Google.* http://www.google.com/about/company/philosophy

3 *How Google Works,* by Eric Schmidt and Jonathan Rosenberg, Grand Central Publishing, 2014. pp.30-31

4 "The Value of Corporate Culture" by Luigi Guiso, Paola Sapienza, and Luigi Zingales, *MIT Economics,* Sept. 2013. http://economics.mit.edu/files/9721

5 "The Untapped Potential of Corporate Narratives" by John Hagel, *Edge Perspectives with John Hagel.* http://edgeperspectives.typepad.com/edge_perspectives/2013/10/the-untapped-potential-of-corporate- narratives.html

6 "It's Not the CEO, It's the Leadership Strategy That Mattes" by Josh Bersin, *Forbes,* June 2012. http://www.forbes.com/sites/joshbersin/2012/07/30/its-not-the-ceo-its-the-leadership-strategy-that- matters/2

Chapter 12: Envisioning Your Culture: Your First Step

1 "A Business and Its Beliefs" by Sam Palmisano, IBM. http://www-03.ibm.com/ibm/history/ibm100/us/en/icons/bizbeliefs
2 "Leading Change When Business Is Good" by Paul Hemp and Thomas A. Stewart, *Harvard Business Review,* Dec. 2004. https://hbr.org/2004/12/leading-change-when-business-is-good/ar/1
3 http://faculty.washington.edu/janegf/buildingvision.html

Chapter 13: LEAD: Building Leaders for Your New Culture

1 "Inside Starbucks $35 Million Decision to Make Brand Evangelists of Its Front-Line Workers, by Sarah Kessler, *Fast Company,* Oct. 2012. http://www.fastcompany.com/3002023/inside-starbuckss-35-million- mission-make-brand-evangelists-its-front-line-workers

Chapter 14: ALIGN: Righting Your Organizational Practices

1 "How Yahoo CEO Mayer fixed 1,000 Problems," by Patricia Sellers, *Fortune,* Oct. 2013. http://fortune.com/2013/10/22/how-yahoo-ceo-mayer-fixed-1000-problems

Conclusion: The End of How and the Start of Why Not

1 "This Wall Street Veteran Is Whipping Google into Shape" by Brian Womack and Michael J Moore, *Bloomberg,* July 2015. http://www.bloomberg.com/news/articles/2015-07-23/google-cfo-ruth-porat-brings-fiscal-discipline
2 "Why Google Is Renaming Itself 'Alphabet'" by Timonty B. Lee, *Vox,* Aug. 2015. http://www.vox.com/2015/8/10/9128375/why-google-is-renaming-itself-alphabet
3 "What the Heck is Angela Ahrendts doing at Apple?" by Jennifer Reingold, *Fortune,* Sept. 2015. http://fortune.com/2015/09/10/angela-ahrendts-apple

INDEX

Sessley, Simeon, 62
Shen, Wei, 61–62
SHIFT Academy, 111
silos, 35, 87, 91, 94, 97, 170, 174, 261
Sinek, Simon, 153–154
Snowden, David, 148–149
social collaboration technologies, 98, 295–296
social media, 19, 66, 129, 132, 171, 225, 252, 267, 282
social network analysis (SNA), 293–294
socialization, 189
Southwest, 109
Southwest Airlines, 208
speed
    hierarchy and, 71–73
    structure for, 277
Spencer, John, 78
Starbucks, 296
startup boot camp, 58–60
storytelling, 286–288
strategy
    clear, 97
    purpose and, 111–114
struggling organizations, 2
Student Maid, 165–167, 171
surveys, 266, 284–285
Swanson, Kate, 128
Swigert, John "Jack," 83–85

T

tasks, open, 89–91
teams
    conversations with, 285–286
    self-organized, 77–80
technology, 19
    consumer expectations and, 19
    embracing new, 15
Tesla, 129–130
Tetzeli, Rick, 98
Thiel, Peter, 23–24
Thomson Reuters, 278
thought, diversity of, 187
Tiedens, Larissa, 71
Tomak, Kerem, 72
TOMS Shoes, 120
Toyota, 63–64, 66
traditional concerns of business, 32
transformation, 249
Triggertrap, 81
triple threats, 55–58
trust, 85
    hierarchy and, 71–73

U

Uber, 24
UCLA Health System, 141–143
Uncertainty Principle, 64–65

uncertainty principle, 147–150
Unilever, 118–119, 229, 278
unison, acting in, 86
US military, 77

V

values, 231
    assessing, 233–234
    celebration of, 190–191
    connection to, 298–299
    courageous leaders and, 153–154
    crafting your, 234
    current, 234–235
    decision making and, 75–77
    envisioning, 221
    future, 234–235
    non-actionable, 232–233
    organizational, 203–208
    rules and, 110–111
    single-word, 232–233
    sprouting new, 233–234
    statements of, 232–233
values of organizations, 203–208
Vernon, Mona, 94–95
vigilance, 5–7
vision, 56, 157–158
"Vox Populi," 93
VUCA (Volatility, Uncertainty, Complexity, Ambiguity), 19, 21, 26, 36, 147, 258

W

Waggl, 285
Wantanabe, Katsuaki, 63
Waterman, Robert, 5
Weiner, Jeff, 128
Welch, Jack, 6–7, 186, 192, 249–250
"what" *versus* "how," 2–3
Whitehurst, Jim, 80
"Who Wants to Be a Millionaire," 93–94
Whole Foods, 79, 278
"Wisdom of Crowds," 93
W.L. Gore, 77–79, 190–191
work environments, 36
Workers' Compensation, 101

X

Xerox, 5, 162

Y

Yahoo!, 266
Yglesias, Matthew, 40–41

Z

Zappos, 66, 80–81, 154–155, 170, 190, 193, 206–207
Zitek, Emily, 71
Zuckerberg, Mark, 32, 33, 40

ACKNOWLEDGMENTS

THIS BOOK SIMPLY WOULD NOT EXIST had it not been for my village consisting of thought partners, co-pilots, wing-people, champions, supporters, nudgers, and risk-takers.

Deepest thanks first and foremost to Peter Carlson, a brilliant man and colleague, who joined my team a few years back and instantly brought my game up ten-fold through his work. Peter, you worked with me patiently to develop this book and bring all our team's ideas, work, and passion to life. This is as much yours as it is mine.

Keith Hollihan, you are such a gifted thinker, talented user of words, and creative developer of stories and concepts. Thank you for working tirelessly and not to mention, quickly, in pushing to make this book and the ideas unfold how I wanted but often couldn't alone. I'm convinced the whole world needs a Keith to make their thinking and writing substantially more cogent, clear, and compelling.

Simeon Sessley, thank you for advocating and encouraging me to put what we were working on together into book form. You have so generously shaped and advanced the thinking behind it. I will be forever grateful for the opportunity to have worked with a client like you. Your belief and passion for this work, paired with your purposeful leadership and example, make me absolutely certain that the practices in the book are true and can be the norm in Corporate America and beyond. I saw it first-hand in how you led and inspired your teams.

Julie Cullinane-Smith and Jenny Clevidence, thank you for being my colleagues for so many years in learning, leading, and shaping these practices. I owe much of how much I have grown professionally over the years to you both. I'm fortunate that I had two of the brightest and most purposeful people I have ever met as part of this journey.

Kate Purmal, thank you for the inspiration and encouraging me to get this out into the world. Without a champion and cheerleader like you, I might not have kept the faith.

Thank you to all the great minds and kind clients and colleagues who were my original NFF sounding board crew. Thank you for helping make these ideas and concepts more real and tangible through your inspiring work. I'm looking at you, David Davidovic, formerly of Genentech, Andy Burtis of McKesson, Dan Cousins of Safeway, Dan Feshbach of LoanPerformance and Measure One, Julie Weinstein of Gap, Inc., Jose Velayos of Genentech Roche, Abby Evans of Dolby Laboratories, Judith Hashimoto of AAA, Liz McGowan of Safeway, Julie Cane of Wells Fargo, Scott Day of Yahoo!, Anish Srivastava of Citi Ventures, Jessica Wilan of Novartis, and Crystal Simon, and Rimma Boshernitsan.

Thank you to my agents who believed in this book, Sheree Bykofsky and Janet Rosen.

Thanks to my publishing team at BenBella Books, especially Glenn Yeffeth and Debbie Harmsen. You impressed me from the get-go. You understood the topic, believed it needed to be out in the world, and have been with me every step of the way.

And last but certainly not least, thank you to my husband, Joerg Schumann, and our young son, Vinn Schumann, for giving me the space, encouragement, and love that was needed to write this book on top of running a business, and trying to still have a life.

ABOUT THE AUTHOR

SARA ROBERTS is a leading authority and "go-to" expert on organizational transformation, culture, and building purpose-led companies.

She's an executive consultant to Fortune 500 leaders, a sought-after keynote speaker, and an entrepreneur. She founded and sold Roberts Golden, a boutique consultancy, where she and her team worked with nearly a quarter of the Fortune 100, over its 12-year span, to help transform their cultures and ability to lead.

Known to spark revolution versus simply evolution, Sara prescribes bold, yet thoughtful shifts in her client's companies to enable them to survive and thrive in this volatile and constantly changing new era. She has been widely recognized for her unique insights on both the emotional and practical sides of business transformation and reveals many of those learnings and approaches she has observed and honed through the years in *Nimble, Focused, Feisty*.

As a speaker, Sara offers a relevant and refreshing take on how organizations can achieve true transformation by capturing the hearts and minds of its employees and customers.

Sara is also the co-author of *Light Their Fire: Using Internal Marketing to Ignite Employee Performance* and *Wow Your Customers* and numerous treatises on building and connecting organizations and employees through purpose.

Learn more at www.nimblefocusedfeisty.com and find her at Sara Roberts on LinkedIn.